THE PUBLIC'S USE OF TELEVISION

PEOPLE AND COMMUNICATION

Series Editors: PETER CLARKE   *University of Michigan*
               F. GERALD KLINE   *University of Minnesota*

Volumes in this series :

THE PUBLIC'S USE OF TELEVISION,

Who Watches and Why

Ronald E. Frank
Marshall G. Greenberg

Foreword by Lloyd N. Morrisett

 SAGE PUBLICATIONS   Beverly Hills   London

For information address:

SAGE Publications, Inc. SAGE Publications Ltd
275 South Beverly Drive   28 Banner Street
Beverly Hills, California 90212   London EC1Y 8QE, England

Printed in the United States of America

Library of Congress Cataloging in Publication Data

Frank, Ronald Edward, 1933-
   The public's use of television.

   (People and communication ; 9)
   Bibliography: p.
   Includes index.
   1. Television audiences—United States.
I. Greenberg, Marshall G., 1935-   joint
author. II. Title.
HE8700.7.A8F7   302.2'3   79-27067
ISBN 0-8039-1389-3

DEDICATION

To those closest to us
who have shared the joys
and the frustrations associated
with a project of this scale.

Iris	*Addy*
Linda	*Paula*
Lauren	*David*
Kimberly	*Karen*
	Kenny

Contents

**Part Four
Conclusion**

Appendices

Foreword

by **Lloyd N. Morrisett,** President
The John and Mary R. Markle Foundation

At 9:00 p.m. on a Wednesday evening in November, forty million Americans are likely to be looking at their television sets. When a Super Bowl, World Series, or presidential debate is scheduled on television, as many as one hundred million people watch. Television audiences are so large that it is hard, almost impossible, to think about them. Who are these people? What programs do they watch? How does television affect their lives? Advertisers, television executives, and scholars have asked these questions for many years and have developed certain ways of answering them.

The problem is that there are many ways to describe the characteristics and behavior of so many millions of people. With television audiences, we are looking for summary descriptions which relate television programming on the one hand to audience characteristics on the other and which will facilitate our ability to think about and answer the relevant questions. The method of description utilized strongly influences the results of our thinking.

To illustrate this point, consider the analogy of a library containing one million books. It would be possible to describe those books in terms of their width, breadth, and height, the color of their bindings, their weight, numbers of pages, and perhaps age. Using these attributes, we would classify all the books in the library into categories. Then, rather than having to think about the almost meaningless figure of "one million," we could think about many smaller categories each with its own set of attributes. It would also be possible to relate these categories to reading and buying habits. Not surprisingly, perhaps, we might find that smaller, newer books were purchased and read more than large, old books. This would tell us nothing, however, about the contents of the books or about how to write a book to interest people. Another classification system would tell much more. Knowing the numbers of fiction and nonfiction books, subdivided by subject and author categories, is much more useful both to the reader and the author.

The traditional way of describing television audiences is in terms of demographic characteristics—age, sex, occupation, income, education, geographic location, and so on. These categories have long been used in the study of human populations, and they have been found to be remarkably useful. Since people have been studied in these terms, there is a great deal known about the behavior of many different sets of people—for example, females of 18 to 49 years of age living in the Northeast and having family incomes of more than $10,000. Work by census experts, sociologists, and economists tells us much about groups defined in this fashion. The principal television rating companies, Nielsen and Arbitron, tell us about their television behavior and buying habits. In fact, we are so used to describing television audiences in these terms that we have come to believe these are natural and complete audience descriptions. However, demographic characteristics, useful as they are, bear little relation to what people think, feel, and care about—just as the size and color of a book bear little relation to its content.

The question addressed in this study by Ronald Frank and Marshall Greenberg is whether it is possible to describe television audiences in ways that will reveal some of the reasons for their use of television and how television fits into their lives. Descriptions of groups in terms of interests and needs have often been applied in other fields, but seldom to television audiences. This book is a pioneering effort to apply a well-proven approach and methodology to the study of television. What has resulted is a set of descriptions of television audiences, readily comprehensible and highly consistent with data analyzing individual use of other media and leisure time. I believe this approach can usefully supplement demographic description and give all those interested in television new means of thinking about audiences. Writers, producers, and schedulers may be able to use these tools in creative ways to facilitate their work.

Preface

The study reported in this book is an investigation of the functions of television, as well as other media behavior, from the viewpoint of their respective audiences. Our primary purpose is to develop new insights into the ways in which audience members use television and other media in their daily lives.

Many studies have been conducted to examine television viewing behavior. In fact, the mass media have become such an integral part of our culture today that most media behavior is monitored on a continuing basis to supply immediate feedback to those involved in strategy, advertising, and production. While our study describes the behavior of television and other media audiences, that is not its principal goal. Our intent is to try to *understand* this behavior better by examining its relationship to other audience characteristics, especially individual patterns of leisure interests and activities and the psychological needs they satisfy.

Toward this end, we conducted a large-scale national survey of individual leisure interests and activities, related needs and behavior with respect to television, radio, newspapers, magazines, books, and movies. A detailed statement of the rationale underlying the project is provided in Chapter 1.

Our intended audience is comprised of academic, industry, and government professionals in many fields interested in better understanding the role of media in general and television in particular. Included are:

(1) Those directly associated with the process of generating, evaluating, and choosing television programming material. This would include people responsible for program development and research in the commercial and public television networks and stations, along with people in similar positions in television production companies.

(1a) The counterparts of the above in radio.

(2) Those responsible for generating, evaluating, and choosing new publications or for marketing existing publications in book, magazine, and newspaper publishing organizations.

(3) Those who comprise the faculties and student bodies in schools of communication, journalism, and business (especially those interested in advertising and mass media).

(4) Those in advertising agencies concerned with media selection and allocation for a particular product or service, as well as those responsible for determining appropriate advertising content.

(5) Those in marketing organizations (manufacturers) responsible for developing the overall marketing strategies and implementation for particular products and services.

(6) Those in special segments of the general public. There are a number of organizations such as ACT whose members might think our findings of interest.

Given these diverse audience objectives, we have reported the findings in what we hope to be a readable style, irrespective of the reader's background or skills (given the inherently technical nature of the research methodology).

The book uses predominantly verbal rather than numerical or statistical language. For example, in the chapters reporting results, we present our findings in tabular form. However, the discussion itself is written so that it is virtually self-contained. The reader who so chooses can understand the text without continually referring to the tables. However, for those who wish to make their own assessment of our conclusions and interpretations, the data are readily accessible.

Finally, while various statistical methods such as factor analysis, cluster analysis, and multiple discriminant analysis have been used in the data reduction and analysis stages, they are deemphasized in the reporting of our findings. Familiarity with these multivariate procedures is not a prerequisite for reading and understanding the book. The study is not intended to be a demonstration project on new or novel research methodology, nor was it designed to illustrate applications of multivariate statistics. If it serves these purposes for some readers, we will be gratified, but, first and foremost, our goal was to gain useful insights into those characteristics of television audiences that have an impact on their viewing behavior.

Our success will be measured not by the reactions of individual readers to the text, but by evidence that the results are being employed by those people and institutions characterized above as the intended audience for this book.

−R.E.F.
−M.G.G.

Acknowledgements

This book and the research upon which it is based represent the culmination of a series of efforts dating back to 1974. This is when we first began to develop the research strategy that led to the interest-based segmentation of television audiences reported in this book. We could never have gotten this far without the considerable individual and organizational support of many others.

First and foremost, we are deeply indebted to The John and Mary R. Markle Foundation for funding the exploratory work, the pilot phase, and the national study described in this book. To Lloyd Morrisett, president of the foundation, and to Jean Firstenberg, program officer, we are indebted for more than their financial support. They had the vision and the willingness to work with us during the early stages when the project had not yet achieved its ultimate focus. They allowed us the freedom and independence to pursue the research as we saw fit, while at the same time providing us with their counsel and encouragement as the project moved forward.

The Corporation for Public Broadcasting generously provided funding for collecting and processing data from a supplementary sample of minority populations for the national study. Leon Rosenbluth was especially helpful in working with us on

17

those issues relating to public broadcasting and in making available a series of program concepts for evaluation by our survey respondents.

We met on numerous occasions with representatives from the television industry to discuss our design, the questionnaire, and finally the results of the project. Those who were particularly generous with their time were Mel Goldberg of ABC, Joe Klapper and Barbara Lee of CBS, Tom Coffin and Bill Rubens of NBC, and Mike Dann of Warner Communications.

A special word of thanks is also due Jerry Wind, Professor of Marketing at The Wharton School, who was a coinvestigator at the very start of the project.

At National Analysts, there were dozens of individuals who contributed to the success of the survey. The project manager was Lyn Wiesinger, who participated actively in all phases from questionnaire development to data analysis and whose role ranged from that of research professional to that of mediator of our disputes. Tony Asmann, director of data collection services, and Mary Henderson drew the sample for the study and developed the weighting model for the data. Nancy Lessin, manager of the field department, and Ethel Trachtenberg supervised the actual interviewing. Jim Clody, director of data processing, supervised the coding, keypunching, cleaning, and processing of all of the data. Finally, there is a group of people, now with blurred vision and callused fingers, who typed the many drafts of the manuscript for this book. They are (in alphabetical order): Jackie Buck, Nettie Massimi, Dotty Robison, Mary Torpey, and Rosemary West.

To all of the above, and to the many others not mentioned by name who contributed to this project, we are most appreciative for their assistance in bringing it to fruition. We, however, bear the full responsibility for any remaining errors of omission or commission.

Part One
Introduction

1
Overview

BACKGROUND

Television's critics are numerous. Many have argued that it is a wasteland. Nevertheless, as of 1977, 98% of U.S. homes owned one or more television sets. Almost half had more than one set. Over three-quarters (76%) had a color set. The average cost of these receivers ranged from $90 for a black and white to $350 for color (Sterling and Haight, 1978: 372). In the average household, at least one set was on for an average of six and a half hours per day (Sterling and Haight, 1978: 375).

Television has accounted for a major part of time usage in U.S. homes for a substantial percentage of the population for over a quarter of a century. As far back as 1955, fully 65% of households owned a set and used it for an average of five hours per day. In spite of its ubiquity, surprisingly little has been published on the uses made of television by the members of its audience. Most of the published material[1] has been concerned with:

(1) *Program Viewing Behavior.* How many people are watching? What do they watch? What are their demographic characteristics? How long do they watch?

(2) *Program Content.* What programs are being aired? What are they about? What content elements do they contain (e.g., violence, sex)?

(3) *Program Criticism.* What is wrong with what is offered on television? What ought to be offered? What role should television play in American society?

(4) *Use and Effects on Special Interest Audiences* (especially children and minorities). How might television better serve special interest audiences? What effects does it have on their attitudes and behavior?

The study reported in this book investigates the uses of television from the viewpoint of its audience. Its principal purpose is to provide new insights into the ways in which audiences use television and other media in their daily lives.

We believe that a better understanding of how people use television will be useful to those with a serious interest in the medium whether they are concerned with its role in society, its effect on certain segments of society, what programs to produce and air, when to air them, or how to evaluate existing programs, stations, or networks.

Our purpose is neither to praise nor to condemn, but simply to understand better the role of this most ubiquitous medium—television.

STUDY OVERVIEW

In developing our approach to understanding the uses of television, we have drawn from experience reported in two traditions of literature:

(1) *Market Segmentation*—appearing almost completely in the field of marketing.

(2) *Needs and Gratifications*—appearing in the fields of sociology and communication.

It is not our purpose to review this material, as this has been done elsewhere (Frank et al., 1972; Wells, 1974; Blumler and Katz, 1974).

The literature of market segmentation is in large part supplemented by our personal experiences gained in conducting numerous proprietary studies of consumers across a wide range of products and services for manufacturing firms and their advertising agencies. This experience supports our contention that one of the most useful ways to study consumer behavior is to obtain data, not only on their product usage and demographics, but also on their attitudes, interests, and opinions (AIOs) specific to the product or service category under investigation. For many food products, this has led researchers to study consumers' attitudes toward meals and meal preparation. For example, knowing how confident a cook is in preparing meals and in trying new foods when company comes, or knowing how important family nutrition is, is extremely helpful in understanding why new convenience food products are more readily accepted by some consumers than are others. Such studies have allowed marketers to develop successful new products and to direct their marketing efforts most efficiently against those target consumer segments likely to be most receptive to such products.

Based on exploratory research conducted by us prior to our national study (discussed in the next section), we concluded that the most relevant AIO context for the study of television would be to include measures of a wide range of leisure interests and activities (e.g., football, opera) and subjects (e.g., astronomy, poetry). For many people, leisure-related activities are the principal complements or substitutes for watching television. Other potential complements or substitutes are other media such as movies, radio, newspapers, books, and magazines. Measures of the usage of these media are included in the present investigation.

As is apparent from the literature on needs and gratifications, to understand the uses of a product or service from the consumer's point of view, it is useful to obtain data on the psychological needs satisfied when it is used. Hence, we have chosen to develop and include a set of need-related questions about which more will be said in the next two chapters.

It is helpful to view the elements of our approach in terms of attempts to answer the following five questions:

(1) What are the patterns of leisure interests and activities that characterize different segments (groups) of the American public? How do they differ in the psychological needs gratified by their leisure interests and activities? How do they differ in their demographic characteristics?

(2) What are the extent and nature of differences in overall television viewing behavior across the various interest segments? By program type? By program?

(3) What are the extent and nature of differences in the television viewing context (i.e., reasons for viewing, sources of influence in program choice, and so on) across the interest segments?

(4) What are the extent and nature of differences by segment in magazine readership? Book readership? Newspaper readership? Movie attendance? Radio listening?

(5) How does the interest segmentation scheme developed in this study compare to the more traditional use of demographic segmentation in explaining media behavior?

Our findings and conclusions are based on a representative nationwide survey of 2476 people age 13 and over. These people were interviewed in person for an average of an hour and a half each. Besides obtaining an extensive description of their television viewing behavior, the interview included questions pertaining to their interests in leisure activities and different subjects, their needs as served by these interests, and their use of other media.[2]

The data on interests were used to assign individuals into segments, so that the members of each segment have a relatively homogeneous pattern of interests, while differences from segment to segment are great. For example, the people in one segment have strong interests in mechanical activities and outdoor life, while those in another are predominantly interested in artistic and cultural activities.[3]

Examining the differences in television and other media usage across these interest segments leads to an increased understanding of the determinants of media behavior and provides a valuable conceptual framework for the development and implementation of strategies for audience attraction.

RELATIONSHIP TO PREVIOUS RESEARCH

The Work of Others

We found only three studies similar in spirit, if not in exact detail, to ours: *The People Look at Television* (Steiner, 1963), *Television and the Public* (Bower, 1973), and "On the Use of Mass Media for Important Things" (Katz et al., 1973).

The first two of these are based on nationwide samples of the U.S. audience, with Bower's study being a virtual replication of Steiner's. The studies provide detailed descriptions of audience demographic and socioeconomic characteristics, but examine only to a modest extent the functions performed by television (e.g., entertainment, education, and so on). The third study is of interest primarily because the authors attempt to develop an overall structure of the functions performed by the mass media, including, but not restricted to, television.

The study reported in this volume goes beyond these investigations principally in three ways:

(1) It focuses on the uses of television, not as an isolated phenomenon, but in terms of its relationship with a broad range of interests in leisure activities and subject matter.

(2) It focuses on the uses of television in relation to uses of other media, again as opposed to studying it in isolation.

(3) It develops a segmentation scheme to describe how different types of audience members with varying interest patterns use television.

We decided to broaden the scope of our inquiry to include a wide range of leisure interests, as well as other media, for the following reasons:

(1) Leisure interests and other media comprise the principal alternatives to television usage. This is reasonably well recognized in the literature on the subject of leisure (e.g., Kaplan, 1975), but it is often ignored in studies primarily concerned with television.

(2) An exploratory study, consisting of a series of group depth interviews and the pilot survey we conducted prior to the national survey, strongly supported the usefulness of including both interests and other media for the purpose of better understanding television usage.

(3) Our combined past experience in designing and conducting dozens of large-scale segmentation studies of this general type for a variety of products and services supports the usefulness of examining the product or service that is the focus of the study in a broader context.

We have used a *people types* analysis rather than a *variables* analysis approach in the study. It is our intent to gain an understanding of the totality of a person's relationship to television, as opposed to intensively studying some limited aspect of a person (say, income) and its relation to viewing behavior. Focusing on understanding people in terms of attitudinal and behavioral patterns, rather than in terms of individual variables, leads one in two fundamentally different directions from the studies mentioned above:

(1) Toward grouping people by their patterns of interests rather than by their responses to a single interest.

(2) Toward interpreting results in terms of each segment's profile of answers across all variables rather than examining them one variable at a time. For example, for our purposes, it is more useful to know that a person is generally interested in cultural activities than to know his interest in any single activity.

One last comment on the relationship of our research approach to the three previously mentioned studies is in order. Though the present study develops interests and needs in considerably more detail than the others do, it has in common with them the fact that the measures included are situationally dependent. That is, they were developed for the express purpose of segmenting media audiences based on interests; hence they have a clear-cut contextual relation to that subject matter. In contrast, we could have used much more generalized scales, such as those found in standard personality tests.

Our use of situationally dependent measures is consistent with the general direction taken by proponents of segmentation research in marketing to increase the chances that their findings will be both interpretable and useful in developing effective marketing strategies (Wells, 1974).

Our Own Research and Development Efforts

Two exploratory studies were conducted prior to the project reported in this book. Their purpose was to contribute to developing and evaluating the methodology to be used in the national study.

The first of these was an exploratory study conducted to generate hypotheses as to what needs are important determinants of leisure interests, especially as they relate to television viewing behavior (National Analysts, 1975). For this purpose, sixteen group depth interviews were conducted in varying geographic locations, with six to eight participants in each. The geographic locations were Philadelphia, Chicago, Los Angeles, Nashville, and Wilkes-Barre, Pennsylvania.

The findings of this study helped to identify the needs to be measured and to define the language to be used in asking about them. This preliminary project was completed in April, 1975.

It was followed by a demonstration project in which the survey procedure under consideration at the time was "dry run" on a sample of 1200 respondents. The purpose of this project was twofold:

(1) To check out the technical aspects of the survey, such as the length of the interview, the willingness of respondents to cooperate, and questions about sequence and wording.

(2) To provide actual data, using our intended analytic approach to demonstrate, in considerable detail, the type of results to be expected from a national study. Had it not been for this objective, a considerably smaller sample size would have been adequate.

This latter objective was necessary to address the concerns expressed by members of an advisory committee that reviewed the results of the exploratory study and our proposal for a national survey. Questions arose as to whether leisure interests and associated needs would be related to viewing behavior at all, let alone in a way useful to the television industry. The demonstration project was successfully completed in November, 1976.

The results led to a 50% increase in the number of interests included in the interest battery of the questionnaire and to an extensive revision of the need items as well. The proposed sample size for the national study was cut from 4500 to 2500. In addition, numerous other changes were made in the content and wording of specific questions. In June, 1977, authorization was given for the national study.

PLAN OF THE BOOK

The remaining two chapters of Part One complete the introduction of the study. Chapter 2 includes a description of the questionnaire and the sample design, as well as the procedures used in collecting the data. Chapter 3 reports our findings related to the structure of the interests and needs used as the foundation of subsequent data analyses.

Part Two contains a description of the interest segmentation scheme and associated media behavior. Chapter 4 introduces the interest segments, and Chapter 5 describes their television viewing behavior. Chapter 6 presents the results on magazine readership, and Chapter 7 the results on books, movies, newspapers, and radio.

Part Three reports our findings related to two special topics. The first of these is public television (Chapter 8), while the second is the television viewing context (Chapter 9). This latter chapter presents an analysis of the degree of viewer involvement with television, the extent of viewing alone or with others, and the degree to which members in different segments influence the decision about what to watch.

Part Four contains two chapters. Chapter 10 compares the interest segmentation scheme developed in this book to the more traditional demographic approach. Finally, Chapter 11 contains a discussion of the implications of our work for the mass media and related industries.

NOTES

1. Those interested in a comprehensive review of television literature should see Comstock (1975), Comstock and Fisher (1975), Comstock and Lindsey (1975), and Katz (1977).

2. Chapters 2 and 3 provide a more detailed description of both the sampling procedures used and the types of data collected.

3. This process of segmenting respondents is explained in more detail in Chapter 3.

REFERENCES

BLUMLER, J. G. and E. KATZ (1974) The Uses of Mass Communication. Beverly Hills, CA: Sage.

BOWER, R. T. (1973) Television and the Public. New York: Holt, Rinehart & Winston.

COMSTOCK, G. (1975) Television and Human Behavior: The Key Studies. Santa Monica, CA: Rand Corporation.

――― and M. FISHER (1975) Television and Human Behavior: A Guide to the Pertinent Scientific Literature. Santa Monica, CA: Rand Corporation.

COMSTOCK, G. and G. LINDSEY (1975) Television and Human Behavior: The Research Horizon Present and Future. Santa Monica, CA: Rand Corporation.

FRANK, R. E. and W. F. MASSY (1975) "Noise reduction in segmentation research," in J. U. Farley and J. A. Howard (eds.) Control of "Error" in Market Research Data. Lexington, MA: D. C. Heath.

――― and Y. WIND (1972) Market Segmentation. Englewood Cliffs, NJ: Prentice-Hall.

KAPLAN, M. (1975) Leisure: Theory and Policy. New York: John Wiley.

KATZ, E. (1977) Social Research on Broadcasting: Proposals for Further Development. London: British Broadcasting Corporation.

――― M. GUREVITCH, and H. HAAS (1973) "On the use of mass media for important things." American Sociological Review 38 (April): 164-181.

MENDELSOHN, H. (1966) Mass Entertainment. New Haven, CT: College and University Press.
National Analysts (1975) Toward the Identification of Special Interest Audiences. Philadelphia: Author.
STEINER, G. A. (1963) The People Look at Television. New York: Knopf.
STERLING, C. H. and T. R. HAIGHT (1978) The Mass Media: Aspen Institute Guide to Communication Industry Trends. New York: Praeger.
WELLS, W. D. [ed.] (1974) Life Style and Psychographics. Chicago: American Marketing Association.

2
Strategy and Scope

The data for the study were obtained from a national survey of television households. The primary data base constitutes a national probability sample of individuals age 13 and older within such households.[1] This chapter describes the content of the questionnaire, the sampling plan, and the statistical projection system used to extrapolate the data from the sample to the entire population of persons over age 13 residing in households owning at least one television set.

QUESTIONNAIRE

The interview content is outlined below. A complete copy of it is contained in Appendix A. It was developed over a period of several years, drawn heavily from the qualitative study completed in 1975 and the pilot survey of more than 1200 interviews completed in 1976. In addition, the questionnaire was pretested prior to conducting the field work to ensure adequate communication with both respondents and interviewers.

The following is a brief description of its contents. As the results are reported in subsequent chapters, where necessary, a more detailed description is provided. The major categories of coverage are as follows:

(1) For 139 leisure interests and activities, the degree of interest respondents had as measured by their response to a four-point scale.

(2) For 59 need items satisfied by these leisure interests (e.g., "to kill time," "to feel I am important to other people"), the importance respondents indicated as measured by a four-point scale. The interest and need items are discussed in more detail in the next chapter.

(3) For 150 specific television programs:
   (a) Program-viewing behavior.
   (b) Decision-making behavior: Who made the decision to watch?
   (c) Viewing participation: Who watched?
   (d) Viewing role: Was it important not to miss? Did it serve as a background for doing other things?

(4) Additional TV-related behavior, including typical viewing hours, sources of information about programming, and reasons for viewing.

(5) Public television awareness, attitudes, and viewing behavior.

(6) Ratings of eight new program concepts. These were provided with the generous cooperation of Mr. Leon Rosenbluth of the Corporation for Public Broadcasting. Their role, along with the measurements of actual program-viewing behavior, is to serve as one means of "validating" the interest/need segmentation scheme to be developed.

(7) Media usage for books, magazines, movies, newspapers, and radio.

(8) Television set ownership, commercial and public broadcasting coverage and awareness, as well as demographic and socioeconomic characteristics.

SAMPLE DESIGN

The sample of 2476 respondents was based on an area probability sample drawn to permit the projection of results to the entire population of the coterminous United States age 13 and over living in households with one or more television sets. What follows in this section and Appendix B is a detailed description of the sample's structure and the procedures used for selecting respondents within the structure.

The sampling frame for the sample was National Analysts' national area probability sample composed of a first stage sample of 114 primary sampling units (PSUs). This is a multi-stage, stratified sample of all private households in the 48 coterminous United States. The structure of the sampling frame is described in detail in Appendix B.

Selection of Area Segments

The second stage of the sampling procedure was the systematic selection of area segments within each of the 114 PSUs. A segment is a cluster of housing units, clearly delineated to field interviewers, from which household sampling units are ultimately selected. These segments were selected with probabilities proportional to their population, based upon the 1970 census of housing information. An exhaustive listing of all housing units within each segment was created by the interviewer, and the sampling procedure automatically updated the sample to a current basis, adjusting for changes since 1970.

Segments were selected using probability methods from an array of all census blocks in areas where block information is published by the Bureau of the Census. In all other areas, the segments were selected using probability methods from an array of census enumeration districts.

Altogether, 250 area segments were selected for the survey, with the number in each PSU depending on the probability of selection of these first stage units.

Selection of Dwelling Units

Dwelling units (DUs) were selected within each segment on a probability basis from a listing of all DUs developed by the field staff at the time of interviewing. Sample households were selected in a systematic random manner designed to maximize the distance among selected households within each segment.

A variable sampling rate was employed within each segment depending upon the relative proportions of Black and non-Black households. In order to obtain an adequate sample size of Blacks for data analysis, segments with relatively high incidences of Black households were sampled at a higher rate than those with relatively few Blacks. Similarly, households with children living at home between the ages of 13 and 21 were also oversampled.

Interviewers were provided with explicit instructions on the procedures for household listing within segments, and the designation of sample households was done by National Analysts' sampling statisticians.

Eligibility Requirements

Within a household, the following requirements were established for an individual to be eligible for an interview:

(1) The household must contain one or more television sets.

(2) The respondent must be either the male or female head of household or a child aged 13 to 21 living at home.

While we recognize that large numbers of children under age 13 are in the television audience and that they exert a significant influence on the leisure interests and television viewing behavior of other household members, the verbal skills required to complete an interview precluded the possibility of including younger children in the survey. Their presence in households was recorded, however, and their influence measured indirectly by comparing data from households with and without younger children.

Within this framework, a rather complex probability procedure was employed for the selection of up to four survey respondents in a given household. In a single-person household, that person was the designated respondent. In a household with male and female heads with no children living at home between the ages of 13 and 21, the interviewer was required to complete interviews with both adults. In households with one or more children living at home between the ages of 13 and 21, a maximum of two such children were designated to be interviewed along with the male and female heads. If more than two eligible children resided in a household, a predetermined systematic selection procedure was employed by the interviewer to determine which two children were eligible.

Callbacks

Interviewers were instructed to make up to three callbacks in a designated household to establish appointments with eligible household members. Callbacks were to be made at different times of the day and days of the week in order to maximize the likelihood of completing interviews in the designated households.

Field Interviewing

The interviewing was conducted during the period beginning October 15, 1977, and ending January 7, 1978.

Interviewers were mailed detailed written instructions on sampling procedures and on the administration of the questionnaire itself. The field work was monitored by members of National Analysts' Field Administration Department, who maintained frequent telephone contact with the interviewers and were available to answer questions as they arose in the field. A thorough check-in and edit was performed on each questionnaire upon receipt in Philadelphia, so that errors or ambiguities could be resolved by contacting the interviewer immediately or by having the interviewer recontact the respondent.

Telephone validations were conducted with 15% of respondent households.

Since large portions of the questionnaires were self-enumerative, the primary role of the interviewer was to implement the sampling plan properly, to determine respondent eligibility, to arrange an appointment for all eligible household members to be present at the same time, and to answer respondent questions during the course of completing the questionnaire.

The completion rate for the first stage of interviewing (screening) in the basic probability sample was 56.6%. For the second stage, the completion rate ranged from 69.4% in households where only one respondent was eligible to 46.5% in households with four eligible respondents. A detailed report of results of calls on households is presented in Appendix C. While these completion rates are somewhat lower than we would have liked, it should be noted that the interview was an extremely lengthy one, averaging about ninety minutes, and that much of the field work was conducted during the holiday season between Thanksgiving and New Year's Day. Furthermore, in order to remove as much variation from the data collection process as possible, interviewers were required to conduct their interviews with all eligible members of a household at the same time. If it was not possible to schedule such a time, no one in the household was interviewed.

DATA PREPARATION

Data from acceptable questionnaires were keypunched and subjected to a 100% keypunch verification. A mechanical edit or "cleaning" of the data was then performed to check the internal consistency of each interview, insuring that proper skip codes and contingency patterns were followed and that no inadmissible codes existed on the data tape. Errors were checked against the questionnaires, and the decisions necessary for resolving problems were made by the appropriate project staff members.

SAMPLE WEIGHTING PROCEDURE

An individual respondent weighting model was developed to adjust the data for variability in response rates and for the oversampling of Blacks and of people in households with children between the ages of 13 and 21.

Within each segment, households with completed screening forms were assigned weights to bring the segments into balance with one another. Additional segment weights were developed to adjust for varying completion rates across segments.

From the weighted household screening form data, estimates were developed within each sampling point for the number of households containing one, two, three, and four or more eligible respondents. These estimates were then used to develop weights for households with completed interviews to bring them into balance with the screening form data.

The weighted individual interviews were then tabulated by race, age, and sex to produce a 2 x 7 x 2 table of incidences.

Finally, weights were assigned to all individuals to bring the 28 cells of the race, age, and sex data into balance with 1977 census data obtained from the Current Population Reports.

NOTE

1. In addition to the sample of 2476 interviews taken from 1133 households, a supplementary sample of 276 Hispanic households was completed. This resulted in a total of 345 interviews conducted with Hispanic respondents. The Hispanic "supplementary" sample is not included in the data upon which this book is based, due to lack of certainty about the comparability of the questionnaire content and the sampling procedures used for this group of persons. The questionnaire was translated into Spanish, and hence it is difficult to be sure that the questions contained in it have the same general meaning. In addition, we were forced to use a quota sampling procedure of this segment in several (15) locations in which relatively high concentrations of Hispanics are located, in contrast to the probability sample used for the main sample of 1133 households.

3

Defining Individual Interests and Needs

One purpose of this study is to better understand television behavior by understanding individual interests in activities and subjects, as well as the needs these interests fulfill. Given this purpose, what interests should be measured? Should sports be included? Should homemaking-related activities, such as food preparation or serving? What needs should be measured? Should we include the need to spend time with friends? To kill time? To learn new thoughts or ideas?

Television viewing reflects an extremely flexible means of individual expression. It can help satisfy an almost endless array of needs in relationship to an almost equally endless array of interests. This flexibility presents a difficult problem to those who wish to analyze, in quantitative terms, the interests and needs that affect viewing behavior. Because of the ubiquity of television, one can make an argument for including virtually any interest or need.

The following sections discuss the interests and needs included in the questionnaire, the reasoning that led to their inclusion, and the "summary" measures, based on responses to the aforementioned interest and need questions, that were actually used to study television and other media behavior. Also discussed is the process by which the "summary" measures of

individual interests were used to group individuals into categories (segments) of people with varying patterns of interests.

The segments resulting from this last process are introduced
in Chapter 4, and their television and other media habits are
analyzed in detail in Chapters 5 to 7.

INTERESTS

Measurement Strategy

All the people participating in the study rated their interests
in each of 139 activities and subjects. Though the list is too long
to reproduce at this point, it is contained in Appendix A,
Part 1.

This set of 139 interests covers an extremely broad range of
activities, including:

(1) Active as well as passive—e.g., camping, listening to radio
(2) Individual as well as group—e.g., auto repair, community social
    functions
(3) Home versus nonhome—e.g., meal preparation, fishing
(4) Popular culture as well as high culture—e.g., visiting friends, opera

Also covered are subjects such as politics, human behavior, and
transportation.

In selecting the final set of 139 items from a virtually infinite
number of possibilities, we tried to be comprehensive in our
coverage of content areas that might be related to television
viewing behavior, while at the same time avoiding the level of
specificity and detail that might be more appropriate to defining
a target audience for a particular program. Our objective was to
develop an interest segmentation scheme that would be sufficiently generalizable to be useful in the context of programming
decisions that cut across a wide variety of content areas, including news, sports, science, crime drama, soap operas, and
many others. Given this objective, we felt it necessary to provide a breadth of coverage with a relatively small number of
items representing each content area examined, recognizing that
this would limit our ability to explore any given content area in
depth.

In developing and implementing this strategy, we benefited considerably from previous research in the fields of marketing (Hawes, 1974; Hawes et al., 1974) and leisure (Ritchie, 1975; McKechnie, 1974; Witt, 1971; Bishop, 1970). Each of these investigations included an effort to measure the degree of interest in a number of activities across some sample of respondents and to analyze the resulting data to develop a typology of interests or activities.

In addition to these studies, we did locate one standardized instrument, the Leisure Activities Blank (LAB) designed to measure leisure activities in certain areas (McKechnie, 1975). However, it was restricted to a range of content too narrow for our purposes, excluding such areas as household care, business, and the sciences. Since several of the studies mentioned above did attempt to span a range of interests as broad as those included in the present study, we found them useful as a check against our inadvertently failing to represent a major category of interest or activity in our own battery.

For each of the 139 items, respondents were asked to indicate their degree of interest on the following scale:

1	2	3	4
Not at All Interested	Not Very Interested	Quite Interested	Extremely Interested

Use of Summary Measures

Though the 139 interest ratings provided the interest category coverage that was desired, there nonetheless were two problems regarding their use in the remainder of the analysis. Working with such a large number of questions renders the interpretation of results difficult and the data processing burdensome. In addition, given our purpose of developing a "generalizable" interest segmentation scheme, it seemed more appropriate to work with some reduced set of summary measures.

Principal components analysis was used to define operationally a set of summary measures (called factor scores) for use in the remainder of the study. In effect, this analysis assisted us in measuring simultaneously the actual pattern of answers to our 139 interest questions and in using the results as a basis for combining questions into a set of summary measures. Rather than use our a priori judgment as to what categories to use, we used data taken directly from the respondents.

The principal components analysis used the simple correlations between the answers to every pair of interest questions (there are 9591 such simple correlations given 139 interest measures) to produce a set of "factors" (summary dimensions) and a set of factor scores (summary measures for each respondent on each factor).[1]

Table 3.1(a) illustrates the first of these outputs. It reports the highlights of the factor (summary dimension) we call "Professional Sports." The "loadings" are the simple correlations between each original question and this new factor (dimension). For example, interest in baseball has a simple correlation with this factor of .75, whereas for golf it is only .39. A simple correlation (factor loading) is computed for each of the 139 interest questions in the questionnaire for each factor. We have reported in Table 3.1(a) only those interests with absolute loadings of .35 or greater. This pattern of loadings can be interpreted as saying that this factor, with its associated set of factor scores, measures respondent interest in Professional

TABLE 3.1   Illustrative Interest Factors

		Loadings
(a)	Professional Sports	
	Baseball	.75
	Basketball	.74
	Football	.67
	Boxing	.39
	Golf	.39
	Hockey	.37
(b)	Community Activities	
	Community social functions	.55
	Charities and civic associations	.53
	Local cultural activities	.42
	Community issues	.35

Sports. In contrast, we have interpreted the factor loadings for Table 3.1(b) as reflecting an interest in Community Activities.

Our factor analysis of the 139 interest questions led to the use of 18 factors as the basis for computing summary measures (factor scores) of individual respondent interests.[2] These are summarized in Exhibit 3.1. The detailed tables of factor loadings supporting it are reported in Appendix D.

Exhibit 3.1 lists the labels we have chosen to use for each summary measure in our subsequent analysis, together with an illustrative list of the highest loading interests for each measure. Items 6 and 12, in Exhibit 3.1, correspond to the two summary measures used for illustrative purposes in Table 3.1. The labels on all 18 factors are virtually self-explanatory except for the first—Comprehensive News and Information. That factor had 52 interest items with loadings of .35 or greater. It summarizes a wide variety of seemingly diverse interests. Yet virtually all of these interests appear to be associated with business, personal finance, government, and politics.[3]

The eighteen factors served as the basis for the interest summary measures (factor scores) used in the segmentation analysis to be reported later in this and succeeding chapters.

Exhibit 3.1

Individual Interest Summary Measures

1. *Comprehensive News and Information*
   National economy, unemployment, tax laws, legal process in U.S. courts, state issues, morality in politics, social security system, preventative medicine.

2. *Athletic Activities—Participant*
   Snow skiing, water skiing, tennis, volleyball.

3. *Household Activities and Management*
   Housecleaning, meal preparation, sewing, needlework, household management.

4. *Classical Arts and Cultural Activities*
   Opera, classical music, ballet, live theater, literature, painting.

5. *Reaping Nature's Benefits*
   Fishing, hunting, agriculture and farming, gardening.

Exhibit 3.1 (Continued)

6. *Professional Sports*
   Baseball, basketball, football, boxing, golf, hockey.

7. *Science and Engineering*
   Chemistry, electronics, medical sciences, engineering, geology.

8. *Popular Entertainment*
   Visiting friends, radio, travel/sightseeing, popular music, dining out.

9. *Religion*
   Religious organization activities and religion.

10. *Popular Social Issues*
    Sex education, sexual attitudes and behavior, rights of minority groups, women's rights, the occult.

11. *Indoor Games*
    Board games, crossword/jigsaw puzzles, chess/checkers, playing cards.

12. *Community Activities*
    Community social functions, charities and civic associations, local cultural activities.

13. *Investments*
    Real estate investment, managing a business, stock market.

14. *International Affairs*
    Arms race, balance of trade, conflict in the Middle East.

15. *Camping Out*
    Camping, backpacking, hiking, boating.

16. *Crime and Society*
    Capital punishment of criminals, abortion vs. right to life issue, causes and prevention of crime.

17. *Mechanical Activities*
    Auto repair, auto racing, model building, engineering, electronics.

18. *Contemporary Dancing*
    Modern dance, dancing.

NEEDS

A battery of 59 need questions was constructed to help understand the motivations behind the pursuit of various leisure interests and activities as well as television behavior. The items themselves were drawn from a wide variety of sources, including the earlier group depth interview phase of the present project and selected items from other studies. The battery was modified after the completion of the pilot study to eliminate items that were highly redundant and to include additional items where they appeared necessary to flesh out our understanding of the dynamics of leisure interest patterns.

The earlier study consisted of a series of group depth interviews conducted among individuals with a diversity of age and sex characteristics (National Analysts, 1975). A major purpose of that study was to develop a conceptual framework and a set of working hypotheses for understanding the relationship between patterns of leisure interests, the needs addressed by them, and television behavior. Based on that study, a paradigm was developed that provided guidance in developing the 48 items employed in the pilot study and the 59 items used in the national study reported here. The paradigm is presented in Exhibit 3.2.

The need-satisfaction items were written to ensure that they dealt with knowledge, action, and feelings, as well as:

(1) Basic Maintenance—needs associated with a person's minimum requirements for normal existence. These needs serve to protect one from a state of extreme psychological deprivation or from pronounced psychological stimulation.

(2) Social—needs related to one's interactions with other people.

(3) Self-actualization—needs related to self-development and growth, maturity, and the broadening of one's horizons.

The literature on television, as well as that associated with leisure interests, was of little help in developing the battery of 59 items. The most relevant article was one by Katz et al. (1973) which reported the results of a study on the use of mass media.

Respondents were asked to rate the importance of each of the 59 need items as reasons for their degree of interest in the leisure interests and activities battery they had just completed. Each of the needs was rated on a scale from 1 to 4 as follows:

46

Exhibit 3.2 Need Satisfaction Paradigm

Knowledge Orientation

Basic Maintenance

- Knowing what is going on around me
- Being aware of the many things there are to do and places there are to see

Social

- Understanding why people do things
- Knowing how people different from myself live and think
- Knowing about places and things different from what I am used to
- Being interesting and stimulating to other people

Self-Actualization

- Being exposed to new thoughts and ideas
- Learning how to be more competent. Developing skills and abilities
- Knowing about hings as they really exist
- Understanding myself better

Action Orientation

Basic Maintenance

- Doing things; being active; not being bored

Social

- Helping other people
- Having friends and social interactions
- Matching my mental or physical skills against others

Self-Actualization

- Being creative, doing unique things

Emotion Orientation

Basic Maintenance

- Relaxing and forgetting my problems for awhile
- Feeling good and positive about life in general
- Being entertained, amused
- Being reminded of events and places I enjoyed in the past
- Having intense emotional experiences

Social

- Feeling someting in common with other people
- Imagining being someone else
- Feeling independent, free from the authority of others
- Feeling unique, different from other people

Self-Actualization

- Getting a feeling of accomplishment for doing something
- Having a sense of direction and purpose in life

Source: National Analysts, "Toward the Identification of Special Interest Audiences for Public Television: A Conceptual Framework" (1975: 15).

1	2	3	4
Not at All Important	Not Very Important	Quite Important	Extremely Important

These 59 need items were factor analyzed using the same method as was applied to the interest items. This led to the use of 9 factors as the basis for computing our summary measures.[4] These are summarized in Exhibit 3.3.

Because the labeling of these factors is less straightforward than for the interest factors, a brief discussion of each is provided in the following paragraphs. The detailed tables of factor loadings supporting our interpretations are reported in Appendix E.

(1) *Socially Stimulating.* Persons scoring high on this factor appear to have an above average need to interact with others and to be seen as interesting and stimulating by them. Note that the need expressed here is oriented toward being the kind of person who is stimulating to others rather than toward receiving social stimulation.

(2) *Status Enhancement.* The need expressed in this factor is to gain self-respect and self-confidence by impressing others and influencing them. Presumably those scoring high on this factor pursue their leisure interests and activities with an eye toward how they will be perceived by those people they seek to impress.

(3) *Unique/Creative Accomplishment.* This factor appears to reflect a need to "pull away from the pack" through the achievement of excellence in some domain. The items focus on a need to strengthen one's sense of individuality and identity by engaging in and succeeding in creative activities. This factor differs from the previous one in that the present need satisfaction appears to be dependent less upon the perceptions of others and more upon the individual's feelings about himself.

(4) *Escape from Problems.* This factor is relatively self-explanatory. People scoring high are using their leisure interests and activities to relax and get away from the

Exhibit 3.3

Individual Need Summary Measures

1. *Socially Stimulating*
   To find that my ideas are often shared by others, to be interesting and stimulating to other people, to do things with which I am familiar, to feel good about life in general.

2. *Status Enhancement*
   To impress people, to feel more important than I really am, to have more influence on other people, to be like other people, to compete against others.

3. *Unique/Creative Accomplishment*
   To really excel in some area of my life, to be more of a leader, to feel unique and different from other people, to feel creative.

4. *Escape from Problems*
   To get away from the pressures and responsibilities of my home life, to get away from pressures of work, to relax, to forget my problems for a while.

5. *Family Ties*
   To feel closer to my family, to spend time with my family, to develop strong family ties.

6. *Understanding Others*
   To better understand how other people think, to better understand why people behave the way they do.

7. *Greater Self-Acceptance*
   To lift my spirits, to understand myself better, to overcome loneliness, to feel I am using my time in the best way possible.

8. *Escape from Boredom*
   To be entertained, to kill time, to escape from the reality of everyday life, to experience again events and places I enjoyed in the past.

9. *Intellectual Stimulation and Growth*
   To find out more about how things work, to learn new thoughts and ideas, to learn about new things to do, to learn about new places to see.

stresses and responsibilities of everyday life at home and at work.

(5) *Family Ties.* All of the highest loading items on this factor concern the need for strengthening the bonds with one's family.

(6) *Understanding Others.* People scoring high on this factor appear to be seeking greater insight into the thought processes and the behavior patterns of others, possibly as a vehicle to better self-understanding.

(7) *Greater Self-Acceptance.* The need expressed here seems to be one of mood elevation. High scorers presumably view their leisure interests and activities as a means of lifting their spirits and enhancing their feelings of self-worth and self-acceptance.

(8) *Escape from Boredom.* Unlike Factor 4, the need for escape here focuses on relief from boredom rather than from the problems of work and home life.

(9) *Intellectual Stimulation and Growth.* While this factor has a large number of items with high loadings, it is almost self-explanatory. The pattern clearly reflects the need for continued learning and growth. One gets a sense of intense curiosity and concern for a continuing pattern of self-development among those who score high on this factor.

THE INTEREST SEGMENTATION PROCESS

The objective of the interest segmentation process we used was to classify the 2476 respondents in the sample into subgroups that would be relatively homogeneous with respect to their patterns of leisure interests and activities. This was done using a cluster analysis procedure developed by Howard and Harris (1966).[5]

While this computer program is not well documented at present, it has been used in dozens of segmentation studies. Brief descriptions of it may be found in Green and Carmone (1970) and Howard and Harris (1966).

This procedure starts by splitting the entire sample of 2476 respondents into two mutually exclusive and exhaustive clusters (segments) in a way that makes the patterns of responses to the 18 interest summary measures as different as possible *between* the two groups in relation to the differences among people within the *same* group. The procedure then continues in a similar manner to arrive at three mutually exclusive and exhaustive segments of respondents, and so on, up to the maximum number of groups specified by the user.

The input data for the analysis consisted of the factor scores for each of the 2476 individual respondents in our sample on the 18 interest factors.

We calculated cluster solutions from two to fifteen clusters (segments) and examined the structure of all of these before selecting the fourteen-group solution. The detailed character of the fourteen interest segments is described in Chapter 4. Prior to examining these segments, a brief discussion is in order to describe the thinking that went into the selection of this particular solution and how it relates to our overall conceptualization of the segmentation process.

First, it should be noted that our goal was to develop a segmentation of the television audience in terms of their leisure interests and activities. It was hoped that given such a segmentation system, we would be able to better understand differences among the segments in terms of the needs satisfied by these interests, demographic characteristics, and, most importantly, television viewing and other media behavior. The measure of our success in accomplishing this goal lies in the empirical data to follow.

We were not seeking to *discover* some preexisting number of interest segments in the population with a reality of their own. Rather, we were seeking to *invent* a segmentation structure that would be useful in understanding television audience behavior. Consequently, the decision as to the number of clusters to employ, while based on rational considerations, is almost as much art as science. The computer algorithm can produce optimal two to fifteen group solutions, but it does little to tell us which of these solutions will best serve our needs. Asking how many television audience segments exist is like asking how many regions there are in the United States. Clearly, the answer to both questions depends on the purposes of the segmentation.

We rejected all solutions of size less than ten clusters (the number in the 1976 pilot survey), because with the diversity of the sample in terms of age and sex, we wanted a larger number of segments to ensure that the resultant segments were not overly dominated by simple demographic correlates.

In examining the ten to fourteen cluster solutions, we found an increasing richness of interpretation in terms of interests. We felt that with an average sample size of almost two hundred per segment, we could afford the finer structure offered by the larger number of segments. The final cluster to emerge in the fifteen-group solution was highly resistant to interpretation and did little to clarify the structure of the remaining fourteen clusters, so we decided to use the fourteen-group solution in all subsequent analyses and discussions. And now for the results. . . .

NOTES

1. The 139 x 139 correlation matrix was subjected to a principal components analysis, followed by a varimax rotation of factors having eigenvalues greater than or equal to 1.00. This relatively common data reduction sequence is often referred to in the literature as Kaiser's "Little Jiffy" method (Harman, 1967).

2. The analysis yielded 20 principal components or factors with eigenvalues equal to or greater than one. These accounted for 58% of the variance in the correlation matrix. After examining the total factor structure, we decided to delete the seventeenth and twentiety factors. The former was dropped, because its highest loading items were Golf (.39) and Hockey (.38), and both of these had comparable loadings on the Professional Sports factor. The twentieth factor was basically a one-item factor, Ceramics/Pottery with a loading of .38, and it had a higher loading of .46 on the Household Activities and Management factor.

3. See Appendix D for a complete list of all 52 items.

4. The resulting nine need factors accounted for 55% of the variance in the correlation matrix, and all nine factors with eigenvalues of one or greater were retained for further analysis.

5. The Howard-Harris method is hierarchical and seeks to maximize the ratio of the between cluster variance to the within cluster variance of distances between the objects or people in a Euclidean space. The dimensionality of the space is the number of attributes employed in the input data. The algorithm begins by splitting the population into two mutually exclusive and exhaustive subgroups or clusters, and then shifts individuals from one cluster to the other until the optimal allocation is achieved. A similar procedure is then followed to create the optimal three-cluster solution, and so on, up to the maximum number of clusters specified by the user.

REFERENCES

BISHOP, D. W. (1970) "Stability of the factor structure of leisure research: analyses of four communities." Journal of Leisure Research 2: 160-170.

FRANK, R. E., Y. WIND, and M. G. GREENBERG (1975) "Audience segmentation for public television program development." Report for the John and Mary R. Markle Foundation, July. (unpublished)

GREEN, P. E. and F. J. CARMONE (1970) Multidimensional Scaling and Related Techniques in Marketing Analysis. Boston: Allyn & Bacon.

HARMAN, H. H. (1967) Modern Factor Analysis. Chicago: University of Chicago Press.

HAWES, D. K. (1974) "An exploratory nationwide mail survey of married adult leisure-time behavior patterns and the satisfactions derived from leisure-time pursuits." College of Commerce and Industry Research Report 56, University of Wyoming, Laramie, October.

——— R. D. BLACKWELL, and W. W. TALARZYJ (1974) "Consumer satisfactions from leisure time pursuits." College of Commerce and Industry Research Report 59, University of Wyoming, Laramie, December.

HOWARD, N. and B. HARRIS (1966) A Hierarchical Grouping Routine FORTRAN IV Program. Philadelphia: University of Pennsylvania Computer Center.

KATZ, E., M. GUREVITCH, and H. HAAS (1973) "On the use of mass media for important things." American Sociological Review 38 (April): 164-181.

McKECHNIE, G. E. (1974) "The psychological structure of leisure." Journal of Leisure Research 6 (Winter): 27-45.

——— (1975) Leisure Activities Blank Manual: Research Edition. Palo Alto, CA: Consulting Psychology Press.

National Analysts (1975) "Toward the identification of special interest audiences for public television: a conceptual framework." Report for the John and Mary R. Markle Foundation, April. (unpublished)

RITCHIE, J.R.B. (1975) "On the deprivation of leisure activity types: a perceptual mapping approach." Journal of Leisure Research 7: 128-140.

WITT, P. A. (1971) "Factor structure of leisure behavior for high school age youth in three communities." Journal of Leisure Research 3: 213-219.

Part Two
Interest Segmentation and Media Behavior

4

The Audience Interest Segmentation

INTRODUCTION

This chapter introduces the reader to the interest segments found as a result of the cluster analysis of the interest factor scores described in the concluding pages of the previous chapter. Based on that analysis, the U.S. population has been divided into fourteen interest segments, each of which represents a different type of individual.

The reader will meet fourteen new friends, each of whom has, to some extent, a differentiated set of interests, needs, demographic and socioeconomic characteristics. The introduction to these friends is accomplished in two stages. First, a brief thumbnail sketch of each segment is presented to provide an overview of the people in it. This is followed by a section containing a more detailed analysis of the characteristics of people in each segment. This chapter presents our general conclusions about the segments first, followed by a detailed discussion of the supporting data.

It is especially important for the reader to understand thoroughly the nature of each of the fourteen segments, as subsequent chapters focus on their television viewing and other media behavior.

INTRODUCING
THE INTEREST SEGMENTS

Table 4.1 provides labels for each of the 14 segments, together with data on segment size, and age and sex characteristics. In order to understand the nature of the people in each segment, it is helpful to organize them in terms of their age and sex composition; hence they are classified into four "supra" categories: Adult Male Concentration, Adult Female Concentration, Youth Concentration, and Mixed. First, the supra categories are defined in terms of their age and sex composition, and then the individual segments within them are discussed. Unless indicated to the contrary, the data reported in Table 4.1 and in all subsequent tables in the book, are statistically weighted to represent the U.S. population (48 coterminous states) of persons 13 years of age and older.

The fourteen segments are grouped into these four supra categories as they contain persons who have quite different sex and age characteristics. This is true despite the fact that only interest data were used as the basis for creating the segments.

As shown in Table 4.1, the *Adult Male Concentration* category consists of three segments whose members' average age ranges from 29 to 53 years and who are 77% to 96% male. The four *Adult Female Concentration* segments, in contrast, contain from 69% to 87% female members whose average age ranges from 35 to 61 years. The last supra category in the table, *Mixed,* also consists of four adult segments (average age ranging from 34 to 47 years). However, their sex composition is nowhere near as extremely skewed toward either sex as the other two adult categories. This leaves only one other category in the table, namely the *Youth Concentration.* The average age of its members, ranging from 19 to 22 years, is much younger than those for the other segments. The three segments within the Youth Concentration do, however, differ with respect to their sex composition. One of them is predominantly male (95%), while the other two are predominantly female, 83% and 91%, respectively.

TABLE 4.1   Overview of Fourteen Interest Segments

	Population Percentage	Average Age	Percent of Females in each Segment	Percent of Females in Total Population
	%		%	%
Adult Male Concentration				
Mechanics and Outdoor Life	8%	29 yrs.	4%	1%
Money and Nature's Products	6	53	23	3
Family and Community Centered	6	47	17	2
Adult Female Concentration				
Elderly Concerns	8	61	71	11
Arts and Cultural Activities	9	44	69	11
Home and Community Centered	8	44	84	12
Family Integrated Activities	10	35	87	16
Youth Concentration				
Competitive Sports and Science/Engineering	7	22	5	1
Athletic and Social Activities	4	19	83	7
Indoor Games and Social Activities	4	22	91	7
Mixed				
News and Information	5	47	43	4
Detached	9	46	47	8
Cosmopolitan Self-Enrichment	8	36	59	9
Highly Diversified	8	34	51	8
Entire Population	100%	40 yrs.	52%	100%

SEGMENT SKETCHES

Adult Male Concentration

The three segments in the Adult Male Concentration are labeled Mechanics and Outdoor Life, Money and Nature's Products, and Family and Community Centered. These labels were chosen with the objective of connoting to the reader the general character of the interests and activities of the people who comprise them. The same is true of the labels used for the remaining eleven segments.

People in the Mechanics and Outdoor Life segment tend to be young, adult, blue-collar males whose interests focus on noncompetitive activities emphasizing personal physical accomplishment such as auto repair, fishing, and camping. These are interests which do not place substantial requirements on interpersonal cooperation or support. Interpersonal relations are not a primary component of either their interests or their needs. They score well above average on their needs to escape and for unique, creative accomplishment, and their interests appear to provide a vehicle to satisfy these needs.

The members of the Money and Nature's Products segment are older males with a somewhat above-average representation of rural retirees. Their interests are related to activities providing some form of tangible return or product, such as fishing, hunting, or investments. They are less interested in active, physical activities, such as camping out and professional sports, and in those that are culturally upscale or abstract, such as classical arts and international affairs. These are somewhat complacent people, who nonetheless do feel a need for interpersonal contact and support, especially from their families.

The last segment in the Adult Male Concentration category, the Family and Community Centered segment, consists of people whose interests include many of those of the Money and Nature's Products segment, but incorporate a broader range of activities related to home and community. These people have a much stronger need for family ties than do those in either of the other two segments. They include a mixture of blue-collar and white-collar employees with a relatively large percentage living in nonmetropolitan areas.

Adult Female Concentration

As one would expect, the segments in this category have quite different interest profiles from those just described. There are four segments: Elderly Concerns, Arts and Cultural Activities, Home and Community Centered, and Family Integrated Activities.

The members of the Elderly Concerns segment are older than those in any of the other segments. A much higher proportion are retirees, widowed, and without children. They have relatively few interests. Those areas in which they are interested, namely religion and news and information, appear to help them maintain a sense of social integration and belonging in the absence of very much direct interpersonal contact. Their needs to overcome loneliness and to lift their spirits are quite high. They report relatively little need for creative outlets or for intellectual stimulation.

In sharp contrast are the people comprising the Arts and Cultural Activities segment. They are for the most part highly educated women, who either are themselves or are married to a household head who is a manager or professional. They are interested in a broad range of intellectually upscale activities and subjects, especially the classical arts. They have little need to escape, nor are they particularly concerned with improving their peer group status. They do report strong needs for intellectual stimulation and growth and for understanding others.

As the title suggests, people in the Home and Community Centered segment tend to be married, adult female homemakers. Their interests are associated almost exclusively with home and community activities. Their greatest needs are for maintaining family ties and being socially stimulating. They report relatively low needs for creative accomplishment or for intellectual stimulation.

The last of the four Adult Female Concentration segments is called Family Integrated Activities. This segment has the highest proportion of adult women with young children. They are interested in a broad range of home and family activities (e.g., indoor games, as well as home maintenance). In their homes, the presence of young children appears to have an important influence on adult interests. People in this segment score high on the need for maintaining family ties.

It is important to note that while these segments contain a substantial majority of females, they are far from the only segments in which women are found. In fact, only half the women in the total population fall into these four segments. Fully 29% of all women are in the Mixed category, with the remainder in the Youth segments (15%) and in the Adult Male segments (7%).

Males and teenagers also are quite dispersed across the four-teen segments. At this stage of our discussion, it is important to note these findings. A potential misinterpretation is to assume that all women fall in the Adult Female Concentration. They do not. We are not suggesting that all women can be put into four segments and are like all other women when it comes to their interests. Nor can all men be placed in three categories with only other men. On the contrary, the interests of males and females of all ages tend to be overlapping, and hence members of any major demographic group are found in virtually every one of the fourteen interest segments.

What are the implications of this? Though there is an association between these demographic characteristics and segment membership, it is a far from perfect relationship. The interest segmentation complements the demographic segmentation scheme traditionally used for studying audiences for television and other media. In Chapter 10, a comparison of these two segmentation schemes is presented.

Youth Concentration

The three segments in this category are labeled: Competitive Sports and Science/Engineering, Athletic and Social Activities, and Indoor Games and Social Activities. The first of these three consists primarily of teenage males, while the latter two are comprised principally of teenage females.

Members of the Competitive Sports and Science/Engineering segment are interested in mechanical activities such as auto repair, as well as in competitive sports, both participant and professional. They score quite high on the need to escape from boredom and relatively low on the needs for understanding others and achieving greater self-acceptance.

The teenage females in the Athletic and Social Activities segment are from high-income families. Their interests are or-iented toward active, away-from-home activities such as parti-cipant athletics and popular entertainment. They have above-average needs to be socially stimulating and the highest need to escape from problems, along with the lowest need for family ties.

In contrast, the females in the Indoor Games and Social Activities segment come from lower-income families. Somewhat older than those in the previous segment, their interests and needs are more home and family related, as they have "cut the apron strings" and are in the process of establishing their own households. They report a high need for status enhancement, but are quite low in their need for unique/creative accomplishments.

Mixed

Each of the four segments in this category is comprised of a more balanced mixture of male and female adults. The segments are labeled: News and Information, Detached, Cosmopolitan Self-Enrichment, and Highly Diversified.

News and Information segment members tend to be physically passive adults whose interests center around the collection and dissemination of information on a wide range of subjects and issues. Their needs are focused on family ties and on being socially stimulating.

The Detached segment members are characterized by their extremely low levels of interest across each of the eighteen interest factors. These people have a downscale socioeconomic profile. They score relatively low on all of the need factors as well. The leisure interests and activities studied in this project are probably of little relevance in their struggle for economic and social survival.

In contrast, people in the Cosmopolitan Self-Enrichment segment are upscale in their demographic and socioeconomic characteristics. They report broad interests spanning intellectual and cultural activities and subjects, and they are physically active. They are high on the needs for intellectual stimulation, unique/creative accomplishment, and for understanding others. They are especially low in their needs for status enhancement and for escape from boredom.

The last of the fourteen segments is entitled Highly Diversified. Members of this segment are disproportionately Southern, black adults in homes with children. They report very broad interests, especially relating to activities involving personal participation with family and other informal small group settings. Their strongest need appears to be for intellectual stimulation and growth.

This is the reader's initial introduction to each of these fourteen friends. Some of them should be recognizable in that they represent one way of characterizing the American population of which almost every reader is a member and an observer.

In the following section, these segments are discussed once again. This time, however, the discussion of the interests, needs, and demographic and socioeconomic characteristics of their members is more detailed in an effort to develop an in-depth profile of each of them.

THE INTEREST SEGMENTS IN DETAIL

In the following discussion, a detailed description of the membership of each segment is reported. The data upon which this section is based are contained in Tables 4.2 to 4.5, which report for each interest segment the interest factor scores and the need factor scores along with demographic and socioeconomic characteristics. The discussion centers on the *membership of each segment,* not on *individual variables* such as income. Our purpose is to paint fourteen portraits, in words and numbers. This is quite different from focusing on variables one at a time, for the purpose of evaluating their relationship to interests. The emphasis is on the description of people, not variables.[1] Hence, the discussion of each segment covers the relevant data from all of the tables at once.

In the discussion, we have chosen to deemphasize the citing of specific tables and values within them. The tables, however, have been retained in the body of the text, so that the reader who wishes to check our reasoning or to determine the specific numerical values that serve as the basis for statements may do so with relative ease.

Each of the measures for which findings are reported in Tables 4.2 to 4.5 have been subjected to statistical testing (using the univariate F-ratio) to determine the likelihood that the overall variation in scores across all fourteen segments is due to chance fluctuations. With only one exception, all of the F-ratios

TABLE 4.2 Average Interest Factor Scores by Interest Segment[a]

	Entire Population	Adult Male Concentration				Adult Female Concentration			Youth Concentration					Mixed	
		Mechanics and Outdoor Life	Money and Nature's Products	Family and Community Centered	Elderly Concerns	Cultural Activities and Arts	Home and Community Centered	Family Integrated Activities	Competitive Sports and Science/Engineering	Athletic and Social Activities	Indoor Games and Social Activities	News and Information	Detached	Cosmopolitan Self-Enrichment	Highly Diversified
Comprehensive News/Information	.09	.04	.35	.25	.43	.48	-.60	-.27	-.30	-.38	-.30	1.20	-1.22	.53	.42
Athletic Activities-Participant	-.02	-.02	-.46	-.29	-.72	-.42	-.54	.07	.90	1.44	.55	-.71	-.42	.34	.76
Household Activities and Management	-.00	-.57	-.54	-.61	.18	-.23	.94	.92	-.65	-.25	.04	-.12	-.21	-.19	.61
Classical Arts	.11	-.39	-.38	-.34	-.16	1.96	-.03	-.30	-.38	-.12	.17	-.60	-.16	1.30	.39
Reaping Nature's Benefits	-.00	.40	1.04	.82	-.20	-.38	-.26	-.12	-.41	-.20	-.38	-.35	-.30	-.11	.40
Professional Sports	-.07	-.58	-.01	.30	-.49	.10	.13	-.40	.78	-.30	-.24	-.19	-.19	-.41	.07
Science and Engineering	-.05	-.14	-.29	.02	-.72	-.14	.22	-.59	.48	-.28	.25	.56	.09	-.09	-.37
Popular Entertainment	.00	.32	.10	-.64	-.27	.08	.81	.13	.44	.61	.55	.29	-1.32	-.04	-.34
Religion	-.15	-.63	-.26	.46	.52	.21	.02	-.46	-.36	.00	.46	-.29	-.26	-1.14	-.07
Popular Social Issues	-.07	-.28	-.27	.00	-.78	-.06	-.29	.15	-.30	.56	-.14	.10	-.18	.41	.37
Indoor Games	-.01	-.17	-.38	-.04	-.17	.23	-.49	.92	.25	-.85	1.09	-.24	-.15	-.68	.31
Community Activities	-.05	-.17	-.17	.31	-.44	-.27	.38	-.03	-.25	-.01	-.66	.00	.11	.09	-.18
Investments	.02	.10	.86	.43	-1.25	.41	.29	.39	-.15	-.70	-.03	-.06	.05	-.30	-.05
International Affairs	.04	.37	-.47	.05	-.42	.39	-.52	.06	.03	-.39	-.23	1.09	.29	.01	-.08
Camping Out	.03	.51	-.27	.42	-.49	-.12	.01	.39	-.16	.06	.67	-.12	-.26	.95	.98
Crime and Society	.01	-.01	-.93	.70	-.37	.20	.33	.43	-.02	.54	-.37	.06	-.26	-.20	.07
Mechanical Activities	-.01	1.34	-.38	-.02	-.16	-.18	-.20	-.20	.63	-.58	-.89	-.44	-.17	-.38	-.78
Contemporary Dancing	-.09	.27	-.17	-.52	-.42	-.18	-.24	-.25	-.99	.41	.74	.49	.25	-.37	.32

a. The statistical significance of each of the 18 interest factors contained in this table was evaluated based on univariate F-ratios with 13 and 2,462 degrees of freedom. All 18 ratios were significant at the .005 level or better.

b. Average factor scores for entire sample based on unweighted data are zero by definition. However, reweighting of sample to population results in nonzero values reported in this column.

63

TABLE 4.3 Average Need Factor Scores by Interest Segment[a]

	Entire Population[b]	Adult Male Concentration				Adult Female Concentration			Youth Concentration				Mixed		
		Mechanics and Outdoor Life	Money and Nature's Products	Family and Community Centered	Elderly Concerns	Arts and Cultural Activities	Home and Community Centered	Family Integrated Activities	Competitive Sports and Science/Engineering	Athletic and Social Activities	Indoor Games and Social Activities	News and Information	Detached	Cosmopolitan Self-Enrichment	Highly Diversified
Socially Stimulating	-.01	-.06	.20	-.14	.26	-.00	.17	-.04	-.10	.33	.22	.29	-.73	-.18	.05
Status Enhancement	-.10	.01	.11	.07	-.25	-.50	-.12	-.38	.21	.13	.34	-.11	.04	-.70	-.24
Unique/Creative Accomplishment	.01	.34	-.12	.13	-.57	-.03	-.25	.05	.33	.28	-.30	-.04	-.37	.45	-.22
Escape from Problems	-.01	.21	-.20	-.16	.10	-.29	-.13	.09	.00	.50	.10	-.19	-.09	.10	-.05
Family Ties	.02	-.11	.19	.48	-.11	-.04	.17	.38	-.06	-.52	-.10	.34	-.37	-.25	-.08
Understanding Others	.01	-.28	-.08	.04	.17	.42	.12	.10	-.68	.01	-.26	.08	-.09	.21	-.14
Greater Self-Acceptance	-.02	-.27	-.31	-.11	.22	.17	.11	.17	-.31	.11	.17	.18	-.43	.00	.12
Escape from Boredom	-.04	.22	-.11	-.21	.05	-.18	.02	-.11	.18	-.05	.14	.12	-.00	-.53	-.07
Intellectual Stimulation and Growth	.02	.07	-.08	-.10	-.58	.33	-.16	.01	.21	.16	.11	.16	-.77	.70	.35

a. The statistical significance of each of the nine need factors in this table was evaluated based on univariate F-ratios with 13 and 2,462 degrees of freedom. All nine ratios were significant at the .005 level or better.

b. Average factor scores for entire sample based on unweighted data are zero by definition. However, reweighting of sample for projection to population results in nonzero values reported in this column.

TABLE 4.4 Demographic Characteristics by Interest Segment[a]

	Entire Population	Adult Male Concentration				Adult Female Concentration			Youth Concentration				Mixed		
		Mechanics and Outdoor Life	Money and Nature's Products	Family and Community Centered	Elderly Concerns	Arts and Cultural Activities	Home and Community Centered	Family Integrated Activities	Competitive Sports and Science/Engineering	Athletic and Social Activities	Indoor Games and Social Activities	News and Information	Detached	Cosmopolitan Self-Enrichment	Highly Diversified
Sex (percent female)	52	4	23	17	71	69	84	87	5	83	91	43	47	59	51
Age (years)	40	29	53	47	61	44	44	35	22	19	22	47	46	36	34
Marital Status (percent)[b]															
Married	64	60	82	92	56	79	71	81	29	13	29	75	60	72	61
Widowed	8	0	10	2	35	10	10	3	1	0	3	10	15	3	6
Adults in Segment with Children															
Percent	46	37	41	64	18	52	54	75	21	14	37	41	48	51	56
Children's age (years)	11	11	13	12	12	12	11	9	13	14	12	10	10	10	10
Race (percent)[c]															
Black	11	2	7	6	12	10	12	4	8	4	21	13	19	2	33
Spanish	4	0	1	0	3	4	3	4	3	6	12	2	5	8	7
White	83	93	92	93	83	86	84	91	86	87	66	85	74	86	56
Urban/Non-urban (percent)															
Central City	25	20	12	15	23	24	20	22	23	27	30	24	41	33	25
Suburb	41	38	35	39	30	49	48	49	51	43	36	40	36	45	33
Non-Metro	34	42	53	46	47	27	32	29	26	30	34	36	23	22	42
Region (percent)															
Northeast	24	20	25	13	21	31	21	31	38	22	17	24	29	27	15
Central	24	25	18	23	25	19	25	34	19	31	26	29	26	21	19
South	35	40	41	44	40	26	33	27	27	29	34	40	38	23	49
West	17	15	16	21	14	24	21	9	16	17	23	7	8	29	18

a. The statistical significance of each of the demographic variables in this table was evaluated based on univariate F-ratios with 13 and 2,462 degrees of freedom. All but one, the Central region, were statistically significant at the .005 level or better.
b. Does not add to 100% due to omission of single, divorced, and separated.
c. Does not add to 100% due to omission of American Indian and other categories.

TABLE 4.5 Socioeconomic Characteristics by Interest Segment[a]

	Entire Population	Adult Male Concentration				Adult Female Concentration			Youth Concentration				Mixed		
		Mechanics and Outdoor Life	Money and Nature's Products	Family and Community Centered	Elderly Concerns	Arts and Cultural Activities	Home and Community Centered	Family Integrated Activities	Competitive Sports and Science/Engineering	Athletic and Social Activities	Indoor Games and Social Activities	News and Information	Detached	Cosmopolitan Self-Enrichment	Highly Diversified
Income ($000)	14.2	14.9	14.6	14.2	6.9	16.6	14.3	16.1	16.6	16.8	11.7	14.3	10.6	18.8	12.7
Employment Status (percent)[b]															
Full-time	40	64	41	63	17	46	25	36	31	25	17	48	39	45	52
Retired	15	4	39	23	40	17	18	5	3	0	0	23	22	3	3
Occupation (percent)															
Blue Collar	25	55	36	43	36	11	13	17	19	7	4	32	35	10	30
White Collar	21	8	13	17	21	31	29	31	5	23	18	32	16	25	20
Managerial/Professional	20	20	35	33	6	34	18	12	12	5	4	24	12	38	15
Homemaker	19	1	10	7	34	17	35	34	0	6	25	10	18	18	21
Student	15	17	4	4	3	8	4	5	63	60	49	2	10	8	14
Education (percent)															
Grammar School	12	8	21	13	31	1	14	4	16	6	18	5	26	1	8
High School	55	63	44	48	60	30	62	68	66	74	67	58	50	34	62
College	33	29	35	39	9	69	24	28	18	20	15	37	24	65	30

a. The statistical significance of each of the socioeconomic variables in this table was evaluated based on univariate F-ratios with 13 and 2,462 degrees of freedom. All were significant at the .005 level or better.
b. Does not add up to 100% due to omission of part-time, temporary, unemployed, armed forces, students, and homemakers.

for all of the variables in all four tables are significant at the .01 level (i.e., if there were, in fact, no differences, there is less than one chance in one hundred that segment differences as large as we found would have occurred by chance). Most of the differences are significant at the .005 level (i.e., fewer than five chances in one thousand). These results for needs, Table 4.3, and for demographic and socioeconomic characteristics, Tables 4.4 and 4.5 respectively, serve to provide confirmation that the general pattern of differences across segments is "real" and not simply the result of chance.

However, the F-ratios for Table 4.2 need to be taken "with a grain of salt." They are, at best, just one more set of descriptive statistics and are not legitimate statistical tests. The segments were originally formed via cluster analysis based on precisely the same interest measures evaluated by the F-ratios. Hence, the observed differences in interests across the fourteen segments are, by definition, not due to chance.[2] The needs data and the demographic and socioeconomic measures were not used as part of the input to the cluster analysis, however, and so the F-ratios are independent of the method for creating the segmentation scheme.

Adult Male Concentration

The three segments in this category are named:

- Mechanics and Outdoor Life
- Money and Nature's Products
- Family and Community Centered

Though all three are comprised predominantly of adult males, their patterns of interests, needs, and demographic characteristics diverge considerably. For purposes of brevity, section titles in this chapter covering both demographic and socioeconomic results will be labeled "Demographics."

MECHANICS AND OUTDOOR LIFE

Young adult, blue-collar males whose interests focus on noncompetitive activities emphasizing personal physical accomplishment—e.g., auto repair, fishing, camping—interests which, by their very nature, do not require emphasis on interpersonal cooperation or support. High on needs for escape and unique/creative accomplishment.

Interests. People in this segment score higher than those in any other on their interest in Mechanical Activities, and lower than any other on their interest in Professional Sports. This latter finding is especially surprising in that it conflicts with the usual association of males with athletic interests. These individuals are also well above average on their interest scores on the factors of Reaping Nature's Benefits and Camping Out.

Virtually all of the interests that load highly on the Reaping Nature's Benefits, Camping Out, and Mechanical Activities factors emphasize physical accomplishment in a noncompetitive mode. Such activities include fishing, camping, and auto repair.

Though their interest in competition as modeled by professional sports is low, they show considerable interest in competitive forces in the international arena. Their interest score on International Affairs is well above average. All of the items that load highly on this factor relate to military, economic, and political competition, namely the arms race, the balance of trade, and conflict in the Middle East.

Needs. The members of this segment score well above average on their needs to Escape from Boredom and Problems, as well as on their need for Unique/Creative Accomplishment. At the opposite extreme, they score quite low on the needs for Understanding Others and for Greater Self-Acceptance.

In general, their pattern of needs appears nonintrospective, and relatively individualistic (i.e., few needs are tied to relationships with other people).

Demographics. A full 96% of this segment's members are male. They have an average age of 29, and, as such, they are the youngest of the adult segments. They are more apt to be employed full-time than the average for the population (64% versus 40%) and are more apt to be blue-collar workers (55% versus 25%). In addition, they are much more likely than the other two adult male segments to have completed at least some high school, but less likely to have attended college.

MONEY AND NATURE'S PRODUCTS

Older males with a higher proportion being rural and retired. Interests in passive activities that obtain some form of tangible return or product—fishing, hunting, investments. Low interest in active physical activities—camping out, participant sports—as well as culturally upscale or abstract—classical arts, international affairs. Somewhat complacent, but need interpersonal contact and support, especially from their families.

Interests. Fourteen of the eighteen interest factor scores for people in this segment are below the average for the total population. Members of only two other segments, the Elderly Concerns and Detached segments, have as many interest scores below average.

Of the four interest factors ranked above average for this segment (Comprehensive News and Information, Reaping Nature's Benefits, Popular Entertainment, and Investments), two factors, Reaping Nature's Benefits and Investments, are especially high for this group. The one element these interests appear to have in common is that both involve a seeking of some tangible return for one's efforts.

In general, the interests of this segment reflect relatively low levels of physical activity. On those interest factors involving personal participation in relatively more strenuous activities, such as participating in athletics, camping out, mechanics, and dancing, the members of this segment score well below the average for the total population.

They are also below average on their interest in Classical Arts as well as some of the other more abstract intellectual content areas, such as Science/Engineering, International Affairs, and Crime and Society.

Needs. The need factors on which they are highest are those associated with social interaction and support, in both family and nonfamily contexts, namely Family Ties, Socially Stimulating, and Status Enhancement. On the other hand, they score well below average on Escape from Problems and Greater Self-Acceptance. These seem to be people whose needs are directed toward maintaining interpersonal contact and support, but who at the same time are relatively satisfied with themselves and their rather narrow span of interests and activities.

Demographics. The only segment with a higher average age than this one (53 years) is the Elderly Concerns segment, whose members average 61 years. Compared with the other adult segments, they are more likely to be married and to live in suburban or rural areas. They are below average in education, but not in household income, despite the fact that a relatively large number are retired.

Their age, education, residence, and retirement characteristics are quite consistent with their interests and needs. The one surprising finding concerns their disproportionate participation in both blue-collar and managerial or professional occupations. The interests and needs common to members of this segment are readily accessible to its dominantly male constituents, irrespective of the character of their occupational activities, income, and other socioeconomic characteristics.

FAMILY AND COMMUNITY CENTERED

Employed, blue-collar/white-collar adult males. Married, living in nonmetropolitan areas. Broad interests, including outdoor activities, investments, and home and community centered activities as well as religion. Very strong need for family ties.

Interests. The members of this segment have broad interests relative to the others; they score above average on ten of the eighteen interest factors. This is matched by only one other group, namely the Highly Diversified segment.

The seven interest factors on which these people score the highest are Camping Out, Crime and Society, Reaping Nature's Benefits, Religion, Community Activities, Investments, and Professional Sports. In addition, compared to the members of the other two predominantly adult male segments, they have relatively high scores on Indoor Games, Popular Social Issues, and the Science and Engineering factors.

Their high scores on Reaping Nature's Benefits and Investments constitute a level of interest similar to members of the Money and Nature's Products segment. However, their interests transcend those of the latter segment in being much broader.

One gets the impression that the Family and Community Centered people attempt to integrate successfully a diverse set of interests and activities with their home life. In contrast, the members of the Money and Nature's Products segment limit themselves to just a few interests that can be pursued on a more individualistic basis.

Needs. It is not surprising that the people in this segment score higher than any other on the need for Family Ties. Their lowest need scores are with respect to Escape from Problems and Boredom.

Demographics. As reflected in their family orientation, the adults in this segment are more apt to have children than those in the population as a whole (64% versus 46%). Only one other segment has a higher proportion of adults with children; that is the Family Integrated Activities segment (75%).

Family and Community Centered segment members are better educated than most, and almost two-thirds are employed (64%). As many as 92% are married, and 46% live in nonmetropolitan areas. Both these figures are well above average for the population.

Adult Female Concentration

The four predominantly female segments are:

- Elderly Concerns
- Arts and Cultural Activities
- Home and Community Centered
- Family Integrated Activities

The percentage of females in these segments ranges from 69% to 87%.

ELDERLY CONCERNS

Oldest segment, high percentage of retirees, widowed, few children. Very few interests include religion and news and information. Focus on maintaining sense of social integration and belonging in absence of direct interpersonal contact. Needs to overcome loneliness and lift spirits. Low need for intellectual stimulation.

Interests. The most striking characteristic of the members of the Elderly Concerns segment is that they are below the population average for fifteen of the eighteen interest factors. They are, however, higher than the members of any other segment on one interest factor, Religion. On one other, News and Information, they are the second highest segment. The only other interest factor on which they have an above-average score is Household Activities and Management.

Needs. The members of this segment rank higher than any other on the need for Greater Self-Acceptance factor. This factor includes items involving overcoming loneliness and the need to lift one's spirits. They also score above average on the need to be Socially Stimulating. Also notable are the extremely low scores on the needs for Unique/Creative Accomplishment and for Intellectual Stimulation and Growth.

In other words, these people are struggling with the normal problems of aging. Unlike some, who are able to take advantage of the freedoms offered by diminished work and family responsibilities by broadening their horizons, the members of this segment appear to be somewhat passive in accepting and adjusting to a more circumscribed lifestyle as they turn their world inward upon themselves.

Demographics. People in this segment average 61 years of age. They include, by far, the highest percentage of retirees, 40% versus 15% for the population as a whole. Fully 35% of them are widowed. Only 18% are adults with children remaining at home. Slightly fewer than one-third (31%) have no more than a grammar school education.

ARTS AND CULTURAL ACTIVITIES

> Highly educated, adult women in households with manager or professional as head. Broad range of intellectual and cultural interests—especially classical arts. Low interest in household activities and management. High needs for intellectual stimulation and growth and for understanding others, with low needs for status enhancement or escape.

Interests. The members of this segment rank considerably higher than any other on the Classical Arts factor. They report a broad range of interests, scoring above average on thirteen of the eighteen interest factors, including interest scores which place them among the top three segments for Investments, International Affairs, and Comprehensive News and Information. They are well below average in their interest scores in Participant Athletic Activities, Community Activities, Reaping Nature's Benefits, and they report by far the lowest interest level in Household Activities and Management of the four adult female segments.

Needs. These people are below average on their need scores for Status Enhancement, Escape from Problems, and Escape from Boredom. In contrast, they rank higher than any other segment on the need to Understand Others, and they are among the three highest segments in their need for Intellectual Stimulation and Growth.

Demographics. The pattern of their demographic characteristics is quite consistent with that of their interests and needs. A full 69% of them have at least some college education, as compared to 33% for the population, and 65% of those employed are either managers, professionals, or white-collar workers. They are overrepresented in the Northeast and West and underrepresented in the Central and Southern regions of the country. They also tend more than the rest of the population to live in suburban areas and are less often found in nonmetropolitan areas.

A large percentage, 79%, are married, compared to 64% for the population as a whole.

HOME AND COMMUNITY CENTERED

Adult females with a relatively high percentage of married home-makers. Home and local community interests. Highest needs for family ties and understanding others. Lowest needs for intellectual stimulation and for unique/creative accomplishment.

Interests. People in this segment rank higher than those in any other on three interest factors, Household Activities, Popular Entertainment, and Community Activities. The activities associated with the Popular Entertainment factor, such as visiting friends, radio, travel/sightseeing, popular music, dining out, and movies, are in marked contrast to those "entertainment activities" associated with the Classical Arts factor, which include opera, classical music, ballet, and live theater.

The Home and Community Centered segment members are well below average on their interest scores for International Affairs, Comprehensive News and Information, Participant Athletic Activities, Indoor Games, and Popular Social Issues. With respect to all of these interests, they score among the lowest three segments.

Needs. None of their need scores are extremely high or low in relation to the other segments. Nonetheless, their highest and lowest need scores are consistent with their interests. The highest two scores for people in this segment are for the need for Family Ties and the need to be Socially Stimulating. Their lowest scores are for Unique/Creative Accomplishment and for Intellectual Stimulation and Growth.

This segment appears to comprise primarily women, who even in today's changing world are filling the role of homemaker in a rather narrow, traditional manner.

Demographics. A below-average percentage of the members of this segment are employed full-time (25% versus 40% for the population). A full 35% of the members of this segment are homemakers compared to the 19% average across all groups. With these exceptions, none of their demographics tend to distinguish them clearly from the other predominantly adult female segments.

FAMILY INTEGRATED ACTIVITIES

> High percentage of adult women with young children. Strong interest in home and in family interactive activities—household activities and management and indoor games. High need for family ties. Child presence influences adult interest patterns.

Interests. As with the Home and Community Centered segment, the members of this segment are also well above average on their interest score for Household Activities. However, the interests of this segment's members are somewhat broader. They are also well above average with respect to their scores on Investments, Camping Out, and Crime and Society. In addition, they exhibit a much stronger interest in Comprehensive News and Information, but a lesser interest in Professional Sports and in Science and Engineering. The Family Integrated Activities segment members are sharply differentiated from the Home and Community Centered segment by the former's strong interest in Indoor Games.

Needs. People in this segment are well above average on their need score for Family Ties and well below average on their need score for Status Enhancement.

Demographics. Of the persons belonging to this segment, 87% are women. The only other predominantly adult female segment with anywhere near this proportion of female members is the Home and Community Centered segment, which consists of 84% women. Of the adults in this segment, 75% have children, by far the largest percentage of any of the segments. Their average age is 35, the youngest of the adult female groups. Their children are also on average younger (9 years of age) than those of any other segment. Members of this segment are disproportionately white and tend to reside in suburban areas (49% versus 41% for the entire sample) and in the central United States (34% versus 24%).

Youth Concentration

The three segments in this category are labeled as follows:

- Competitive Sports and Science/Engineering
- Athletic and Social Activities
- Indoor Games and Social Activities

Members range in age from an average of 19 to 22 years. The first of them is 95% male, while the latter two are 83% and 91% female respectively.

COMPETITIVE SPORTS AND SCIENCE/ENGINEERING

Teenage male students with interests in male-associated mechanical activities and competitive athletics. Avoidance of female-oriented subjects and interests. High on needs for unique/creative accomplishment, intellectual stimulation and growth, status enhancement, and escape from boredom. Low needs for understanding others and for greater self-acceptance.

Interests. There are four interest factors on which this segment's members are among the top two in the study. They are Professional Sports, Participant Athletic Activities, Science and Engineering, and Mechanical Activities. At the opposite extreme, there are five interest factors on which they rank among the bottom two: Household Activities, Classical Arts, Reaping

Nature's Benefits, Popular Social Issues, and Contemporary Dancing.

The people in this segment are attracted by interests involving traditional male-related, competitive interactions and those associated with competence in mechanical or technological areas. They have little interest in activities or subjects that tend to be associated with female roles, such as Household Activities and Contemporary Dancing. They also exhibit low levels of interest in current events, as evidenced by their low scores on Comprehensive News and Information and on Popular Social Issues. In addition, they are also less attracted to more abstract subject matters, such as the Classical Arts.

Needs. The need scores for people in this segment are above average for Status Enhancement, Unique/Creative Accomplishment, Intellectual Stimulation and Growth, and Escape from Boredom. They are among the bottom two segments on the Understanding Others and Greater Self-Acceptance factors.

In general, the segment is comprised of adolescent boys whose interest patterns appear to be rather narrow and recreational. They have not yet begun to expand their horizons toward more abstract, intellectually oriented content areas. Their pattern of needs reflects the adolescent struggle for identity as they prepare to move into the world of adults.

Demographics. Consistent with their interests and needs, the members of this segment are 95% male with an average age of 22. This segment has the largest proportion of students (63%). They disproportionately reside in the suburbs and in the Northeast.

ATHLETIC AND SOCIAL ACTIVITIES

Teenage females from high-income families. The youngest of all the segments. Interests in active, away-from-home, face-to-face activities. High need to escape from problems and to be socially stimulating. Low need for family ties.

Interests. There are five interest factors on which this segment is well above average: Participant Athletic Activities, Popular Entertainment, Contemporary Dancing, Popular Social Issues, and Crime and Society. It is our hypothesis that the common denominator of these interests and subjects, especially the first three, is that they involve active, face-to-face interaction, in nonhome settings. The latter two represent subject matter that may provide the basis for interpersonal conversation among peers.

Interests such as Indoor Games, which tend to be home-based vehicles for face-to-face interaction, score well below average. Persons in this segment rank lowest on this interest score.

Interests which extend beyond members' immediate sphere of influence, such as Comprehensive News and Information, Investments, and International Affairs receive interest scores well below average.

Needs. The importance of peer group relationships to the members of this segment is further signaled by their scores on the need to be Socially Stimulating, on which they have higher scores than any other segment, and on the Status Enhancement factor, where their score is above average, ranking third.

The away-from-home orientation of their interests is consistent with the fact that their need score for Family Ties is lower than that for any other segment, and their score on the need to Escape from Problems is higher than that for any other segment. The highest loading item on this latter factor was: "To get away from the pressures and responsibilities of my home life."

This segment consists primarily of active adolescent girls, who appear to be breaking away from the pressures of home and family and who are channeling their energy into physical and social activities with their peers.

Demographics. This segment is 83% female. Besides their average age (19 years) and related characteristics, the only other demographic or socioeconomic characteristic that sharply differentiates members of this segment is the average family income of the households to which its members belong. This is $16,800, compared to $14,200 for the entire sample, ranking the members of this segment among the top two segments.

INDOOR GAMES AND SOCIAL ACTIVITIES

Young, low-income females. Interests in activities, especially indoor games. Low interest in most subject matter areas. Nonintellectual.

High needs for status enhancement and the need to be socially
stimulating.

Interests. The members of this segment share with those in
the Athletic and Social Activities segment high interests in
Popular Entertainment and Contemporary Dancing, with low
interest in Mechanical Activities.

The single interest factor that most sharply differentiates
people in this segment from those in the Athletic and Social
Activities segment is Indoor Games. The members of this segment have the highest score of any segment on this factor, while
those in the Athletic and Social Activities segment have the
lowest. The next most important interest factor differentiating
them is Participant Athletic Activities, on which they score
much lower than the other segment. This segment has no high
interest scores on any of the factors that emphasize intellectual
content, although they exhibit by far the highest interest in
Religion among the youth groups.

Needs. Like the Athletic and Social Activities segment, this
group scores high on the need for Status Enhancement and the
need to be Socially Stimulating. The Indoor Games and Social
Activities segment, however, is distinguished by much lower
needs for Unique/Creative Accomplishment and for Understanding Others. The latter group has a below-average need for
Family Ties, but not nearly so much as the former group.

Demographics. This segment's members are young (average
age 22) and primarily female (91%). Their lack of an away-
from-home orientation is, at least in part, due to the fact that
37% of the members of this segment are adults in families with
children, compared to 14% for the previous segment.

In addition, the average family income of members of this
segment is $11,700 versus $16,800 for those in the Athletic and
Social Activities segment. The people in this segment are also
disproportionately black (21% versus 11% for the population)
or Hispanic (12% versus 4% for the population).

Compared to the previous segment, whose members are primarily older adolescents, the women in the Indoor Games and
Social Activities segment tend to be young adults. Their interests and needs reflect the changing patterns associated with the

three-year age differential. There is less of a need to focus on seeking independence from parental authority and more of a need, having gained some of that independence, to establish a new household and an identity as an adult household head.

Mixed

These segments include:

- News and Information
- Detached
- Cosmopolitan Self-Enrichment
- Highly Diversified

The four segments discussed in this section are predominantly adults whose average age ranges from 34 to 47. Their composition of males and females is much more balanced than that of the ten segments previously discussed. For example, the percentage of females in these four segments ranges from 43% to 59%, whereas in the four predominantly adult female segments it ranged from 71% to 87%. The corresponding percentages for males are 41% to 57% among the four segments to be discussed, and 77% to 96% among the three predominantly adult male segments previously presented.

NEWS AND INFORMATION

Passive interests related to keeping informed on a broad range of subjects and activities. Needs are focused on being socially stimulating and maintaining family ties.

Interests. As the label suggests, the people in this segment are interested in being informed on a wide range of subjects. They rank among the top two segments on the following five interest factors: Comprehensive News and Information, International Affairs, Professional Sports, Science and Engineering, and Contemporary Dancing. The interests of this segment are quite broad in relation to subject matter. They do not, however, encompass the more abstract, cultural interests, as evidenced by their score on the Classical Arts factor, which places them as the least interested of all the segments.

In addition, they appear to be more oriented toward observing and knowing, rather than directly participating. The only segment whose members rank lower on the Participant Athletic Activities factor is the Elderly Concerns segment. They also rank well below average on the Reaping Nature's Benefits factor.

Needs. This segment's members exhibit relatively high scores on the need for Family Ties and the need to be Socially Stimulating. Their scores are not very low on any of the other seven needs measured. Their lives appear to center around making themselves both collectors and distributors of a wide variety of information.

Demographics. For the most part, neither the demographic nor the socioeconomic characteristics of this segment tend to set it apart from the others. Members have an average age of 47, and 57% of them are male. Their occupations are quite diverse, reflecting the relatively heterogeneous age and sex composition of the segment. They do have the highest percentage of white-collar workers (32%) among all fourteen segments.

DETACHED

> Low socioeconomic profile. Extremely few interests and activities and few psychological needs satisfied by them. Low scores on needs related to both intellectual stimulation and interpersonal contact and support.

Interests. People in this segment score well below average relative to other segments on thirteen of the eighteen interest factors. They do not rank first or second on any factor. They rank third on only one, Community Activities, and fourth on another, International Affairs. Members in only two other segments have a span of interests as narrow, namely the Elderly Concerns and the Money and Nature's Products segments, with fifteen and fourteen interest factor means below average respectively. In both cases, these segment members have at least one interest factor on which they score higher than all other segments. The Detached segment's members not only have a narrow range of interests, they also tend not to score as high on the few interests which they do rate above average. In addition, they are the lowest scoring segment on their interest in both Comprehensive News and Information and Popular Entertainment. That is, they show little evidence of any desire to stay in touch with day-to-day events in the world around them.

Needs. The profile of need factor scores for people in this segment reveals a picture consistent with their interests. On none of the nine need factors do the members of this segment rank higher than sixth out of the fourteen segments. The two needs on which they have the highest relative position are Status Enhancement and Escape from Boredom. For five out of the nine need factors, they have the lowest, or the second lowest, need scores of all the segments. The five are Socially Stimulating, Unique/Creative Accomplishment, Family Ties, Greater Self-Acceptance, and Intellectual Stimulation and Growth. The members of the Detached segment have few, if any, strongly felt needs that we have been able to identify.

Demographics. This segment has the highest percentage of central city residents (41% versus 25% for the population). They are about evenly divided between men and women and above average in age (46 versus 40 years old). They rank third in the percentage of black members (19% versus 11%), with a higher percentage being widowed (15% versus 8%).

They have the second lowest average income ($10,600 versus $14,200) and the second highest percentage of members who did not complete high school (26% versus 12%).

It appears that this segment comprises those members, of society who are quite low on the socioeconomic ladder and whose interests, activities, and needs are more fundamental than those investigated in this study. The types of leisure interests and psychological needs investigated in this project are probably of little relevance to people concerned with providing the more basic needs of food, clothing, and shelter for themselves and their families.

COSMOPOLITAN SELF-ENRICHMENT

Extremely high socioeconomic profile. Diverse pattern of intellectual and cultural interests. Physically active. High needs for intellectual stimulation, unique/creative accomplishment, and understanding others. Low needs for status enhancement and for escape from boredom.

Interests. Members of this segment and the Arts and Cultural Activities segment have in common exceptionally high interest scores on the Classical Arts and Comprehensive News and Information factors. They share an interest in abstract and culturally upscale subject matter.

The differences between people in the two segments are as informative as their pattern of similarities. Based on a comparison of their relative positions among the fourteen segments:

(1) The members of the Arts and Cultural Activities segment rank notably higher than those in the Cosmopolitan Self-Enrichment segment with respect to their scores on the following interest factors: Professional Sports, Religion, Indoor Games, Investments, International Affairs, and Crime and Society.

(2) The members of the Cosmopolitan Self-Enrichment segment rank notably higher than those in the Arts and Cultural Activities segment on Participant Athletic Activities, Popular Social Issues, Community Activities, and Camping Out.

The Cosmopolitan Self-Enrichment segment's members have interests that appear to involve more active participation than do those in the Arts and Cultural Activities segment. The mix of their interests spans not only interests related to intellectualizing and abstraction, but also interests related to people and community. The members of the Cosmopolitan Self-Enrichment segment, in general, appear to have a set of interests that are more highly developed and require a greater sense of involvement and participation.

Needs. Members of both segments are well above average (among the top two) on their need scores related to Intellectual Stimulation and Growth and Understanding Others. They are both well below average on their need scores for Status Enhancement and Escape from Boredom. They diverge, too, however. The Cosmopolitan Self-Enrichment segment members are (1) well above average, ranking first, on the Unique/Creative Accomplishment factor, where the members of the Arts and Cultural Activities segment register a slightly below average score, and they are (2) above average, ranking third, on the Escape from Problems factor, where those in the other segment have a score that ranks them lower than any other.

In contrast, persons in the Arts and Cultural Activities segment score higher than those in the Cosmopolitan Self-Enrichment segment on such people-related needs as Socially Stimulating, Family Ties, and Greater Self-Acceptance.

Demographics. Common to the members of both segments is an exceptionally high educational level: 65% with some college or more for the Cosmopolitan Self-Enrichment segment and 69% for the Arts and Cultural Activities segment. Both segments also contain a disproportionate number of people who are managerial and professional. They both comprise people with above-average household incomes, $18,760 on average for members in the Cosmopolitan Self-Enrichment segment and $16,570 for those in the Arts and Cultural Activities segment. The former segment, however, averages 36 years of age, while the latter averages 44 years.

This segment comprises a group of well-educated, relatively affluent men and women whose interests and activities include a broad spectrum of intellectual and cultural areas. They are active. They participate in their family and community, although not in religion.

HIGHLY DIVERSIFIED

Southern, black, adults with children. Broad range of interests, especially those permitting personal participation with family and/or other informal small group settings. High need for intellectual stimulation and growth.

Interests. Of the eighteen interest factors, the people in this segment are above average on eleven. No segment has a larger number of above-average interest factor scores than this one. The two closest segments are the Family and Community Centered segment, with the same number, and the Family Integrated Activities segment, with ten.

The members of this segment rank first on only one activity, namely Camping Out, but they rank well above average on the following six: Participant Athletic Activities, Household Activities, Reaping Nature's Benefits, Classical Arts, Popular Social Issues, and Indoor Games. With the exception of Popular Social Issues, all of the interests on which they score high involve some form of active personal participation.

There are three interest factors on which the people in this segment score well below average: Science and Engineering, Mechanical Activities, and Popular Entertainment. The first two of these factors involve interests in technical subjects. The third tends to be highly oriented toward today's youth with low intellectual or cultural content. The interests of this group tend to be either more intellectually upscale or to involve some form of active participation.

Needs. This segment reports a high need for Intellectual Stimulation and Growth and relatively low needs for the remaining factors.

Demographics. The Highly Diversified segment is most notable demographically for its large percentage of blacks (33% compared to 11% in the population), by far the largest of all the segments. Geographically, it includes the largest representation from the South and the second smallest from the Northeast. Full-time employment is among the highest of all the segments, although household income averages only $12,700 compared to $14,200 for the population.

This segment appears to comprise a group of people, who, without the benefit of the educational and social advantages of others in the population, are seeking to expand the intellectual and cultural horizons of themselves and their families.

CONCLUSIONS

The fourteen interest segments that have been introduced in this chapter are used in subsequent chapters as the focal point for the analysis of television, as well as other media behavior.

We believe that this particular interest-based segmentation scheme will provide a useful complement to the more traditional demographic segmentation based on age and sex that is often used in practice. Clearly, our solution is not unique. Other interest-based segmentation models might be developed that would be equally useful or even more so. We have not *dis-*

covered a segment structure which existed among media audiences just waiting to be found. Rather, we have *invented* a structure, one of many possible ways of looking at such audiences. Similar taxonomies could be built with fewer segments or with more. We chose fourteen in an effort to balance the need for differentiation in interest patterns (which increases with the number of segments) with the need for conceptual simplicity and manageability (which decreases with the number of segments).

The potential value of the interest classification system presented here depends upon its relationship to differential behavior patterns and its usefulness in understanding the public's use of television, as well as upon the ability to use this relationship to develop and target media content more effectively for its appropriate audiences.

Relationship to Past Research in a Similar Vein

Very few persons have published empirical research findings (we could locate only four articles) relating to the development of people-oriented classification systems based on interest profiles. Those published differ substantially from the present study in their coverage of items upon which the segmentation is based or in the survey design and analytical techniques used. As the questionnaire content is the most clear-cut area of difference, the four previous studies are briefly discussed only in terms of this characteristic.

The earliest effort is an article by two psychologists Stein and Lenrow (1970), who developed an interest segmentation system based on a limited range of interests and activities, for the sole purpose of developing a psychological test entitled Motoric Ideational Sensory Test (MIST) for measuring motoric, ideational, and sensory-perceptual dimensions. Two other articles are more similar to ours in purpose, namely those by Perrault et al. (1977) and Duncan (1978). The first of these reports the development of an interest segmentation focused almost exclusively on vacation-related activities and interests. For example, the segment labels include the Homebodies, Budget Travelers, and Adventurers. Their work, while very much in the spirit of ours, is not directly comparable, as they studied a narrower domain of interests and activities. Duncan, on the other hand, attempted to develop a classification system for describing overall patterns of leisure behavior. Though his purpose was similar to ours, the differences in the domain of interests explored is appreciable. Duncan focused his measurements upon activities and did not include interests in a number of content areas explored in the present research (e.g., engineering, astronomy). His questionnaire included 59 items compared to our 139. Lastly, he attempted to measure *participation* in various activities, while we measured *degree of interest* in various activities and subject matters. A study published by the Newspaper Advertising Bureau (1973) also comes close in spirit to the present research, but diverges in purpose and content coverage. Their questionnaire covers some 300 items, loosely divided into three categories: personality, personal aspirations, and social role.

Most of the items used to establish the clusters were not related to leisure interests and activities in the areas that form the basis for our segmentation scheme.

Though this review of previous efforts has focused primarily on differences in questionnaire content, a more detailed review of research designs leads to essentially the same conclusion. Given the current state of the art regarding the development of interest profiles in building systems for classifying people, the differences in content coverage, survey methodology, and analytic approaches to date have made it impossible to develop an integrated, cohesive body of knowledge to build upon. There is a need for such development, not only to provide the basis for a better understanding of media behavior, but to impose a more structured framework on the study of leisure behavior in general. We hope that the segmentation scheme presented in this chapter will move the field a few steps forward in that direction and provide a foundation upon which future investigators will build.

What Comes Next

In the chapters to follow, separate analyses of each major medium are reported, with the most detailed analysis devoted to television. It includes an analysis of viewing behavior by program type and by programs. In addition to television, magazine reading behavior is discussed with some attention to individual magazines. Analyses are reported for books, newspapers, radio, and movies as well. These are less detailed in that they focus on types of radio programs listened to, sections of newspapers read, and types of movies seen, as opposed to discussions of specific radio programs, newspapers, or movies.

NOTES

1. For a more detailed discussion of the distinction between people type analysis and variables analysis, see Frank and Massy (1975).

2. Fourteen-way multiple discriminant analyses were also performed as part of the process of evaluating the extent of the overall between segment differences in interests, needs, demographic and socioeconomic characteristics. Three discriminant analyses were performed, each using a different set of variables as follows: (1) interest factor scores; (2) need factor scores; and (3) demographic and socioeconomic characteristics. The interest-based discriminant analysis was included simply to provide another set of descriptive statistics and not to evaluate any null hypotheses for the same reasons cited in the text. Based on interest factor scores, 94% of the respondents were correctly classified by the discriminant equations compared to the 7% one could expect from a random assignment to the fourteen segments or the 10% accuracy that would occur if all were assigned to the modal segment. One, of course, would expect this percentage to be extremely high, as the same interest factors used in the discriminant analysis also served as input to the cluster analysis which formed the fourteen segments in the first place. The need and demographic/socioeconomic discriminant runs resulted in 23% and 33% being correctly classified, which is substantially greater than the chance expectations of 7% or 10%. The overall pattern of between segment differences for both of these discriminant analyses was tested using the Wilk's Lambda statistic. Based on the appropriate F-ratio approximation, the results for both discriminant analyses were significant beyond the .005 level.

REFERENCES

DUNCAN, D. J. (1978) "Leisure types: factor analyses of leisure profiles." Journal of Leisure Research 10 (Spring): 113-125.

FRANK, R. E. and M. G. GREENBERG (1976) "Audience segmentation analysis for public television program development: evaluation and promotion." Prepared for the John and Mary R. Markle Foundation, November. (unpublished)

FRANK, R. E. and W. F. MASSY (1975) "Noise reduction in segmentation research," pp. 145-205 in J. U. Farley and J. A. Howard (eds.) Control of "Error" in Market Research Data. Lexington, MA: D. C. Heath.

Newspaper Advertising Bureau, Inc. (1973) Psychographics: A Study of Personality, Life Style and Consumption Patterns. New York: Author.

PERRAULT, W. D., D. K. DARDEN, and W. R. DARDEN (1977) "A psychographic classification of vacation life styles." Journal of Leisure Research 9 (Summer): 208-224.

STEIN, K. B. and P. LENROW (1970) "Expressive styles and their measurement." Journal of Personality and Social Psychology 16: 656-664.

5

Television Viewing Behavior

INTRODUCTION

This chapter describes the television viewing behavior of each of the fourteen interest segments.

The previous chapter developed a segmentation scheme based upon leisure interests and activities and enhanced the segment descriptions by examining the psychological needs and the demographic and socioeconomic correlates of the segment structure. In order for this taxonomy to be useful in the development and implementation of television programming strategies, it is necessary that the segments, at least to some extent, exhibit differential *behavior* in their use of television.

In this chapter, we first report overall television viewing behavior, followed by an analysis of behavior with respect to program types and individual programs. Subsequent chapters in Part Three report findings related to the use of public television and the context in which television is viewed.

OVERALL VIEWING BEHAVIOR

Television Viewing and In-Home Availability

Table 5.1 reports overall television viewing behavior and in-home availability data by interest segment. In analyzing tele-

vision viewing behavior, it is useful to distinguish between
segment differences associated with in-home availability and
those associated with the proportion of in-home time spent
watching television.

The first column of Table 5.1 reports overall television
viewing by interest segment. Viewing behavior was measured by
having respondents indicate, by day of week and time of day,
the time periods during which they typically watched television.

Across the population, respondents reported watching television sometime during an average of 35.7 hours per week. This
is greater than their actual viewing time, as it includes a count
of all time periods during which they watched, even if it was
only for a portion of that time. The data entries are the ratios
of the average number of hours of television exposure of persons in each segment to the population average multiplied by
100 to convert to percentages. Hence, the index of 134% for
persons in the News and Information segment indicates that
their television exposure is 134% of the average for the population, or 34% above average. In contrast, the index of 75% for
members of the Cosmopolitan Self-Enrichment segment means
that they are below average. They view television only 75% as
often as does the average individual.

To obtain the in-home availability results (the second column
of Table 5.1), respondents were asked during what time periods
on weekdays and Saturdays and Sundays they were usually at
home. On an average, they report being home 107.2 hours a
week. This is also undoubtedly an overestimate, as, if people
indicated they were usually home from midnight to 6:00 a.m.
on weekdays, a 30 hour count (6 hours times 5 days) was
included in tabulating their weekly in-home hours.

As with television exposure, the data on in-home availability
are reported in the form of ratios of each segment's average
availability to that of the population as a whole.

For our purposes, it is less important that the absolute levels
of hours watching television or staying at home be precisely
reported, than that the relative magnitudes of these numbers
across segments be approximately correct.

We have no external way of validating these self-report data
by segment. However, the high and low television usage seg-

TABLE 5.1   Overall Television Exposure and In-Home
Availability by Interest Segment

	Television Exposure Index*	In-Home Availability Index*	Television Share of In-Home Time Index*
Adult Male Concentration			
Mechanics and Outdoor Life	89%	87%	103%
Money and Nature's Products	98	100	100
Family and Community Centered	87	99	88
Adult Female Concentration			
Elderly Concerns	118	123	97
Arts and Cultural Activities	97	104	94
Home and Community Centered	92	102	91
Family Integrated Activities	106	111	97
Youth Concentration			
Competitive Sports and Science Engineering	101	90	115
Athletic and Social Activities	80	84	94
Indoor Games and Social Activities	114	100	115
Mixed			
News and Information	134	106	127
Detached	93	95	100
Cosmopolitan Self-Enrichment	75	96	79
Highly Diversified	120	89	136
Entire Population	(35.7)	(107.2)	(33.3%)
	(hours/ week)	(hours/ week)	(share of in-home hours exposed to television)

*All percentages are indexed against a figure of 100% for the average individual.

ments demonstrate considerable face validity in the light of the interests, needs, and demographics data reported in the preceding chapter.

The last column of Table 5.1 is a measure of the relative share of in-home time spent watching television across segments. The raw data were ratios of television exposure: in Column 1, to in-home availability, in Column 2, for each segment. On average, across all segments, one-third of the reported in-home availability time is associated with watching television. Here again, for comparative purposes, the ratio of each segment's television share to that of the population is reported. For example, people in the Highly Diversified segment are 36% above average in their share of in-home time devoted to television and, as such, rank higher than any other segment on this measure.

At this stage, the focus of discussion is on in-home availability and television share as they relate to overall television viewing. The major portion of this chapter, to follow, analyzes the relationships between segment composition and viewing behavior by program type and program.

Above-Average Viewing

There are six segments that report above-average levels of television exposure. Ranked by viewing as a share of in-home availability, they are:

	Television Exposure	In-Home Availability	Television Share
Highly Diversified	120%	86%	136%
News and Information	134	106	127
Indoor Games and Social Activities	114	100	115
Competitive Sports and Science/ Engineering	101	90	115
Elderly Concerns	118	123	97
Family Integrated Activities	106	111	97

Of these six, people in the first four are predominantly above-average television viewers due to relatively high television shares combined with in-home availability near or below average for the population. Members of the latter two, the Elderly Concerns and Family Integrated Activities segments, are above average in their television exposure largely due to high levels of in-home availability rather than because of large shares of time devoted to television.

Those in the high in-home time segments are probably there for different reasons. People in the Family Integrated Activities segment are primarily adult women with young children, while those in the Elderly Concerns segment have low incomes combined with relatively few interests or social contacts to draw them out of their homes.

Below-Average Viewing

Eight of the segments are below average in their overall time spent viewing television. From the most to the least below average in television *share*, they are as follows:

	Television Exposure	In-Home Availability	Television Share
Cosmopolitan Self-Enrichment	75%	96%	79%
Family and Community Centered	87	99	88
Home and Community Centered	92	102	91
Arts and Cultural Activities	97	104	94
Athletic and Social Activities	80	84	94
Detached	93	95	100
Money and Nature's Products	98	100	100
Mechanics and Outdoor Life	89	87	103

Members of three of these eight segments are below average in their television viewing, principally because a relatively low share of their in-home time is spent watching television. These are people in the Cosmopolitan Self-Enrichment, Family and Community Centered, and Home and Community Centered segments.

Given the upscaled nature of the interests of the members of the Cosmopolitan Self-Enrichment segment, it is not surprising that their television share of in-home time is as low as it is. In the case of people in the Family and Community Centered and the Home and Community Centered segments, there are strong home-related and community-related interests that compete for in-home time and attention.

While the Athletic and Social Activities segment and the Mechanics and Outdoor Life segment have higher television shares, their exposure to television is also well below average as a result of their relatively low levels of in-home availability.

Based on the earlier discussion of interests, needs, and demographics in Chapter 4, it should come as no surprise that those in both the Athletic and Social Activities segment and the Mechanics and Outdoor Life segment spend substantially less time than average at home.

The remaining three segments exhibit levels of television exposure, in-home availability, and television shares that are relatively close to the population averages.

VIEWING BEHAVIOR BY PROGRAM TYPE
AND PROGRAM

This discussion is based upon a summary of respondent ratings of their frequency of viewing of each of 149 programs or program categories during the four-week period preceding the interview. The programs have been grouped into 19 program types. The 19 types and the programs included in each are listed in Exhibit 5.1. We recognize that some of these program types are not as homogeneous as we would like them to be and that some real anomalies exist, but we felt constrained for conceptual reasons to limit the number of categories as much as possible. Certainly *Fernwood 2 Night* is different from other programs in the Talk Show category and might indeed be sufficiently unique to constitute a category of its own. The variety of types of music in the Musical Performances category is clearly great. However, rather than allow our preconceived notions about the types of audiences that would be attracted to a program to influence our categorization, we elected to use the system outlined in Exhibit 5.1 and to account for apparent anomalies in segment viewing in the course of the discussion if and when they emerged.

The reader should also be aware that the data include some

sources of variation resulting from the nature of the television industry and the method of data collection in this project.

The survey was fielded shortly after the 1977 fall schedule was initiated, and most of the interviews were collected over a three-month time period. Respondents were queried on their program viewing over the past four weeks. The fall of 1977 produced one of the most fiercely competitive battles for audiences among the networks in the history of the television industry. There was frequent and significant shifting of programs from one time period to another, as well as unusually heavy early cancellations of series and substitutions of new programs. As a result, the programming available to audiences during any given four-week period varied even more than usual.

Such differences should, however, average out across segments, particularly at the level of program *types,* where the mix available during any given week is more stable than the individual programs themselves.

Table 5.2 reports the relative viewing frequency of each of the 19 types by interest segment. The first column contains the average viewing frequency by program type for the population. For example, situation comedies were watched on an average of 19.14 times during the preceding four weeks, while documentaries were watched on average only one-third of a time (i.e., approximately once every three weeks).

In order to facilitate comparing the relative frequency of viewing of each program type across segments, the body of Table 5.2 contains the percentaged ratio of each segment's score for the program type to the corresponding average for the population as a whole. The ratios serve as indices to be read in the same manner as those in Table 5.1. The score of 124 for Adventure programs, among persons in the Mechanics and Outdoor Life segment, indicates that their average frequency of exposure to adventure programming is 24% higher than the population average.

The variation in viewing frequencies across all segments for each of the nineteen program types has been tested for statistical significance using the univariate F-ratio statistic. All of the nineteen tests were significant at the .005 level.

Exhibit 5.1

Television Programs by Type

Adventure
Nancy Drew and the Hardy Boys
The Wonderful World of Disney
Six Million Dollar Man
Young Dan'l Boone
The Life and Times of
    Grizzly Adams
The Bionic Woman

Children's Programs
Captain Kangaroo
Captain Noah
Sesame Street
Mister Rogers
Electric Company
Children's Cartoons

Crime Drama
Kojak
Police Woman
Charlie's Angels
Baretta
Chips
Hawaii Five-O
Barnaby Jones
Rosetti and Ryan
Switch
The Rockford Files
Quincy
Starsky and Hutch

Documentary
Age of Uncertainty
Nova
Last of the Wild

Drama
Little House on the Prairie
Rafferty
The Fitzpatricks
Lou Grant
Family
Oregon Trail
Big Hawaii
The Waltons

Game Shows
Hollywood Squares
The Price Is Right
Wheel of Fortune

Family Feud
It's Anybody's Guess
Gong Show
Tattletales
20,000 Dollar Pyramid
Match Game '77

Movies
Sunday Night
The Big Event
Monday Night
Wednesday Night
Friday Night
Saturday Night
Late Night

Musical Performances
Evening at Symphony
Opera
Evening at Pop's
American Bandstand
Soul Train
Music Hall America

News/Commentary
Sixty Minutes
Washington Week in Review
Wall Street Week
Black Perspective on the News
Evening Magazine
MacNeil/Lehrer Report
Face the Nation
Meet the Press

News Shows/Daily
Local News
National Network News
    (ABC, CBS, NBC)

Science Fiction
The Man from Atlantis
The New Adventures of
    Wonder Woman
Logan's Run

Situation Comedy
Rhoda
On Our Own
All in the Family
Alice
The San Pedro Beach Bums

Exhibit 5.1 (Continued)

The Betty White Show
Maude
Happy Days
Laverne and Shirley
Three's Company
Soap
M*A*S*H
One Day at a Time
Mulligan's Stew
Eight Is Enough
Good Times
Bustin Loose
Welcome Back, Kotter
What's Happening
Barney Miller
Carter Country
Sanford Arms
Chico and the Man
Bob Newhart
We've Got Each Other
Fish
Operation Petticoat
The Jeffersons
Tony Randall
The Love Boat

Soap Operas
Love of Life
The Young and the Restless
Search for Tomorrow
All My Children
Days of Our Lives
As the World Turns
The Doctors
One Life to Live
The Guiding Light
Another World
General Hospital

Specials
Washington Behind Closed Doors
The Trial of Lee Harvey Oswald
Kill Me If You Can—
  Caryl Chessmen Story

Sports
NFL Football
Wide World of Sports
Football
Basketball
Hockey
Baseball
Other

Talk Shows
Fernwood 2 Night
Johnny Carson
Today
Good Morning America
Phil Donahue
Joel A. Spivak
Dialing for Dollars
Women
Mike Douglas
Dinah
Merv Griffin Show

Theatrical Performances
Dickens of London
Visions
Upstairs, Downstairs
In Pursuit of Liberty
Great Performances
The Best of Families
Masterpiece Theater
Once Upon a Classic

Variety Shows
The Richard Pryor Show
Redd Foxx
Donnie and Marie Osmond
The Carol Burnett Show
Lawrence Welk
Saturday Night Live
Andy Williams

Others
The French Chef
Any Religious Programs
Any Spanish Programs

TABLE 5.2 Viewing Frequency Ratios by Program Type and Interest Segment[a]

	Entire Population	Adult Male Concentration				Adult Female Concentration				Youth Concentration			Mixed		
		Mechanics and Outdoor Life	Money and Nature's Products	Family and Community Centered	Elderly Concerns	Arts and Cultural Activities	Home and Community Centered	Family Integrated Activities	Competitive Sports and Science/Engineering	Athletic and Activities	Indoor Games and Social Activities	News and Information	Detached	Cosmopolitan Self-Enrichment	Highly Diversified
Adventure	4.14	124	104	92	111	56	91	107	109	90	145	102	85	42	164
Children's Programs	1.36	82	46	46	34	46	111	224	119	121	132	81	71	103	165
Crime Drama	7.70	109	100	85	109	81	96	100	105	139	139	118	97	51	139
Documentary	.34	76	129	59	88	171	91	126	94	3	44	132	59	129	126
Dramas	4.42	81	109	90	134	81	113	129	72	87	105	126	83	66	119
Game Shows	3.56	60	69	62	169	89	121	123	103	58	166	141	79	48	123
Movies	5.45	108	92	77	81	84	84	123	88	108	90	133	93	79	147
Musical Performances	1.02	52	57	30	75	192	90	77	48	91	162	106	72	94	211
News/Commentary	2.37	58	160	113	133	157	84	64	71	35	27	233	66	102	112
News Shows – Daily	5.19	70	113	117	126	127	99	96	131	40	46	134	80	134	103
Science Fiction	1.25	127	62	63	75	70	80	86	130	115	184	94	93	71	174
Situation Comedy	19.15	93	77	33	105	87	114	103	122	86	149	121	82	80	118
Soap Operas	3.64	25	77	71	196	76	180	146	29	64	154	140	99	26	127
Specials	.89	85	119	131	81	153	113	112	65	69	96	118	39	117	137
Sports	5.79	72	132	72	73	101	79	51	205	42	86	167	73	127	121
Talk Shows	2.90	29	113	68	139	143	119	96	19	76	76	182	78	86	92
Theatrical Performances	.63	29	68	56	73	386	46	70	19	19	60	124	46	216	100
Variety Shows	3.63	79	117	82	140	86	108	90	83	79	131	154	73	72	133
Others	.67	13	136	133	191	94	164	48	39	64	64	154	100	31	164

a. The statistical significance of each of the nineteen program type measures contained in this table was evaluated based on univariate F-ratios with 13 and 2,462 degrees of freedom. All nineteen F-ratios are significant at the .005 level.

Though the analysis of television viewing behavior is based primarily on the results reported in Table 5.2, reference will sometimes be made to data for individual programs as well. Because of the number of tables involved, this set of data is reported across all interest segments in Appendix F.

Adult Male Concentration

MECHANICS AND OUTDOOR LIFE

> Young adult, blue-collar males whose interests focus on noncompetitive activities emphasizing personal physical accomplishment—auto repair, fishing, camping. Interests which, by their very nature, do not require emphasis on interpersonal cooperation or support. High on needs for escape and unique/creative accomplishment.

People in this segment are above-average viewers of only four program types, namely: science fiction (27% above average), adventure (24%), crime drama (9%), and movies (8%). The common denominator of the first three of these is that they provide vehicles for escape and fantasizing. It is also likely that their television movie selection is consistent with this pattern. We do not know about the specific content of the television movies they watch, as they were not asked to describe them. However, as will be seen in Chapter 7, their viewing of movies away-from-home is oriented to escapist material of the sort contained in the preceding three television program types.

This interpretation of their viewing pattern is further reinforced by their choices of programs within each of the three types as described below:

(1) *Science Fiction.* Though they are above-average viewers of all three programs in this category, they are especially high on *Logan's Run,* next on *The New Adventures of Wonder Woman,* and least on *The Man from Atlantis.* That is, the closer the program is to reality, the less they deviate from the average viewing frequency.

(2) *Adventure.* The two programs which the people in this segment view most, in relation to the average for the population, are *Six Million Dollar Man* and *The Bionic*

Woman. They report their lowest relative frequency for *Young Dan'l Boone.*

(3) *Crime Drama.* The higher ranking programs for these people are *Chips, Charlie's Angels, Baretta,* and *Rockford Files* as opposed to *Switch, Barnaby Jones, Police Woman,* and *Quincy.*

In general, the Mechanics and Outdoor Life segment concentrates its relatively heavy viewing on programs that involve the elements of adventure, drama, and suspense in vehicles in which the forces of good and evil are clearly drawn. These shows are relatively fast-paced and focus upon hero-figures who inevitably triumph in the end. One would hypothesize that members of this segment would have been heavy viewers of Westerns during the 1950s and 1960s when such programs were abundantly available.

There are, of course, many forms of escape, depending upon an individual's personality and needs. For some people, situation comedies provide an outlet for escape. For others, soap operas or game shows may perform the same function. One can learn as much about a segment by noting the types of programs they elect *not* to watch as well as those they do.

Members of this segment score well below average when it comes to program types that contain more upscaled intellectual content or abstract subject matter. They rank among the lowest three segments in their viewing of:

- Other (religion)—13% of average
- *Soap Operas—25%
- Theatrical performances—29%
- Talk shows—29%
- Musical performances—52%
- *Game shows—60%
- News shows/daily—70%
- Sports—72%

The two program types marked with asterisks contain shows that are aired at times when the adult, male, employed members who constitute a clear majority of this segment are typically not at home. However, the low scores on the other types do not appear to be explainable by schedule considerations. All of the remaining types contain programs predominantly shown during nonworking hours. In the case of talk shows, available during both the day and late evening, this segment exhibits below-average viewing during both time periods. All of the remaining program types listed, with the exception of sports, contain intellectual or cultural content.

Even their low viewing rate for sports is consistent with their expressed interests and needs. It was shown in Chapter 4 that people in this segment tend to have low levels of interest in competitive, as opposed to noncompetitive, activities. All of the programs contained in the sports category are competitive in nature.

MONEY AND NATURE'S PRODUCTS

Older males with a higher proportion being rural and retired. Interests in passive activities that obtain some form of tangible return or product—fishing, hunting, investments. Low interest in active physical activities—camping out, participant sports—as well as culturally upscale or abstract—classical arts, international affairs. Somewhat complacent, but need interpersonal contact and support, especially from their families.

The program types with above-average viewing by the members of this segment reflect three distinct elements associated with their interests, needs, and demographic characteristics:

(1) Interest in outdoor and nature-related activities.

(2) Need for social contact, support, and respect.

(3) Interests in investment and business-related subject matter.

Though it is useful to conceptualize their viewing behavior in terms of these three categories, programs in any one category serve some of the same needs and interests as those in others.

Outdoor content. Their above-average viewing of adventure, documentary, and drama program types is principally accounted for by programs associated with nature-related settings, namely:

(1) Adventure—*The Life and Times of Grizzly Adams* and *Young Dan'l Boone* as opposed to *Six Million Dollar Man, Nancy Drew,* or *The Hardy Boys.*

(2) Documentary—*Last of the Wild* as opposed to *Age of Uncertainty.*

(3) Dramas—*Oregon Trail* and *The Waltons* as opposed to *Family* and *The Fitzpatricks.*

(4) Sports—Above average on all professional sports—as spectators, not players.

Social contact, support, and respect. Associated with this set of needs is the above-average viewing by this segment of crime-drama, talk shows, and variety shows. In the programs for which they are relatively heavy viewers, the story tends to be focused on a single personality, close in age to the members of this segment, who is socially integrated both in terms of contact, support, and respect, namely:

(1) *Crime-Drama. Kojak, Hawaii Five-O, Barnaby Jones* as opposed to *Starsky and Hutch, Rossetti and Ryan,* and *Baretta.*

(2) *Talk Shows.* Johnny Carson is viewed more often by this segment than by any other except for the News and Information segment. Less frequently viewed programs in this category are confounded with scheduling differences, as many talk shows are on during the daytime when the large majority of this segment is unavailable for watching television.

(3) *Variety Shows.* Lawrence Welk, Carol Burnett, and Andy Williams as opposed to Redd Foxx and *The Richard Pryor Show.*

Some of the same need satisfactions are probably also derived from several of the outdoor-related programs previously mentioned, such as *Grizzly Adams* and *Dan'l Boone.* The heavy viewing of *Lou Grant,* a drama, most likely also serves functions similar to those associated with programs discussed in this section, even though it is classified under a different program type. Last but not least, members of this segment are above average in their viewing of the "other" program category, primarily due to their heavy viewing of religious programs. These, too, probably help to satisfy their needs for support and contact.

It is also our hypothesis that one of the common needs of persons in this segment is a need for the continued support and reinforcement of the more traditional values associated with American life. Virtually all of the main characters in the programs discussed in this and the preceding section tend to personify some or all of these values.

Investment/business content. Though they are above-average viewers of news shows—daily programs (13% above average)—they are considerably higher in their viewing of news/commentary programs, on which they are 60% above average in viewing.

Their viewing of these program types is related to their interests in financial matters and business, as described in Chapter 4. In addition, there is some tendency for them to be somewhat higher than average on programs that emphasize particular personalities and their evaluations rather than the issues per se. Examples are *Wall Street Week, Meet the Press,* and *Face the Nation.*

Given the nature of this segment's interests in business, much of their nonfictional television viewing can be explained by a desire to be knowledgeable about what is going on in the world around them. In today's economy, success in business and investment is often related to one's ability to be tuned in to the social and political trends of our society as well as the economic trends. This segment's above-average viewing of daily news, news commentary, documentary shows, talk shows, and even sports programs all help to maintain a high level of awareness of these trends.

FAMILY AND COMMUNITY CENTERED

Employed, blue-collar/white-collar adult males. Married, living in nonmetropolitan areas. Broad interests, including outdoor activities, investments, and home and community centered activities as well as religion. Very strong need for family ties.

The breadth of interests of people in this segment, combined with their family orientation, might cause one to expect them to be heavy television viewers. However, as was shown previously in Table 5.1, they have the second lowest share of in-home time devoted to television. They are not among the top three segments in their viewing of any of the nineteen program types. They rank fourth on only one, sports, and fifth on two, news/ commentary and daily news shows. For eleven of the types, they are among the lowest four segments in viewing frequency.

It is likely that their relatively low television usage is due in large part to other family and community activities that compete for their time. This segment also shows evidence of a high degree of involvement with religion, and this may cause them to find much of what is aired on television objectionable. Their involvement in religion is evidenced by the following:

(1) Their interest factor score for Religion (Chapter 4) places them among the top three segments on this interest.

(2) Their television viewing of programs with religious content is well above average.

(3) Their usage of religious material in books, movies, and radio ranks them second out of fourteen on *each* of these three media (see Chapter 7).

(4) The television program types on which they rank the highest, sports and news, are apt to be the least offensive in light of their religious beliefs.

The involvement of this segment in religion is not, however, a totally satisfactory explanation for their restricted viewing of television, even if it is partially responsible. Certainly, there are many program types other than news and sports that do not contain objectionable material. Also, there are several other segments which evidence equally great involvement in religion, but which spend a much larger portion of their in-home time viewing television.

Adult Female Concentration

ELDERLY CONCERNS

> Oldest segment, high percentage of retirees, widowed, few children. Very few interests include religion and news and information. Focus on maintaining sense of social integration and belonging in absence of direct interpersonal contact. Needs to overcome loneliness and lift spirits. Low need for intellectual stimulation.

The people in this segment have higher levels of viewing behavior than any other segment for dramas, game shows, soap operas, and religious programming. In addition, they are substantially above average for the population (20% or more) in their viewing of news/commentary, daily news shows, talk shows, and variety shows.

At the opposite extreme, they are extremely light viewers of children's programs (viewing only 34% as frequently as the entire sample), and they are well below average on their viewing of sports, theatrical performances, science fiction, musical performances, movies, and specials.

Their above-average viewing of news and religious programming comes as no surprise, as these subject matter areas match their expressed interests. Both their interests and viewing of these two types of programs probably help to satisfy their needs for social integration and acceptance.

Their exceptionally high levels of viewing of the other program types listed above also appear to reflect these same needs. A common denominator of these program types is that they provide vehicles for vicarious participation. Heavy viewers of soap operas are known to become involved in a very personal way with the characters in the stories and with the problems in their lives. The hosts and celebrities of game shows and talk shows provide a kind of vicarious relationship. They tend to be stable, accepting figures with highly predictable (bordering on ritualistic) patterns of behavior. As such, they appear to offer surrogate friends, or at least acquaintances, for this segment, whose members appear lonely and spend much of their time isolated from real-life support groups.

Many of the lead personalities associated with the programs viewed by this segment can be characterized as nonthreatening in that they exhibit an interest in, and an almost uncritical acceptance of, others. For example, *The Waltons* and *The Lawrence Welk Show* feature very nonthreatening personalities to a group of people very much in need of acceptance at this point in their lives.

There are, of course, other factors, in addition to needs, that have an impact on their overall viewing behavior. For example, the above-average television viewing by the people in this segment is in part a result of the fact that they are more apt to be at home and available for viewing than those in any other segment. Their light viewing of some of the talk and variety shows is related not only to their content, but also to their scheduling. As people in the Elderly Concerns segment have an average age of 61, it is reasonable to assume that they are less apt to stay awake to watch late night shows such as *Fernwood 2 Night* and *Saturday Night Live,* even if their content were attractive to them.

In the following paragraphs, each of the program types with above-average viewing by this segment, except for news and religion, is commented upon:

(1) *Dramas.* The fact that this segment has the highest viewing index for dramas is principally due to their exceedingly heavy viewing of two of the eight programs in this category, *Little House on the Prairie* and *The Waltons.* In contrast, they view *Rafferty* and *The Fitzpatricks* to a lesser extent than do members of any other segment. Both of the more heavily viewed programs emphasize family solidarity and acceptance.

(2) *Soap Operas.* Members of this segment watch daytime soap operas considerably more than the average for the population. This attraction to soaps is broad-based. There are eleven programs in this category, and they are above average in their viewing of all, ranking first on six programs and fourth or above on the remaining programs.

(3) *Game Shows.* As in the case of soap operas, people in this segment are well above average in their viewing of all nine

programs in this category. Of these, they rank first on
three of them and fifth or higher on the remaining ones.

(4) *Talk Shows*. Within this category, there are substantial
differences in this segment's viewing behavior from program to program. They rank first in their viewing of Merv
Griffin, Mike Douglas, *Dialing for Dollars*, and *Woman*.
They are below average in their viewing of *Fernwood 2
Night*, Johnny Carson, and Phil Donahue. There appears
to be a pattern of watching personalities who tend to be
less critical and more accepting of others.

(5) *Variety Shows*. The one variety show which the people in
this segment watch more than people in any other segment is Lawrence Welk. Next in their above-average
viewing are Carol Burnett and Andy Williams. They
watch *Saturday Night Live* less often than any other
segment and are well below average in their viewing of
The Richard Pryor Show.

ARTS AND CULTURAL ACTIVITIES

Highly educated, adult women in households with manager or professional as head. Broad range of intellectual and cultural interests—
especially classical arts. Low interest in household activities and
management. High needs for intellectual stimulation and growth and
for understanding others, with low needs for status enhancement or
escape.

The people in this segment are well above average in their
viewing of seven of the nineteen program types. The seven types
are:

- Theatrical performances—286% above average
- Musical performances—92%
- Documentary—71%
- News/commentary—57%
- Specials—53%
- Talk shows—43%
- News Shows/daily—27%

In contrast, the people in this segment are at least 20% below average in their viewing of adventure programs, children's programs, science fiction, and soap operas.

This profile of viewing behavior is quite consistent with the earlier discussion of their interests, needs, and demographics in Chapter 4. The program types on which they rank high tend to be upscale in their intellectual and cultural content.

In general, members of this segment appear to be rather selective in their television viewing, choosing programs which they see as contributing to their intellectual and cultural development, as opposed to programs which satisfy needs for escape or interpersonal support. For them, television is used like other media, to satisfy informational needs and to broaden their intellectual and cultural horizons.

In three of the above-average program types, differences in the viewing of particular programs within a type provide further insight into this segment's behavior:

(1) *Musical Performances.* The overall viewing of programs in this category is extremely high (286% above average). This percentage is higher than for most of the other 266 program type/segment combinations included in Table 5.2. There are 6 programs in this category. Of these, 3 are watched by the members of this segment more than any other: *Evening at the Symphony, Opera,* and *Evening at Pops.* With respect to the others (*American Bandstand, Soul Train,* and *Music Hall America*), they are below average in their viewing.

(2) *News/Commentary.* Within this category, the people in this segment have higher viewing levels for those programs which tend to focus on (a) analysis rather than description and (b) issues rather than personalities. They are average or above average in their viewing of all the category's eight programs. However, they rank among the *top three* segments in their viewing of *Sixty Minutes, Washington Week in Review, Wall Street Week,* and *The MacNeil/Lehrer Report.* In their viewing of *Black Perspective on the News, Evening Magazine, Face the Nation,* and *Meet the Press,* their relative position is some-

what lower, ranking them between fourth and sixth out of the fourteen segments.

(3) *Talk Shows.* The three programs they watch more often than does any other segment are *Today,* Phil Donahue, and *Dinah.* The three programs on which they rank lowest are *Fernwood 2 Night, Good Morning America,* and *Dialing for Dollars.* The most striking discrepancy here is that between their viewing of *Today* and *Good Morning America,* which are on at the same time on competing networks. It seems reasonable to hypothesize that this difference is related to program content and format. *The Today Show* is more serious in its orientation and less folksy in terms of the demeanor of its principal personalities than *Good Morning America.* Even the physical stage settings support this distinction in orientation, with the program set of *Good Morning America* suggesting a homelike context and the *Today Show*'s set clearly serving the function of a speaker's platform.

HOME AND COMMUNITY CENTERED

> Adult females with a relatively high percentage of married home-makers. Home and local community interests. Highest needs for family ties and understanding others. Lowest needs for intellectual stimulation and for unique/creative accomplishment.

Members of this segment are well above average, ranking second out of fourteen, on their viewing of only two program types, namely soap operas (80% above average) and the "other" program category which is heavy on religious programming (64% above average). In addition, they are above average in their viewing of seven other program types. On five of these, they are within only 13% of average; on two, game shows and talk shows, they are 21% and 19% above average respectively. There appears to be no clear systematic pattern of viewing of these seven program types or the programs in them.

However, with respect to soap operas and religious programming, there is an element of systematic behavior. About 35% of the members of this segment are homemakers, which is well above the population average of 19%. They tend to be home during the day and to be taking care of children. In addition, these people have relatively narrow interests and needs focused on their family and community.

In many ways, their viewing pattern is similar to the pattern for the Elderly Concerns segment. A major difference, of course, in daytime viewing is reflected in the above-average index for children's programs among the Home and Community segment, while the Elderly Concerns segment has the lowest index of any group on this program type. It is likely that the present segment, relatively cut off from adult companionship during the day, finds that the soap operas, game shows, religious programs, and talk shows satisfy a need for social integration in much the same way as the Elderly Concerns segment does.

The Home and Community segment members appear to use television primarily for social integration during the day and for entertainment during the evening hours, with little effort to use it as a medium for gaining information or broadening their cultural exposure. Their viewing pattern is almost diametrically opposed to that of the Arts and Cultural Activities segment, for example, if one compares the relative high and low scores for these two segments in Table 5.2.

FAMILY INTEGRATED ACTIVITIES

> High percentage of adult women with young children. Strong inter-
> est in home and in family interactive activities—household activities
> and management and indoor games. High need for family ties. Child
> presence influences adult interest patterns.

Individuals in this segment rank among the top three in their viewing of three program types, children's programs, dramas, and movies. Their relative exposure to children's programs is exceedingly high, 224% of average, the third highest index in Table 5.2. In addition to these three program types, they are also more than 10% above average in their viewing of documentaries, game shows, soap operas, and specials.

Their high viewing index for children's programs is to be expected. Members of this segment are 87% female, and 75% are adults with children. On both statistics they are higher than any other segment. Furthermore, the average age of their children is nine, the youngest of any segment. The programs in this category they watch most often relative to the population are those that combine entertainment with educational material, namely *Sesame Street, Mister Rogers,* and *Electric Company.* This segment's viewing rate for each of these programs is at least three and a half times the average for the population studied. Parents in this segment, we hypothesize, watch these programs with their children and tend to direct their children's viewing toward those program alternatives they see as contributing to their children's development.

In addition, these are people who tend to select programs stressing family-oriented subject matter, even with programming that is not solely child-oriented. For example:

(1) *Dramas.* Two of the three dramas on which the people in this segment rank among the top two segments in viewing frequency are *Little House on the Prairie* and *Family.*

(2) *Soap Operas.* Two of the three soap operas they watch well above average are *All My Children* and *The Young and The Restless.*

(3) *Miscellaneous.* Across all program types, there are seven other programs on which people in this segment rank among the top two segments, namely:

- Once Upon a Classic
- Wonderful World of Disney
- Love Boat
- Quincy
- Rossetti and Ryan
- Soap
- Late Night Movies

The first three of these programs are appealing to both adults and children; thus they lend themselves to family viewing. The latter four are not available for viewing until after the bedtimes of young children.

With few exceptions, the extremely high levels of viewing behavior of the adults in this segment are attributable to programs which are either:

(1) Aimed toward the intellectual and social development of young children.

(2) Focused on family participation or about young families.

The behavior of the members of this segment is quite consistent with the previous characterization of their interests, needs, and demographics. Their television viewing behavior appears to be influenced more by children than that of any other segment. This finding is more than a reflection of the fact that this segment contains households with children and teenagers, as other segments share this characteristic. What makes this segment unique is the extent to which the children have an impact on the behavior of the adult members of the segment.

Television appears to play a very definite and focused role in the households of the Family Integrated Activities segment. Through the selection of programs whose content has a broad range of appeal across age groups, they are able to use television as a means of bringing parents and children together when they share the viewing experience, at least during the hours when the children are awake. This is markedly different from those households in which television is used as a "babysitter" or as a vehicle for keeping children out of the way while their parents pursue separate interests and activities.

Youth Concentration

COMPETITIVE SPORTS AND SCIENCE/ENGINEERING

Teenage male students with interests in male-associated mechanical activities and competitive athletics. Avoidance of female-oriented subjects and interests. High on needs for unique/creative accomplishment, intellectual stimulation and growth, status enhancement, and escape from boredom. Low needs for understanding others and for greater self-acceptance.

The most distinguishing characteristic of the television viewing behavior of members of this segment is that their viewing of sports programming is 105% above average. This is extreme, not only in relation to their own viewing of other program types, but also in comparison to that for other segments. Their ratio of above-average sports viewing is the sixth highest index reported in Table 5.2. They rank first on all seven of the sports programs included in the category.

In addition to sports, they have viewing indices that exceed 115% on three other program types, children's programs, situation comedies, and science fiction. In the case of children's programs, persons in this segment are especially heavy viewers of cartoons. They are above average on all three programs which comprise the science fiction category, although they rank some-what higher on *Logan's Run* and *The Man from Atlantis* than on *The New Adventures of Wonder Woman.*

Of the thirty programs in the situation comedy category, they rank first or second in their viewing of the following ten:

- All In the Family
- Barney Miller
- Bustin Loose
- Carter Country
- Good Times
- Happy Days
- M*A*S*H
- San Pedro Beach Bums
- Welcome Back, Kotter
- What's Happening

The five lowest ranking situation comedies for the people in this segment are:

- Sanford and Son
- The Betty White Show
- Maude
- Rhoda
- The Tony Randall Show
- We've Got Each Other

All ten of their heavily viewed situation comedies incorporate one or more of the following characteristics:

(1) The absence of strong male or female authority figures (e.g., *Good Times, Happy Days*).

(2) Mocking of male authority figures (e.g., *All in the Family, Barney Miller*).

(3) Strong male teenage heroes (e.g., *Happy Days, Good Times, Welcome Back, Kotter, San Pedro Beach Bums, What's Happening*).

The low ranking situation comedies have, with one possible exception, one of two characteristics:

(1) Female personalities in strong assertive roles (e.g., *Betty White, Maude, Rhoda*).

(2) Male figures in weak roles (*We've Got Each Other*).

In general, the types of situation comedies most appealing to this segment bear in some way upon the adolescent male's conflicts with his struggle for independence from parental and other adult authority figures. The heavily viewed programs in this category tend to provide a light and humorous treatment of this conflict, and, in doing so, they may provide considerable tension release to those whose lives are constantly affected by it.

The people in this segment are among the lowest three segments in their viewing of the following program types:

- Theatrical performances—19%
- Soap operas—29%
- Other (religion)—39%
- News/commentary—48%
- Talk shows—76%
- Dramas—72% of average

The general characteristics indicated by their below-average viewing of these program types are:

(1) An avoidance of intellectual, cultural, informational, or abstract material, especially reflected in their light viewing of news/commentary, talk shows, theatrical performances, and religious program types.

(2) Possible discomfort with family shows depicting traditional authority relationships within the family and cooperative coping with life's more serious problems. Such presentations of family life may be threatening to a group

whose members are often in the midst of family conflict and having great difficulty resolving it. This interpretation is supported by the fact that within the general drama category, the people in this segment are among the lowest three segments in their viewing of *Little House on the Prairie, Big Hawaii,* and *The Waltons,* while they are among the top three segments in their viewing of *Lou Grant* and *The Fitzpatricks.*

Persons in this segment appear to be attracted to male-dominated program content in which young male figures are admired and looked up to because of their physical and/or social prowess. They tend to avoid programming involving traditional authority relationships (unless treated as comedy), whether they are male- or female-related. For them, television appears to be an entertainment or recreational medium with little use dedicated to seeking information or broadening their intellectual or cultural horizons.

ATHLETIC AND SOCIAL ACTIVITIES

Teenage females from high-income families. The youngest of all the segments. Interests in active, away-from-home, face-to-face activities. High need to escape from problems and to be socially stimulating. Low need for family ties.

Persons in this segment are 20% below average in their total amount of television viewing. In large part, this is due to the fact that they are well below average in their in-home availability (84%).

They are above average in their viewing on only four of the nineteen program types as follows:

- Science fiction—22%
- Children's programs—21% above average
- Situation comedy—15%
- Movies—8%

At the opposite extreme, their viewing index is below 50% of the average for the population in the following categories:

- Documentary—3% of average
- Theatrical performances—19%

- News/commentary—35%
- News shows/daily—40%
- Talk shows—42%

As in the other Youth Concentration segments, these people are well below average in their viewing of information-oriented or cultural subject matter.

We believe that the need to escape from problems at home, combined with a low need for family ties, on the part of members of this segment is met by immersing themselves in away-from-home interests and activities. In addition, part of their above-average viewing behavior also serves an escape function:

(1) *Children's Programs.* They rank among the top four segments in their viewing of *Mr. Rogers, Captain Kangaroo,* and *Electric Company.*

(2) *Science Fiction.* They are above average in their viewing of all three programs in this type, though they rank somewhat higher on *The New Adventures of Wonder Woman* than on either *The Man from Atlantis* or *Logan's Run.*

(3) *Movies.* Television movie content was not specifically covered in the questionnaire; however, we do know the viewing habits of these persons when it comes to attending movies. Members of this segment will be seen in Chapter 7 to be heavy viewers of escape films, such as science fiction, horror, and disaster films.

(4) *Situation Comedies.* Their situation comedy viewing appears to serve related, but somewhat different, functions. They are among the two top segments in their viewing of:

- Laverne and Shirley
- Love Boat
- One Day at a Time
- Operation Petticoat
- San Pedro Beach Bums
- Soap
- Three's Company

Common to all of these programs are light-hearted treatments of male-female relationships in nontraditional family (or household) relationships. As such, they may provide the same sort of tension release for the members of this youth segment as provided to the Competitive Sports and Science/Engineering segment by their preferred situation comedies as discussed above. Consistent with this interpretation is the fact that the Athletic and Social Activities segment ranks first in its viewing of *Soap*, the ultimate satire on family life.

For this, the youngest of all the segments (average age of 18 years), television is clearly used as an entertainment medium and not as a means of keeping informed or broadening exposure to the arts. The difference in preferences among the situation comedies selected most often by this predominantly female youth segment and those selected by their male counterparts is interesting. This difference appears to reflect a subtle difference in the nature of the adolescent's conflict for boys and girls. The boys are struggling to establish their independence from authority figures and to exert their own authority. Their situation comedy viewing is concentrated on programs that poke fun at traditional authority figures and roles. The girls, on the other hand, while confronted with a similar struggle, seem more oriented toward simply escaping from the problems of home life. Their viewing of situation comedies is focused on programs that treat family life in general in a humorous vein.

INDOOR GAMES AND SOCIAL ACTIVITIES

Young, low-income females. Interests in activities, especially indoor games. Low interest in most subject matter areas. Nonintellectual. High needs for status enhancement and the need to be socially stimulating.

Members of this segment watch a substantial amount of television. In terms of average hours per week (Table 5.1), individuals in this segment are 14% above average, ranking fourth out of fourteen. In addition, they view considerably more television than do members of the Athletic and Social Activities segment, which is also comprised primarily of young women.

These individuals are above-average viewers of ten of the nineteen program types. On only six program types are they more than 20% below the average for the population in their viewing behavior. The six types are:

- Talk shows—76%
- Others (religion)—64%
- Theatrical performances—60%
- News shows/daily—46%
- Documentary—44% *below* average
- News/commentary—27%

Like the previous segment, they clearly avoid program content that is information-oriented or culturally enriching. While their viewing of musical performances is quite high, this is attributable to their ranking first on the frequency of watching *American Bandstand* and second on *Soul Train*. Otherwise, their general viewing pattern is less selective than that of almost any other segment. They watch an above-average amount of virtually every other type of programming aired on television.

The average person in this segment is a female adult in a major transitional stage of her life. At age 22, she has usually moved from her parents' home and completed her schooling; she is in the early stages of establishing her own home. The diversity of viewing behavior for this segment undoubtedly reflects a mixture of young women, some of whom are teenagers, and some of whom are married with young children and many hours available at home.

In particular, they are well above average in their viewing of:

(1) Youth-oriented program types, such as science fiction, musical performances (due to their heavy viewing of *Soul Train* and *American Bandstand*), adventure, crime drama (highest ranking are *Charlie's Angels, Starsky and Hutch, Switch*), and children's programs.

(2) Daytime programs, such as game shows and soap operas.

(3) Situation comedies, including an unusually broad variety of programs.

This segment has by far the highest viewing index for situation comedies of all the segments, and they rank high in their viewing of virtually all of them.

It is also notable that 21% of this segment's members are Black. This percentage is the second highest among the fourteen segments and no doubt contributes in large part to its high rating for musical performances (*Soul Train*) and for its above-average viewing of variety shows, which include *The Redd Foxx* and *The Richard Pryor Shows.*

It is clear that television plays a significant role in the lives of the Indoor Games and Social Activities segment. They appear to be at a stage in their lives when their away-from-home social activities are restricted and when, at least for the time being, television viewing of a broad variety constitutes one of their major sources of entertainment.

Mixed

NEWS AND INFORMATION

Passive interests related to keeping informed on a broad range of subjects and activities. Needs are focused on being socially stimulating and maintaining family ties.

The members of this segment watch television during more time periods on average than does any other segment. Their overall television exposure index, reported in Table 5.1, is 134%, and they rate above average on all but two of the nineteen program types as shown in Table 5.2. These are children's programs and science fiction. They rank first or second in their viewing of seven of the nineteen program types as shown below:

Rank First

- News/commentary—133% above average
- Talk shows—82%
- Sports—67%
- Variety shows—54%

Rank Second

- News shows/daily—34%
- Movies—33%
- Documentary—32% above average

Their desire to keep informed on a broad range of subjects pervades at least five, if not all seven, top ranked program types. The only two types for which this interpretation is not obvious are movies and variety shows, although both represent vehicles for keeping up-to-date on what is happening in the entertainment world, an integral part of our social structure.

Because the viewing behavior of people in this segment is so consistently high, an analysis of individual programs adds little to understanding them.

Members of the News and Information segment clearly use television heavily both as an entertainment medium and as a means of keeping informed about the society in which they live. As indicated in Chapter 4, the members of this segment do not appear to be social or political activists, and their broad need for information is not reflected in their demographic or occupational characteristics. Rather, they seek to be knowledgeable about a wide range of subjects in order to make themselves more socially stimulating and better able to converse with others.

DETACHED

Low socioeconomic profile. Extremely few interests and activities and few psychological needs satisfied by them. Low scores on needs related to both intellectual stimulation and interpersonal contact and support.

Members of this segment are average or below average in their viewing frequency of all nineteen program types. They do not rank above seventh in their viewing of any program type. This finding is especially interesting in the context of Table 5.1, which indicates that the Detached segment has a television exposure index which, while below the population average, is larger than that of five other segments. The other segments, however, tend to be much more selective in their television viewing; thus they score high on some program types and very low on others. The Detached segment is relatively nondiscriminating in its program selection; as a result, their below-average viewing frequency is reflected in all categories.

Their highest scoring four program types are crime drama with an index of 97%, movies (93%), science fiction (93%), and soap operas (99%). Their lowest are news/commentary (66%), theatrical performances (46%), documentaries (59%), and specials (39%).

In addition to being oriented to less intellectually demanding or informative program content, the people in this segment use television to a large degree as a vehicle for escape. Though their need scores for Escape from Boredom and Problems, as discussed in Chapter 4, were neither exceptionally high nor low in relation to the *other segments,* these, along with the need for Status Enhancement, were among the top three needs for *people in this segment.*[2]

COSMOPOLITAN SELF-ENRICHMENT

Extremely high socioeconomic profile. Diverse pattern of intellectual and cultural interests. Physically active. High needs for intellectual stimulation, unique/creative accomplishment, and understanding others. Low needs for status enhancement and for escape from boredom.

The people in this segment make less overall use of television, 75% of average, than do those in any other. This results from the fact that they have the lowest television share of in-home time (79%), rather than from a lack of in-home availability.

In contrast to the Detached segment, their lower level of television exposure reflects considerable selectivity in their viewing behavior as evidenced by the fact that they are at least 20% above the population average (ranking fourth or higher) in their viewing behavior of the following program types:

- Theatrical performances—116%
- News shows/daily—34%
- Documentary—29% *above* average
- Talk shows—27%

In order to interpret their selective use of television, it is useful to "get ahead of our story" and relate it to their use of other media. The members of this segment are among the heaviest users of all forms of print media—books, magazines, and newspapers. Their use of all three types tends to be oriented toward seeking information, knowledge, and culture, and their use of television reinforces this pattern.

Their viewing of theatrical performances consists in large part of book-related programs such as *Once Upon a Classic* and *Dickens of London.* Their documentary, news programs, and talk show preferences closely mirror their newspaper and magazine reading habits.

This is a segment of highly literate individuals, likely intellectuals in the truest sense of the word, who are selective in their exposure to all the mass media, choosing only that material they believe will be informative or intellectually stimulating.

HIGHLY DIVERSIFIED

Southern, Black, adults with children. Broad range of interests, especially those permitting personal participation with family and/or other informal small group settings. High need for intellectual stimulation and growth.

Members of the Highly Diversified segment were seen in Chapter 4 to have the highest television share of in-home time (136%). Consistent with their interest pattern, they exhibit an extremely broad range of exposure to television programming. They are average or above average in their viewing of eighteen of the nineteen program types measured. Those on which they rank higher than any other segment are:

- Musical performances—111%
- Adventure—64% *above* average
- Movies—47%
- Crime drama—39%

Those on which they rank second are:

- Science fiction—74%
- Children's programs—65% *above* average
- Others (religious)—64%
- Specials—37%

The Highly Diversified segment, both in terms of its interest pattern and its use of television, appears to be the polar opposite of the Detached segment previously discussed. Its high levels of reported interests and television viewing of all types is as varied as the low levels reported by the Detached group.

Insight into the interest pattern and viewing behavior of the Highly Diversified segment does not come readily, although, as noted in Chapter 4, their demographics are quite distinctive. One third of the members of this segment are Black, and the South is disproportionately represented.

Certainly, the television set plays a major role in their family lives. The mixture of heavily viewed programs includes those typically associated with children and adults, males and females, entertainment and education, and both "highbrow" and "lowbrow" material. This pattern leads to the hypothesis that television viewing in these households is a family affair, in which the entire household participates as a group, with program selections alternating from time to time to fit the preferences of different family members. This hypothesis will be further evaluated by the data reported in Chapter 9, which deals with the viewing context and set control.

CONCLUSIONS

Exhibit 5.2 contains a "thumbnail sketch" of the television viewing behavior of each of the fourteen interest segments. From these profiles, it is clear that the programs and program types are related in an interpretable and meaningful fashion to the interests, needs, and demographic characteristics of the fourteen segments.

In Chapters 6 and 7, similar analyses are reported on magazines and other media (books, movies, newspapers, and radio).

While the primary focus of this book is the use of television, there is of course a relationship between the use of television and the use of other media. In fact, an examination of how each of the segments uses other media is helpful in gaining insights into the relationships between interest and need patterns and television viewing.

Exhibit 5.2

Television Viewing Behavior
Interest Segment Characteristics

A. *Adult Male Concentration*

Mechanics and Outdoor Life
Below-average television exposure and in-home availability. Relatively high on escape/fantasy-related adventure, science fiction, crime, movies. Low on programming containing intellectual content. Quite low on sports programming, especially for a predominantly male segment.

Money and Nature's Products
Average viewing level. Attracted to programming associated with one or more of the following four elements: outdoor nature-related activities; need for social contact, support, and respect; interest in money/business; need to be knowledgeable about events and trends in the world around them. Support of traditional American virtues.

Family and Community Centered
Below-average television viewers, with family and community activities competing for time. Religious convictions may limit use of television. Program types favored tend to be least offensive—religious, sports, news.

B. *Adult Female Concentration*

Elderly Concerns
Above-average viewers. Highest in-home availability. Needs for vicarious participation, social integration, and acceptance appear to be common denominators of above-average viewing behavior. Favored program types—dramas, game shows, soap operas, religious programming, as well as news, talk shows, and variety shows. Typical programs—*The Waltons,* Merv Griffin, Lawrence Welk.

Arts and Cultural Activities
Average viewing level. Selective viewers satisfying informational needs and seeking to broaden intellectual and cultural horizons. Extremely high on theatrical performances, musical performances, documentaries, news/commentary.

Home and Community Centered
Slightly below-average overall viewing. Focus on family relations. Favored program types—soap operas, religious programs.

Exhibit 5.2 (Continued)

Family Integrated Activities
Slightly above-average viewing rate. Focus on family entertainment and child development. Program types—children's programs, dramas, and movies. Exceptionally high on educational children's programs such as *Sesame Street, Mister Rogers.* Dramas tend to be nonviolent with family content. Also true of programs in other categories—*Once Upon a Classic, All My Children, Family Feud.* Television used as a means to bring together adults and children for shared viewing experiences.

C. *Youth Concentration*

Competitive Sports and Science/Engineering
Average level of viewing. Heavy viewers of programs and program types with male personalities, especially young men who are admired because of their physical and/or social prowess. Programs mocking authority figures. Low on programming that is intellectually upscaled or abstract, copes with problems that do not yield to immediate solutions, or features female personalities in assertive roles. Generally avoid traditional authority relationships that appear to threaten their need to establish personal independence.

Athletic and Social Activities
Well below average television viewers. Lowest level of in-home availability. Heavy viewers of escape programming and programming involving male-female relationships in nonfamily, light-hearted contexts. Need to get away from problems of home life.

Indoor Games and Social Activities
Well above average viewers of television. Low on informational or cultural program types. Above average on virtually all others. Overall profile reflects combination of youth- and young home-maker-oriented programming. Both roles coexist in segment. Television a major source of entertainment for this segment.

D. *Mixed*

News and Information
Highest of any segment in overall television viewing. Second highest on television share of in-home time. Favor news shows, talk shows, variety shows, documentaries, movies, sports. Good subjects for day-to-day casual conversation. Need to be socially stimulating and conversant with many subjects.

Exhibit 5.2 (Continued)

Detached

Below-average viewing. Less intellectually demanding, somewhat escape-oriented. Crime dramas, movies, science fiction, soap operas are high for the segment, but not compared to other segments.

Cosmopolitan Self-Enrichment

Lightest television viewing segment. Highly literate, print-oriented persons. Television viewing is highly selective. Favored program types/programs resemble print preferences. Theatrical performances (*Once Upon a Classic, Dickens of London*), news shows, talk shows, documentaries. Avoid escape, general entertainment-oriented program types such as adventure and crime drama.

Highly Diversified

Second highest viewing segment. Highest share of in-home time watching television. Average or above average on eighteen of nineteen program types. General family fare viewing reflects diversity of family member interests. Highest scoring types—adventure, crime drama, movies, musical performances (*Soul Train, Music Hall America*). Also high on children's programs (cartoons), science fiction, specials, religion.

NOTES

1. A fourteen-way multiple discriminant analysis was also performed as part of the process of evaluating the extent of overall segment differences in viewing frequency by program type. The nineteen viewing frequency measures were used as independent variables. Based on the results of this analysis, 26% of the respondents were correctly classified compared to the 10% one could expect from a random assignment to the fourteen segments or the 10% accuracy that would occur if all were assigned to the modal segment. The overall pattern of between segment differences was tested using the Wilk's Lambda statistic. Based on the appropriate F-ratio approximation, the results of this discriminant analysis were significant beyond the .005 level.

2. The appearance of a Detached segment in this study is not unique. Based on our involvement in dozens of market segmentation projects spanning a wide range of categories of products and services, it would have been more surprising had such a segment not emerged. Almost universally, we have encountered a portion of the population whose interests, needs, and attitudes associated with a particular product

category are uniformly low with respect to the remainder of the population. In almost all cases, their consumption behavior reflected this pattern as well, through low levels of purchase and little brand differentiation.

In previous work, these segments have been labeled with titles such as "Nonintrospective," "Uninvolved," "Low Involvement," "Detached," "Unconcerned," and others. In the present study, as indicated in Chapter 4, it is highly likely that for the members of this segment, the interests and needs measured (as well as the desire to watch television) are simply of lower salience than for the rest of the population.

6

Magazines

INTRODUCTION

Though this chapter is primarily concerned with readership by type of magazine, results relating to individual magazines are reported where these serve to clarify the discussion. The data are based on answers to one question in the study, in which respondents were asked to identify which of 77 magazines they read regularly. For analytical purposes, the 77 magazines are grouped into 15 types. The types, and the magazines that comprise them, are reported in Exhibit 6.1.[1] The list of magazines includes virtually all of the principal national monthlies and weeklies. It spans a wide range of general and special interest subject matter.

OVERALL READERSHIP

Overall magazine readership is measured on the basis of the average number of magazines respondents report reading regularly. Table 6.1 reports the findings by segment. The datum for each segment is the ratio of the segment's average to that for the entire population multiplied by 100. For example, the ratio of 132 for people in the Family Integrated Activities segment

Exhibit 6.1

Individual Magazines by Type

Automotive
  Car and Driver
  Hot Rod
  Motor Trend
  Road and Track

Black
  Black Enterprise
  Ebony ⌐
  Essence
  Jet ⸺

Business/Finance
  Business Week ⸺
  Forbes
  Fortune ⸺
  Money
  Moneysworth
  Nation's Business

Fashion
  Glamour
  Mademoiselle
  Vogue

General
  People
  Reader's Digest
  TV Guide
  Us

Home Service/Home
  American Home
  Apartment Life
  Better Homes and Gardens
  House Beautiful
  House and Garden

Mechanics
  Mechanix Illustrated
  Popular Mechanics
  Popular Science

Men
  Esquire
  Penthouse
  Playboy ⸺
  True

News
  Newsweek
  Time ⸺
  U.S. News and World Report

Outdoor
  Argosy
  Field and Stream
  Guns and Ammunition
  Outdoor Life
  Sports Afield

Romance
  Modern Romances ⸺
  Modern Screen
  Photoplay
  True Story ⸺

Select
  Harper's
  National Geographic
  Natural History
  New Yorker
  Psychology Today
  Gourmet
  Scientific American
  Smithsonian
  Travel and Leisure
  Rolling Stone
  New Times

Sports
  Flying
  Golf
  Golf Digest

Exhibit 6.1 (Continued)

Sport
Sports Illustrated
Tennis
Yachting
Motorboating and Sailing

Women's Services
Cosmopolitan
Family Circle
Good Housekeeping

Ladies Home Journal
McCall's —
Ms.
Parent's Magazine
Redbook —
Woman's Day
Baby Talk
Mother's Manual

Miscellaneous
Popular Photography
National Lampoon

indicates that the number of magazines they report regularly reading is 32% greater on average than for the population.

People in the Highly Diversified, Cosmopolitan Self-Enrichment, and Family Integrated Activities segments are the heaviest users of magazines. They range from 32% to 50% above average in their usage. In addition, members of three other segments are above average but to a lesser degree (6% to 14%), those in the Arts and Cultural Activities, Indoor Games and Social Activities, and Competitive Sports and Science/ Engineering segments.

At the other extreme, the lightest users are the members of the Elderly Concerns and Detached segments, both of which are slightly over 50% of average. Next are those in the Money and Nature's Products and Family and Community Centered segments, which are 72% and 80% of average respectively.

The heavy usage segments tend to be those with strong intellectual and cultural interests and those whose interests include people, places, and things outside of their immediate families and communities. In contrast, light magazine usage is associated with segments characterized by narrow ranges of interests.

READERSHIP BY MAGAZINE TYPE

Table 6.2 reports the percentage of people by segment regularly reading at least one magazine of a given type. These percentages are measures of net readership. In this chapter, the

phrases net readership and regular readership are used synony-
mously.

Detailed tables reporting readership of individual magazines
are presented in Appendix G. The discussion draws upon data in
Table 6.2 as well as data contained in the Appendix. These
tables have been placed in the Appendix, as they are quite
lengthy, and relatively little of the information in them is used
in the course of this discussion.

The variation in readership across all segments for each of the
fifteen magazine types has been tested for statistical significance
using the univariate F-ratio statistic. All fifteen of the tests are
significant at the .005 level.[2]

TABLE 6.1   Overall Magazine Readership by Interest
Segment

	Average Number of Magazines Read by Segment As Percentage of Population Average
	%
Adult Male Concentration	
Mechanics and Outdoor Life	92
Money and Nature's Products	72
Family and Community Centered	80
Adult Female Concentration	
Elderly Concerns	56
Arts and Cultural Activities	114
Home and Community Centered	100
Family Integrated Activities	132
Youth Concentration	
Competitive Sports and Science Egineering	106
Athletic and Social Activities	98
Indoor Games and Social Activities	108
Mixed	
News and Information	96
Detached	52
Cosmopolitan Self-Enrichment	134
Highly Diversified	150
Population mean	(5.0) (magazines)

TABLE 6.2 Percentage of Persons Frequently Reading at Least One Magazine by Magazine Type and Interest Segment[a]

	Entire Population	Adult Male Concentration			Adult Female Concentration					Youth Concentration		Mixed			
		Mechanics and Outdoor Life	Money and Nature's Products	Family and Community Centered	Elderly Concerns	Arts and Cultural Activities	Home and Community Centered	Family Integrated Activities	Competitive Sports and Science/Engineering	Athletic and Social Activities	Indoor Games and Social Activities	News and Information	Detached	Cosmopolitan Self-Enrichment	Highly Diversified
Automotive	9%	30%	7%	8%	6%	3%	2%	2%	32%	6%	3%	1%	3%	4%	16%
Black	7	3	2	5	5	7	10	4	5	2	13	6	6	2	27
Business/Finance	10	5	11	13	2	16	12	7	9	7	4	10	9	21	17
Fashion	9	2	0	2	1	13	12	15	3	27	20	5	4	12	13
General	53	54	49	50	44	61	51	67	46	45	66	69	30	56	56
Home Service/Home	28	11	20	20	25	40	44	47	6	27	43	21	9	33	39
Mechanics	11	27	14	17	4	6	1	6	28	3	4	6	12	4	19
Men's	24	53	25	21	10	19	11	18	33	11	27	28	16	31	33
News	26	13	18	23	13	39	19	23	35	15	16	40	20	57	29
Outdoor	15	31	29	28	2	3	6	8	25	12	5	15	12	12	27
Romance	9	5	2	2	8	6	13	13	5	20⁻	20⁻	8	5	4	17
Select	30	22	22	27	16	53	20	25	26	20	24	29	18	66⁻	36
Sports	20	18	18	23	3	15	15	11	54	20	15	20	15	27	28
Women's Service	42	13	20	27	41	54	61	77	10	57	58⁻	37	15	55	55
Miscellaneous	5	11	2	2	3	4	2	3	9	5	3	3	1	9	9

a. The statistical significance of differences in segment readership of each of the fifteen magazine types contained in this table was evaluated based on univariate F-ratios with 13 and 2,462 degrees of freedom. All fifteen tests are significant at the .005 level.

133

Adult Male Concentration

MECHANICS AND OUTDOOR LIFE

People in this segment rank first in their readership of three types of magazines, men's, outdoor, and miscellaneous. On two other types, automotive and mechanics, they rank second. They do not rank above seventh in their readership of any of the other ten types of magazines.

They are among the lowest three segments in their reported readership of women's services, home service/home, and fashion. In addition, members of this segment are light readers of business/finance and news magazines.

These results are consistent both with the expressed interest patterns of this segment and with its demographic composition.

These people's readership of outdoor, automotive, and mechanics magazines reflects their reported interests in mechanical and outdoor activities. Their low readership of women's service, home service/home, and fashion magazines is not surprising, given that this segment contains the lowest percentage of females (4%) of any of the fourteen segments. It also contains by far the highest percentage of blue-collar workers (55%), which undoubtedly is related to their low readership of business/finance and news magazines.

There are four magazines in the men's category. On two of these, *Playboy* and *Penthouse,* this segment ranks highest in regular readership. On the other two, *True* and *Esquire,* they rank fourth and sixth respectively. They rank second in their readership of both *Popular Photography* and *National Lampoon,* the two magazines that comprise the miscellaneous category.

In general, the magazine readership of this segment appears primarily to satisfy entertainment and recreational needs of a highly individualistic nature. It concentrates on personal interests and hobbies with little sense of family integration or of broader involvement in community, national, or world affairs.

MONEY AND NATURE'S PRODUCTS

The only magazine type ranked above fifth for people in this segment is outdoor, on which they rank second with 29%

readership. Of the five magazines in this category (*Argosy*, *Field and Stream*, *Guns and Ammunition*, *Outdoor Life*, and *Sports Afield*), the only one they read more frequently than those in other adult male segments is *Outdoor Life*.

The next three highest ranking readership categories are automotive, mechanics, and business/finance. On the first two of these, this segment's members rank fifth, while on the third they rank sixth.

This magazine usage profile corresponds to their principal interests as reflected in the very name of the segment.

FAMILY AND COMMUNITY CENTERED

In spite of their broad interests, members of this segment are relatively light users of magazines. They do not rank first or second in their usage of any magazine type. They rank third on only one category (outdoor) and fourth on four others: sports, business/finance, automotive, and mechanics. These reading habits are closely associated with a subset of their interests. That is, this segment is composed of people who ranked second on the Reaping Nature's Benefits and Investments factors and third on Professional Sports and Mechanical Activities factors.

Several of their high ranking interests (e.g., Community Activities, Religion, and Crime and Society) either do not correspond closely to existing types of national magazines or are cast in too intellectualized a form to be acceptable to members of this segment. To some extent, this point of view is supported by the discussion of this segment's newspaper usage in Chapter 7. As will be shown, the people in this segment are relatively heavy users of daily and local weekly newspapers. They tend to use them for gaining exposure to much of this type of subject matter. Local newspapers may be better suited to pursuing the aforementioned interests than are currently available magazines.

Adult Female Concentration

ELDERLY CONCERNS

People in this segment make relatively little use of magazines. Their overall readership index is 56%, lower than every other segment but the Detached group. They rank in the bottom three segments on nine of the fifteen magazine types and do not rank above sixth on any type.

The three types on which they rank highest are women's services, home service/home, and romance. On none of these types are they above average in their readership.

The particular women's services magazines on which they have higher ranks (seventh or eighth) are *Good Housekeeping, Family Circle,* and *Woman's Day.* These are all magazines related to home maintenance activities, in contrast to other magazines in this category such as *Ms., Parent's Magazine, Baby Talk,* and *Cosmopolitan,* on which they rank twelfth or lower. This is consistent with the fact that Household Activities was one of the only three above-average interest factors for persons in this segment.

The romance magazines on which they have relatively high ranks (fifth out of fourteen) are *Modern Romances* and *True Story,* in contrast to the tenth ranked *Photoplay,* with *Modern Screen* falling in between with a rank of seventh. Only a small percentage of the people in this segment frequently read any one of the romance magazines (7%); nonetheless, for those who do, we would hypothesize that they are using them to cope with their loneliness in much the same manner they use the soap operas, game shows, and talk shows on television. In both cases, the medium offers a surrogate set of interpersonal relationships in which the reader or viewer can get involved.

ARTS AND CULTURAL ACTIVITIES

The people in this segment score quite high on the Classical Arts, Investments, International Affairs, and Comprehensive News and Information interest factors. The subject matter content, as well as the intellectually upscaled nature of their interests, is consistent with their overall pattern of magazine readership.

A full 53% of the members of this segment read one or more select type magazines regularly. This places them second out of fourteen segments, with only those in the Cosmopolitan Self-Enrichment segment ranking higher with 66% readership. The high relative readership of select type magazines is broadly based, in that they rank among the top three segments in readership of eight of the ten magazines in this category. The two exceptions are *Natural History* and *Rolling Stone*, on which they rank no higher than tenth. This segment is also among the top three in readership of two other magazine types, business/finance and news.

They have lower readership of women's services and home service/home magazines than do people in the other dominantly adult female segments except for those in the Elderly Concerns segment. Their readership of these two types of magazines is consistent with their relative lack of interest in Household Activities, on which they ranked ninth.

HOME AND COMMUNITY CENTERED

The interests of these people are relatively narrowly focused on home and community. In addition, they tend to be directed more toward activities, ideas, and objects than toward other individuals. The members of this segment rank second only to those in the Family Integrated Activities segment in their readership of women's services and home services/home magazines. Within the women's services category, their highest ranking magazines are *Family Circle, Woman's Day,* and *Ladies Home Journal,* while the lowest ranking are *Ms., Mother's Manual, Cosmopolitan,* and *Parent's Magazine.* This aspect of their readership profile is consistent with their interest in Household Activities.

They have interests that are less intellectual than those of the Arts and Cultural Activities or the Family Integrated Activities segment.

Their usage of magazine content is more narrowly focused than that of these other two segments, and they have lower readership on ten of the fifteen magazine types than do those in these segments.

The narrower focus of their magazine usage may also be due to their interest in community activities, along with the fact that none of the magazines included in this study focuses on such activities. This hypothesis is supported by the fact that this segment makes more use of local weekly newspapers than do the other two (see Chapter 7).

FAMILY INTEGRATED ACTIVITIES

The interest of members of this segment in all aspects of home and family life is consistent not only with the fact that they rank first in their readership of both women's services and home service/home magazines, but also with the finding that of the sixteen magazines that comprise these categories, they rank first on eleven of them and second on two.

Of these high ranking magazines, three of them are about children, namely *Parent's Magazine, Baby Talk,* and *Mother's Manual.* This is also consistent with the extremely high percentage of adults with children in this segment (75%) and with the hypothesis that the people in this segment tend to be more responsive to their children than are those in other segments.

The people in this segment have reading habits that transcend traditional female family role activities. They have a somewhat higher proportion of regular readers than does the Home and Community Centered segment for ten of fifteen magazine types. This is also consistent with their broader pattern of interests.

Youth Concentration

COMPETITIVE SPORTS AND SCIENCE/ENGINEERING

Given their high scores on interests in Sports, Participant Athletic Activities, and Science/Engineering, as well as Mechanical Activities, the fact that members of this segment rank higher than any other in their readership of sports, automotive, and mechanics types of magazines comes as no surprise.

In addition, this segment's high ranking readership of men's magazines is consistent with its large percentage of young males.

ATHLETIC AND SOCIAL ACTIVITIES
INDOOR GAMES AND SOCIAL ACTIVITIES

The readership behavior of persons in the Athletic and Social Activities and the Indoor Games and Social Activities segments is best understood by examining the profile of similarities and differences that exist between them across the fifteen types of magazines. Table 6.3 provides such a summary.

TABLE 6.3 Comparison of Readership of Selected
Types of Magazines for the Two Predominantly
Female Youth Concentration Segments

	Athletic and Social Activities		Indoor Games and Social Activities		Population
	Rank	Percent Regular Readers	Rank	Percent Regular Readers	Percent Regular Readers
Similar High Ranking Types					
Women's services	4	57%	3	58%	42%
Romance	1-2	20	1-2	20	9
Fashion	1	27	2	20	9
Similar Low Ranking Types					
Business/finance	7	7%	12	4%	10%
News	12	15	11	16	26
Mechanics	13	3	10	4	11
Athletic and Social Activities Segment Relatively High Ranking Types (higher by at least four ranks)					
Outdoor	7	12%	12	5%	15%
Automotive	7	6	11	3	9
Miscellaneous	5	5	12	2	5
Indoor Games and Social Activities Segment Relatively High Ranking Types (higher by at least four ranks)					
Men's	13	11%	6	27%	24%
Home Service/Home	7	27	3	43	28
General	12	45	3	66	53
Black	12-14	2	2	13	7

The magazine types on which people in both these segments
rank high are women's services (especially *Cosmopolitan, Mc-
Call's*, and *Ms.*), romance, and fashion.

Those they both read to a much lesser extent are business/
finance, news, and mechanics. Given that these segments are
comprised primarily of young females, this profile is to be
expected.

The somewhat higher incidence of readership by persons in
the Athletic and Social Activities segment for outdoor, automotive, and miscellaneous (especially *Modern Photography*) types,

is consistent with this segment's need to develop and maintain away-from-home peer group involvement and support.

The higher readership of home service/home magazines among the Indoor Games and Social Activities segment members is consistent with their interests, which are more oriented to their nuclear family than those of the other segment. To some extent, home orientation is also reflected in their relatively high readership of general magazines. The magazine primarily responsible for this is *TV Guide.* As reported in Chapter 5, members of this segment rank fourth in television viewing. We would hypothesize that one reason for this and the associated *TV Guide* readership is that television is an easily shared in-home medium.

The reason for the above-average readership of Black magazines is obvious, as this segment includes the second highest percentage of Blacks in the study (21%).

Lastly, people in the Indoor Games and Social Activities segment have more than twice as high an incidence of readership of men's magazines than do those in the Athletic and Social Activities segment. As previously stated, the interests of people in the former segment are more oriented to the nuclear family, and within that, to its adult members. As such, we would hypothesize that they are interested in more sophisticated, adult-oriented discussion of the issues surrounding sexual relations and not simply the rudimentary facts of life. The men's magazines for which a higher percentage of regular readers are found in this segment are *Playboy* and *Penthouse.* These magazines may be their most readily available sources of what they perceive as the most sophisticated information on issues related to sex. Being older and more independent, they are also more likely to be able to afford such magazines, and they are less constrained by the influence of their own parents.

Mixed

NEWS AND INFORMATION

The only magazine types on which these people rank in the top three segments are news and general. Within the news category, they rank first in their readership of *Newsweek* and

U.S. News and World Report. Their high rank on general magazines is due to the fact that they rank second on *Reader's Digest* and *TV Guide.*

This profile of magazine usage is consistent with their desire to keep informed on a broad range of issues.

DETACHED

On fourteen of the fifteen magazine types, the percentage of regular readers in the Detached segment is below that for the population. There are no types of magazines on which these segment members rank above fifth. The two highest ranking types are Black magazines, on which they are tied for fifth place, and mechanics, on which they rank sixth.

Their relatively heavy readership of Black magazines is to be expected, as they have the third highest percentage of Black members across all segments.

Their high readership within the mechanics category reflects a "how to do it" orientation, as they are somewhat higher than average on *Mechanix Illustrated* and *Popular Mechanics,* and they are lower than average in their readership of *Popular Science.*

There is an anomaly in the pattern of their readership, namely that they rank first in readership of both *Forbes* and *Fortune.* The reason for this is not obvious based on their interests, needs, demographic and socioeconomic characteristics.

COSMOPOLITAN SELF-ENRICHMENT

There are five types of magazines on which the members of this segment rank among the top three:

(1) Select, on which they rank first with 66% being regular readers versus 30% for the population
(2) News, on which they also rank first with 57% regular readers versus 26% for the population
(3) Business/finance, where again they rank first with 21% versus 10% for the population
(4) Sports, with a rank of third, 27% reading versus 20% for the population
(5) Miscellaneous, where they rank second (9% versus 5%) principally because of their first position with respect to *Popular Photography*

The high ranks for select, news, and business/finance also characterize people for the Arts and Cultural Activities segment. However, in all three categories, the proportion of Cosmopolitan Self-Enrichment persons reading regularly is higher than that for the other segment. For select magazines, 66% of the Cosmopolitan Self-Enrichment segment read at least one magazine regularly, while the percentage for the Arts and Cultural Activities segment is 53%. The corresponding percentages for news readership are 57% and 39%, and those for business/finance are 21% and 16%. The profile of readership for these three types supports the intellectually upscaled nature of the interests of both segments.

The interests of people in this segment, however, go beyond intellectual and artistic interests to include people-related and physical activity interests. This is consistent with their magazine readership, in that they are relatively high in readership of sports publications.

HIGHLY DIVERSIFIED

The diversified nature of the interests of the people in this segment is clearly reflected in the profile of the magazine types they regularly read. Of the fifteen types included in this study, they rank sixth or higher on all fifteen.

There is one magazine type on which they rank first. That type is Black magazines, which 27% read regularly versus 7% for the population. This segment has the highest percentage of Black members, with 33% versus 11% for the population as a whole.

Their general pattern of magazine usage is similar to their pattern of interests, diverse but generally not exceptionally strong (first rank) in many categories.

CONCLUSIONS

Exhibit 6.2 contains a thumbnail sketch of the findings on each of the fourteen segments. As with the discussion of television, the pattern of each segment's magazine usage is generally consistent with their interests, needs, and demographic characteristics.

Exhibit 6.2

Magazine Usage Interest Segment
Characteristics

A. *Adult Male Concentration*

Mechanics and Outdoor Life
Heavy users of men's, outdoor, automotive, mechanics, and miscellaneous (*Modern Photography*). Magazine readership concentrated on entertainment and recreation, especially on personal interests and hobbies.

Money and Nature's Products
Below-average overall magazine readership. Only type on which they are above fifth is outdoor. Next in line are automotive, mechanics, and business/finance.

Family and Community Centered
Below-average readership of magazines. Third on outdoor. Fourth on sports, automotive, mechanics, and business/finance. Breadth and level of interests not well matched to magazines. Better suited to local, daily newspapers.

B. *Adult Female Concentration*

Elderly Concerns
Lightest of all magazine users. Slightly higher levels of usage among women-oriented magazines, romance. Magazine choices seem, in general, to help them cope with loneliness.

Arts and Cultural Activities
Above-average readership. Heavy on select, business/finance, and news. Lower relative to other adult female segments on women's services and home service/home.

Home and Community Centered
Average overall readership. Heavy on women's services, home service/home. Narrow subject matter focus of reading tends to be related to home activities.

Family Integrated Activities
Heavy users. Rank first on women's services and home service/home. Broad home/family readership is reflected in their ranking first on eleven of the sixteen magazines in these categories.

Exhibit 6.2 (Continued)

C. *Youth Concentration*

Competitive Sports and Science/Engineering
Intermediate overall readership. First on sports, automotive, and mechanics. Also high on men's and miscellaneous (*National Lampoon*).

Athletic and Social Activities
Intermediate usage. Heavy, along with Indoor Games and Social Activities segment, on women's services, romance, and fashion. Somewhat more usage than the other segment on outdoor, automotive, and mechanics.

Indoor Games and Social Activities
Above-average readership. Heavy, along with Athletic and Social Activities segment, on women's services, romance, and fashion. Somewhat more usage than the other segment on men's, home service/home, general, and Black publications.

D. *Mixed*

News and Information
Slightly below-average overall readership. Heavy on news and general.

Detached
Second lightest overall readership. Below population average on fourteen out of fifteen types. Highest ranking types are Black and mechanics.

Cosmopolitan Self-Enrichment
Heavy overall readership, especially select, news, business/finance, sports, miscellaneous. Next in line are men's magazines.

Highly Diversified
Heaviest overall readership. Rank sixth or higher on all fifteen types of magazines, especially Black.

NOTES

1. The classification system is similar, though not identical, to what one would get by doing a factor analysis and using its output as the basis for classifying magazines.

2. A fourteen-way multiple discriminant analysis was also performed as part of the process of evaluating the extent of overall segment differences in magazine

readership by type. The fifteen readership measures were used as independent variables. Based on the results of this analysis, 23% of the respondents were correctly classified compared to the 7% one could expect from a random assignment to the fourteen segments or the 10% accuracy that would occur if all were assigned to the modal segment. The overall pattern of the between segment differences was tested using the Wilk's Lambda statistic. Based on the appropriate F-ratio approximation, the results were significant at the .005 level.

REFERENCE

SWANSON, C. E. (1967) "The frequency structure of television and magazines." Journal of Advertising Research 7 (June): 8-14.

7

The "Other" Media: Books, Movies, Newspapers, and Radio

INTRODUCTION

This chapter reports results on the remaining four major media: books, movies, newspapers, and radio. Its purpose is not only to provide more information regarding the public's use of media, but also to validate the interest segmentation.

The measures of reported behavior used for these four media are considerably less detailed in their coverage than are those for television and magazines. For example, while measures were taken of general content areas such as Westerns and comics, no effort was made to measure readership of specific vehicles (i.e., specific books, movies, and so on) as was done for television and magazines.

More detailed viewing data were collected for television, as it is the principal focus of this study. Similar detailed data were obtained for national magazines, as the incremental interviewing and analysis time required were modest. However, in the case of the other media, the number and complexity of offerings posed both data collection and analysis problems well beyond available resources. For example, much of what is aired on radio consists of programs with limited geographic exposure. To obtain relatively comprehensive coverage of specific program usage would require a monumental effort.

The following discussion is organized by segment and describes the general pattern of results simultaneously across all four media, rather than one at a time.

BACKGROUND DETAILS

While the data on book, movie, newspaper, and radio usage are less detailed than those for television and magazines, they require the use of two types of summary tables to facilitate the task of identifying and interpreting segment usage patterns. These summary tables serve as the basis for the discussion of results that follows.

Table 7.1 reports the pattern of overall usage by interest segment for books, movies, newspapers, and radio. The figures in the body of the table are percentaged ratios of a given segment's score for a given medium to that for the entire population. For example, members of the Mechanics and Outdoor Life segment had a reported annual frequency of movie attendance 49% greater (therefore, a ratio of 149) than the average for the entire population, which is 6.1 times attending the movies per year.

Though these usage ratios are computed in the same fashion across all media, the absolute measures of usage do, of course, vary by media. For each medium, the measure used and the average for the entire population are as follows:

(1) Books—average number of books read in past year (15.6 books)
(2) Movie attendance—average number of times gone to movies in past year (6.1 times)
(3) Radio—average number of hours during which some listening occurs in a typical week (18.0 hours)
(4) Sunday papers—percentage who usually read (70.7%)
(5) Sunday supplement—percentage who read at least one regularly (34.8%)
(6) Daily papers—average number of days per week read (4.1 days)
(7) Local weeklies—percentage who usually read (47.6%)
(8) Financial newspapers—percentage who read at least one (*Barrons* or *Wall Street Journal*) regularly (4.2%)

Tables 7.2 through 7.5 report detailed summaries by segment

TABLE 7.1 Overall "Other" Media Usage by Interest Segment

	Books Read	Movies Attended	Radio	Newspaper Readership				
				Sunday Papers	Sunday Supplements	Daily Papers	Local Weeklies	Financial Newspapers
Adult Male Concentration								
Mechanics and Outdoor Life	90	149	134	75	62	80	92	64
Money and Nature's Products	30	38	69	100	72	110	94	69
Family and Community Centered	69	48	72	107	112	115	115	114
Adult Female Concentration								
Elderly Concerns	70	18	69	95	69	98	103	–
Arts and Cultural Activities	154	84	74	117	132	120	102	114
Home and Community Centered	90	98	98	114	93	110	116	83
Family Integrated Activities	92	102	122	98	140	98	102	93
Youth Concentration								
Competitive Sports and Science/Engineering	103	172	95	108	79	95	93	33
Athletic and Social Activities	67	187	161	70	60	63	66	12
Indoor Games and Social Activities	162	131	79	68	83	63	85	74
Mixed								
News and Information	99	70	78	127	132	117	114	171
Detached	49	67	93	95	57	88	74	12
Cosmopolitan Self-Enrichment	238	128	125	116	178	110	104	267
Highly Diversified	83	139	126	92	98	100	121	126
Population Mean	15.6	6.1	18.0	70.7%	34.8%	4.1	47.6%	4.2%
	(books per year)	(movies per year)	(hours listened to per week)			(days read)		

"frequent or regular" p 154

TABLE 7.2 Percentage of Persons Reading Selected Types of Books by Interest Segment[a]

Types of Books	Entire Population	Adult Male Concentration			Adult Female Concentration					Youth Concentration			Mixed		
		Mechanics and Outdoor Life	Money and Nature's Products	Family and Community Centered	Elderly Concerns	Arts and Cultural Activities	Home and Community Centered	Family Integrated Activities	Competitive Sports and Science/Engineering	Athletic and Social Activities	Indoor Games and Social Activities	News and Information	Detached	Cosmopolitan Self-Enrichment	Highly Diversified
Fiction															
Mysteries	44.1	49.1	41.9	20.7	49.1	41.5	36.1	54.2	48.9	58.0	60.9	36.0	44.0	31.4	49.9
Science Fiction	21.3	38.8	11.8	10.1	16.2	17.5	5.9	8.4	37.8	43.1	30.4	22.5	11.5	16.1	39.5
Historical Novels	33.6	15.1	31.8	40.9	37.5	59.9	23.3	25.3	19.1	15.1	14.1	52.8	18.4	50.8	37.2
Other Fiction	45.6	38.8	35.8	30.0	51.9	46.9	43.8	44.9	44.2	50.7	47.9	49.7	44.9	63.6	36.7
Nonfiction															
Biography or Autobiography	39.4	19.3	41.0	34.3	36.8	54.1	39.2	38.0	33.9	26.5	37.5	46.3	21.7	61.9	35.4
Psychology Self-Help	22.8	7.5	4.8	9.1	16.9	28.3	18.0	27.3	8.1	22.2	10.5	20.5	10.3	54.7	37.1
Philosophy, Religion	24.7	3.3	20.7	43.1	43.4	36.4	28.4	25.9	3.7	11.0	18.8	19.8	20.5	27.4	29.0
"How to" Books	30.1	40.0	29.9	31.4	33.8	28.5	25.1	41.0	17.2	14.5	22.7	14.2	23.1	38.1	36.7
Other Nonfiction															
Poetry	13.0	5.9	2.4	2.9	16.0	18.9	9.8	17.3	3.1	15.4	11.5	5.6	2.9	24.7	22.2
Drama (Plays)	10.2	1.4	3.8	3.6	5.8	22.5	6.7	7.0	6.1	9.8	13.7	5.4	5.7	15.7	19.8
Humor	31.1	38.3	24.7	17.2	28.0	35.0	23.3	36.6	39.9	49.4	25.9	21.4	14.5	29.5	37.0
Travel	14.9	13.2	19.2	20.7	12.3	25.2	6.9	8.7	12.7	3.9	6.8	22.1	5.6	21.7	19.2
Other Nonfiction	8.9	9.0	14.9	11.5	7.4	7.3	8.6	5.5	12.6	6.9	5.9	10.2	5.1	16.9	2.8
No Answer/Not Read Books	31.3	40.3	48.1	37.2	51.0	10.6	34.5	20.2	25.9	24.5	18.8	39.9	57.2	6.5	22.9

a. The statistical significance of each of the thirteen book type measures contained in this table was evaluated based on univariate F-ratios with 13 and 2,462 degrees of freedom. All but "other nonfiction" were significant at the .005 level.

TABLE 7.3 Percentage of Persons Viewing Selected Types of Movies by Interest Segment[a]

Types of Movies	Entire Population	Adult Male Concentration				Adult Female Concentration				Youth Concentration			Mixed		
		Mechanics and Outdoor Life	Money and Nature's Products	Family and Community Centered	Elderly Concerns	Arts and Cultural Activities	Home and Community Centered	Family Integrated Activities	Competitive Sports and Science/Engineering	Athletic and Social Activities	Indoor Games and Social Activities	News and Information	Detached	Cosmopolitan Self-Enrichment	Highly Diversified
Love and Romance	32.1	31.5	7.8	14.1	11.9	35.8	40.7	45.6	19.9	69.1	45.9	24.1	19.0	53.7	38.2
Comedies	49.8	62.2	22.1	31.0	17.0	60.3	48.9	58.0	72.4	83.3	74.0	41.0	24.5	66.6	53.0
Westerns	25.3	45.2	25.8	27.1	10.1	22.5	25.5	22.6	29.8	16.7	21.0	27.0	15.6	15.5	46.8
Science Fiction or Supernatural	27.6	45.4	10.1	11.0	2.7	25.2	14.8	27.4	56.5	53.9	38.7	23.2	9.4	42.5	40.6
Horror	18.2	32.8	3.5	4.7	3.6	7.6	8.9	17.7	38.3	40.2	29.1	15.2	12.1	17.6	35.8
Religious	6.9	1.3	2.6	13.2	4.0	12.7	9.1	3.9	3.9	8.3	10.1	4.9	4.3	4.7	15.9
Musical, Opera or Dance	11.6	4.3	10.7	5.8	3.8	34.9	10.1	13.2	4.4	10.0	11.7	10.3	4.5	26.6	5.6
Biographies	10.9	6.2	7.6	11.6	3.0	23.3	10.9	9.9	10.4	8.3	7.1	11.5	2.4	26.2	10.3
Children's Movies	14.5	15.3	2.7	9.8	2.8	15.2	20.6	28.9	10.6	21.1	17.7	10.7	7.9	17.6	18.6
Crime or Spy Thrillers	27.6	40.3	20.2	15.2	4.0	28.2	15.4	27.9	53.6	47.6	18.6	23.0	15.6	40.0	40.7
Documentaries	7.0	8.1	0.8	8.2	—	16.2	4.3	4.3	7.8	1.0	2.7	6.5	2.0	20.3	10.1
Historical or Adventure Film	18.9	20.2	14.1	16.2	5.9	29.9	9.9	9.2	24.7	10.8	13.7	18.2	10.4	47.2	28.9
Disaster Film	20.4	30.2	9.2	8.2	1.1	11.9	11.4	33.4	44.5	46.4	26.8	20.7	9.8	14.3	30.7
Other Films	7.6	17.1	2.5	5.8	1.0	4.3	6.5	6.5	15.3	10.5	6.7	3.7	4.8	14.9	6.7
Never Attend Movies	26.9	8.5	49.5	41.8	72.3	21.5	25.9	20.6	8.6	0.4	7.8	37.9	51.8	4.1	14.7
No Answer	1.3	1.0	2.7	2.3	2.4	—	2.2	1.1	0.7	0.5	—	2.3	1.7	0.5	0.9

a. The statistical significance of each of the fifteen movie types measured contained in this table was evaluated based on univariate F-ratios with 13 and 2,462 degrees of freedom. All were significant at the .005 level.

TABLE 7.4 Percentage of Persons Reading Selected Types of Newspaper Sections by Interest Segment[a]

Newspaper Sections	Entire Population	Adult Male Concentration			Adult Female Concentration				Youth Concentration				Mixed		
		Mechanics and Outdoor Life	Money and Nature's Products	Family and Community Centered	Elderly Concerns	Arts and Cultural Activities	Home and Community Centered	Family Integrated Activities	Competitive Sports and Science/Engineering	Athletic and Social Activities	Indoor Games and Social Activities	News and Information	Detached	Cosmopolitan Self-Enrichment	Highly Diversified
World News	56.2	47.4	66.6	72.6	58.8	81.1	42.2	52.7	41.0	17.3	27.4	81.9	43.9	76.3	55.2
National News	56.7	51.9	60.8	65.4	54.7	80.5	53.1	58.7	46.9	23.1	18.4	85.9	39.7	81.4	47.7
Local News	71.2	60.0	80.4	81.0	74.0	81.8	76.1	76.8	55.6	47.1	36.0	89.5	63.4	79.3	72.8
Editorial Pages	40.0	21.4	46.0	48.0	37.4	60.3	49.6	40.2	21.4	21.9	14.3	68.4	13.4	58.4	27.0
Gardening	24.0	7.5	33.2	25.8	33.4	32.2	36.7	37.9	4.1	2.0	8.4	17.6	13.4	34.6	25.2
Travel	23.3	16.7	28.7	25.3	22.6	42.7	24.6	22.0	12.6	9.0	9.0	26.5	9.6	42.1	21.1
Cooking	27.9	3.6	15.6	14.2	40.8	45.2	51.7	49.0	1.6	5.1	24.5	26.7	16.9	40.1	28.2
Advertising	45.4	41.4	51.8	37.5	48.9	47.0	60.0	60.4	32.1	33.4	29.4	58.2	34.1	37.8	48.8
Social News	31.6	12.3	32.4	22.5	33.8	46.2	46.4	42.1	13.1	15.8	20.3	40.9	19.9	38.3	41.0
Entertainment	46.6	42.3	30.7	26.8	32.2	62.2	61.8	57.0	41.3	50.5	39.4	55.8	26.8	63.6	53.5
Comics	45.2	58.1	39.7	38.0	30.0	45.6	44.7	43.5	65.5	59.7	47.5	40.5	34.8	42.1	51.1
Personal Advice	35.6	19.1	22.1	21.2	35.2	53.0	58.7	53.4	12.3	35.0	25.5	39.6	25.5	42.7	36.5
Sports	42.5	31.6	56.2	67.6	26.1	44.8	35.3	21.0	79.2	35.0	33.4	68.5	36.0	31.8	48.9
Business	25.6	24.9	38.4	34.4	16.7	37.7	24.6	18.7	12.6	4.8	11.1	41.7	18.7	37.5	28.2
Real Estate	19.9	27.4	35.3	20.7	8.3	27.9	18.8	23.7	8.8	6.5	5.4	20.8	12.7	24.0	24.4
Do Not Read Any Newspaper	12.2	21.6	7.7	11.1	14.0	6.0	8.1	10.0	11.7	22.4	28.5	1.0	18.1	10.5	8.6
No Answer	0.9	–	–	1.7	0.7	0.1	2.3	1.1	1.2	2.4	0.4	0.5	1.1	0.0	1.1

a. The statistical significance of each of the fifteen newspaper section types measured contained in the table was evaluated based on univariate F-ratio with 13 and 2,462 degrees of freedom. All were significant at the .005 level.

TABLE 7.5 Average Ratings of Frequency of Viewing[a] for Persons Listening to Selected Types of Radio Programs by Interest Segment[b]

Types of Programs	Entire Population	Adult Male Concentration				Adult Female Concentration				Youth Concentration			Mixed		
		Mechanics and Outdoor Life	Money and Nature's Products	Family and Community Centered	Elderly Concerns	Arts and Cultural Activities	Home and Community Centered	Family Integrated Activities	Competitive Sports and Science/Engineering	Athletic and Social Activities	Indoor Games and Social Activities	News and Information	Detached	Cosmopolitan Self-Enrichment	Highly Diversified
Classical	1.52	1.38	1.01	1.49	1.21	2.32	1.55	1.27	1.32	1.31	1.54	1.30	1.29	2.23	1.82
Country Music	2.02	2.28	1.99	2.31	1.77	1.96	2.35	2.03	1.95	1.87	1.68	2.25	1.82	1.59	2.13
Disco Music	1.89	2.08	1.15	1.46	1.16	1.58	1.74	2.06	2.48	3.09	2.79	1.72	1.45	1.92	2.55
Golden Oldies – From the 50's and 60's	2.12	2.21	1.68	1.98	1.53	2.37	2.34	2.43	2.15	2.18	2.15	2.25	1.70	2.16	2.45
Jazz	1.63	1.74	1.25	1.33	1.06	1.80	1.51	1.61	1.90	1.86	1.80	1.34	1.31	2.03	2.28
Mostly Instrumental – "Background Music"	1.86	1.53	1.52	1.62	1.32	2.35	2.15	2.12	1.73	1.69	1.81	1.88	1.50	2.24	2.27
Popular Music – By Popular Vocalists, Some Current Hits	2.38	2.58	1.84	1.94	1.44	2.40	2.41	2.90	2.86	3.15	2.72	2.36	1.69	2.65	2.76
Rhythm and Blues	1.75	1.68	1.27	1.46	1.28	1.78	1.79	1.83	1.86	2.05	1.79	1.87	1.43	2.15	2.27
Rock Music	2.12	2.68	1.27	1.47	1.20	1.73	1.95	2.55	3.23	3.27	2.53	1.68	1.56	2.36	2.62
Top Hits of the Week	2.23	2.50	1.51	1.74	1.32	1.88	2.25	2.64	2.99	3.24	2.84	2.14	1.75	2.23	2.72
All-News Stations (Local, National, International)	2.03	1.70	2.08	2.48	2.05	2.29	2.13	2.24	1.86	1.64	1.46	2.14	1.67	2.01	2.34
Black Programming	1.21	1.09	0.89	1.12	1.00	1.20	1.22	1.11	1.31	1.29	1.24	1.16	1.22	1.19	1.90
Educational/Instructional Programming	1.38	1.17	1.24	1.47	1.01	1.69	1.56	1.36	1.35	1.16	1.20	1.30	1.07	1.59	1.94
Farm Programs	1.21	1.24	1.54	1.38	1.08	1.14	1.24	1.08	1.19	1.10	1.05	1.09	1.00	1.12	1.63
Radio Drama	1.20	1.21	0.94	1.05	0.91	1.34	1.15	1.20	1.37	1.20	1.42	1.04	1.07	1.35	1.49
Religious Programs	1.49	1.21	1.40	1.76	1.60	1.62	1.75	1.31	1.27	1.30	1.43	1.49	1.38	1.17	2.08
Spanish Programming	1.01	1.01	0.85	0.94	0.84	0.93	1.06	1.02	1.11	1.10	1.09	0.86	1.02	1.05	1.24
Sports Programming	1.70	1.48	1.65	2.16	1.20	1.82	1.40	1.48	2.58	1.52	1.47	1.75	1.50	1.71	2.19
Talk, Phone-in Shows on Radio	1.50	1.52	1.17	1.51	1.12	1.67	1.39	1.61	1.64	1.55	1.56	1.44	1.17	1.63	1.94

153

of the type of content usage that is associated with each of the four types of media.

The original data for these tables are derived from the answers to four sets of questions, one for each medium. For each set, respondents were asked to indicate the types of content they used most often. For example, in the case of movies, they rated such categories as disaster films and Westerns, while, for radio, typical items were rock music and jazz.

For books, movies, and newspapers, in Tables 7.2 to 7.4, the numbers in the body of the tables are the percentages of frequent or regular readers by segment for each content type. In the case of radio programs, in Table 7.5, the numbers in the body of the table are average scores based on a 1 to 4 scale as follows:

1   = Never
2   = Almost never
3   = Sometimes
4   = Very often

The higher the average score, the greater the reported usage.

The variation in usage for each media content type, listed in Tables 7.2 to 7.5, has been tested for statistical significance using the univariate F-ratio statistic. All of the F-ratios except one for all of the content types in all four tables are significant at the .005 level. The one that is not significant at the .005 level is significant at the .01 level.[1]

RESULTS BY INTEREST SEGMENT

In order to minimize redundancy, table numbers are seldom repeated in the following discussion. Statements related to *overall* usage for each of the four media are based on results from Table 7.1 and those related to content type of usage are based on Tables 7.2 to 7.5.

Adult Male Concentration

MECHANICS AND OUTDOOR LIFE

Overall. This segment's members are relatively heavy users of movies and radio, for which their usage is 49% and 34% above average respectively. These are the only two media on which their usage ranks them among the top three of the fourteen segments. For books and all types of newspapers, they rank ninth or lower.

Content. For people in this segment, virtually all of the high ranking media content areas are consistent with their interests in mechanical activities, outdoor activities, or their needs to escape from boredom and problems. As one might expect from their interest in mechanical activities, they are the second highest segment on readership of "how to" books, with 40% reporting themselves as regular readers compared to 30% for the population. They rank fourth in listening to country music and farm programs, which is probably, in part, a function of their interest in outdoor activities and their rural locations.

It is hypothesized that the need to escape from both problems and boredom for the people in this segment is an important determinant of the types of movies they attend and the books they read. For movies, they rank fourth or above in attendance of Westerns, science fiction or supernatural, horror, and crime and spy films. Other than for "how to" books, the high ranking book content categories are science fiction and humor.

It seems likely that their heavy usage of newspaper comics serves a similar escape function. They rank higher on reading the comics (third, with 58% frequently reading versus 45% for the population) than all but two of the Youth Concentration segments.

Members of this segment are quite low in their exposure to religious content and, more generally, in their usage of material with intellectual content such as biographical books, movie musicals, operas, dances, and educational/instructional radio programs.

MONEY AND NATURE'S PRODUCTS

Overall. The people in this segment are not among the top three segments on usage of any of the media studied. The only one for which they have an above-average usage rate is daily papers. Their usage is only 10% in excess of that for the total population. For Sunday papers, it is equal to the population average. They are light users of books, movies, and radio programs, ranking thirteenth or fourteenth on all three.

Content. The only newspaper sections on which their reported readership ranks among the top three segments are real estate, business, and travel. Readership of the first two of these is probably an expression of their interest in investments.

Their readership of travel sections, as well as travel books, on which they also rank high, may relate to travel opportunities associated with their outdoor interests. However, respondents were only asked about travel in general, not about particular types of travel. Hence, one can only hypothesize about the relationship between their interest pattern and readership of travel material.

There appears to be a common need for one important component in the content of the books and movies they use. With the exception of travel and other nonfiction books, all of the higher ranking content categories for books and movies involve settings in which strong male personalities are in positions of power or control, whether they be detectives, Western heroes, or subjects of biographies.

FAMILY AND COMMUNITY CENTERED

Overall. Relative to the entire population, this segment's members are above average in their usage of all types of newspapers, Sunday papers, Sunday supplements, daily papers, local weeklies, and financial newspapers. On all five types, they rank sixth or above. In contrast, they rank eleventh and twelfth on books and movies respectively. This pattern of usage is consistent with their broad range of interests and with their orientation toward family and community activities. Newspapers, more than any other media, contain material tailored to local interests, while at the same time encompassing a relatively broad range of subject matter.

Content. With respect to newspaper section readership, the members of this segment rank among the top four on local news, sports, world news, and national news. With respect to radio programming, they are similarly positioned among the top four in their listening to all-news stations, religious programs, and country music.

Religion is also prominent for these people as subject matter in the three media in which it is included as a content category: books, movies, and radio. They rank second on readership of religious content in all three of these media types. This profile of newspaper and radio content is consistent not only with their broad range of interests, but also with their religious interests. That is, as in the case with television, the content they are relatively heavily exposed to is least apt to be objectionable from a religious point of view.

Adult Female Concentration

ELDERLY CONCERNS

Overall. The highest media usage rates for people in this segment are for Sunday, daily, and local weekly newspapers. Even with respect to these, however, they rank between sixth and tenth with usage rates close to the averages for the entire population.

At the opposite extreme, virtually none of the members of this segment report using financial newspapers. Their movie attendance is only 18% of that for the entire sample. Their usage of books and radio is also low, 70% and 69% of average.

The narrowness of their range of interests is most likely a major contributor to their relatively modest degree of media usage.

Content. The only content types across all four media on which the people in this segment rank higher than those in any other are books on philosophy or religion. These are read regularly by 43% of the members compared to 25% for the population. Though little overall use is made of movies or radio, when they are used, the people in this segment rank higher on religious content than any of the other segments. This is consistent with their score on the Religion interest factor, higher than that for any other segment.

Newspapers and radio appear to play a role in facilitating the efforts of those in this segment to stay in touch with familiar people, places, and things, via listening to all-news radio stations and reading the world news and advertising sections of newspapers.

ARTS AND CULTURAL ACTIVITIES

Overall. The members of the Arts and Cultural Activities segment are relatively heavy users of books, Sunday papers, Sunday supplements, daily papers, and financial newspapers. They are light users of movies and radio. They occupy an intermediate position with respect to usage of local daily papers.

The media which people in this segment use relatively heavily provide either opportunities for exposure to intellectually up-scaled material (books, public television, and magazines, as discussed in other chapters) or a means of efficiently tracking the broad range of their interests (newspapers).

Content. Their breadth of interests, as well as their intensity of media usage, is amply illustrated by the number of media content categories on which they rank in the top three. Out of 61 content categories from all 4 media, they rank in the top 3 on 29. This is a considerably higher number than for any other segment.

The content of these media usage categories is also consistent with the intellectual nature and the breadth of their interests. For both books and movies, the high ranking content categories include historical novels and musicals, operas, or dances, while the low ranked categories are related to fantasy/escape (science fiction books or horror movies) or to mechanical skills ("how to" books).

Newspapers, in contrast, appear to be used as a vehicle for the tracking of news and information. People in this segment rank among the top three on all of the news content categories. Their high rank (second) for the entertainment section is probably related to their interest in attending cultural activities.

The highest ranking usage content categories for radio emphasize intellectual and cultural programming (classical and educational/instructional) or simply its use as a background to some other activity, rather than a principal focus of attention.

HOME AND COMMUNITY CENTERED

Overall. The only media which the membership of this segment use more than the average for the population are local weekly papers, Sunday papers, and daily papers.

Content. The newspaper sections on which they rank among the top three segments are those which provide information about subjects or activities related to the home or local community, such as cooking, social news, personal advice, gardening, advertising, and entertainment.

This is in contrast to their newspaper readership of material related to subjects or activities not immediately associated with the home and community, where they rank low. For example, their readership of world news ranks eleventh. Only 42% of the people in this segment read this section frequently versus 56% for the population. Their national news readership also ranks relatively low (eighth), with a slightly lower than average percentage of the segment's membership frequently reading it.

Their high ranking of religious content for books, movies, and radio programs is to be expected, as people in this segment rank fourth on the Religion interest factor.

Over half the members of this segment are adults with children. When one combines this fact with their home and community orientation, the high rank for children's movies is also quite consistent.

FAMILY INTEGRATED ACTIVITIES

Overall. The people in this segment rank second in their readership of Sunday supplements and fifth in their usage of radio. For all of the other media studied, their usage tends to be quite close to the population average.

Content. They are at a stage in their family life cycle where their interests are influenced by the presence of young children to a greater extent than is true of most segments. The impact of children is reflected in their book, movie, and newspaper content usage. They rank first in their attendance of children's movies. In addition, they frequently read psychology, self-help books, and personal advice columns in newspapers. It is likely that their exposure to this type of material is dictated by their interest in the development of their children and in their emergent family structure. Their frequent readership of "how to" books, as well as the gardening and advertising sections of newspapers, is also consistent with their high degree of involvement in family life.

Youth Concentration

COMPETITIVE SPORTS AND SCIENCE/ENGINEERING

Overall. The three highest ranking media, and the only media which persons in this segment use to a greater degree than the population, are movies, Sunday papers, and books. Their movie attendance is quite high, 72% above average.

Content. The people in this segment favor book and movie content types which appear to provide a means of escape and fantasizing. They have high usage rates of humor and science fiction books, as well as similar categories of movies. In addition, they are also high on such movie types as crime and spy, horror, disaster, and Westerns. Their relatively high readership of newspaper comics may well satisfy the same needs.

Their usage of most newspaper content sections is quite low, ranking thirteenth or fourteenth for nine out of fifteen sections. However, on one other section besides comics, they rank first, namely sports. Sports also receive a rank of one with respect to their radio usage. This is to be expected given their sports-oriented interest pattern.

Members of this segment, like those in the other Youth Concentration segments, frequently listen to disco, top hits of the week, and rock music. Finally, they also rank high on a broad range of radio listening, including ethnic programming, drama, and talk shows. Program types ranked low include news, religion, and "old time" music—golden oldies.

ATHLETIC AND SOCIAL ACTIVITIES

Overall. Members of this segment are well above average in their use of two media, namely movies and radio. Their usage of all types of newspapers is quite low relative to other segments. They are among the bottom three ranking segments for all newspaper types, with usage ratios ranging from a high of 70% of average for Sunday papers to 12% of average for financial newspapers.

Content. They read or view almost all of the same types of escapist science fiction, horror, disaster books and movie types as do people in the previous segment. In addition, 58% are frequent readers of mysteries compared to 44% of the population, placing them second out of fourteen. Unlike their male counterparts (this segment is largely comprised of teenage females), however, they rank first in attending love and romance films and second on children's movies.

Like their male counterparts, they read few newspaper sections frequently. The comics page is their only high ranking category. Their heavy usage of radio is principally oriented toward music. They rank higher than any other segment in listening to disco music, popular music, rock music, and top hits of the week. In addition, they rank third in listening to rhythm and blues. The only other types of radio programs on which they rank as high as third are Black and Spanish programs.

INDOOR GAMES AND SOCIAL ACTIVITIES

Overall. The members of this segment are similar to those in the Athletic and Social Activities segment, in that they are predominantly young (average age is 22 compared to 19 for the previous segment) females (91% female versus 83%). Nevertheless, the overall pattern of their media usage of the four media under discussion is quite different.

This segment's members report the second highest number of books read per year, a figure 62% *above* average, while the comparable figure for persons in the preceding segment is 33% *below* average. Members of both segments are well above average in movie attendance, though the members of the present segment are considerably lower in their usage than those in the former one (31% versus 87% above average).

As readers of Sunday and daily papers, they are below average. Their usage of financial newspapers (*Barrons* and the *Wall Street Journal*) is below average, though greater than that for the Athletic and Social Activities segment (74% of average versus 12%). The same is true of usage of Sunday supplements (83% of average versus 60%) and local weeklies (85% of average versus 66%). Lastly, the radio usage of this segment is considerably less (21% below average versus 61% above average for the preceding segment).

Content. The usage of books for people in this segment is somewhat more intellectually oriented than for persons in the Athletic and Social Activities segment. They rank higher in their reading of biography/autobiography, philosophy, religion, "how to" books, and drama as follows:

	Athletic and Social Activities Segment	Indoor Games and Social Activities Segment
Biography/ autobiography	27%	38%
Philosophy, religion	11%	19%
"How to" books	14%	23%
Drama	10%	14%

Their viewing of escapist movie types is also consistently lower than that for persons in the Athletic and Social Activities segment as follows:

	Athletic and Social Activities Segment	Indoor Games and Social Activities Segment
Science fiction or supermatureal	54%	39%
Science fiction or supernatural	54%	39%
Horror	40%	29%
Crime or spy thrillers	48%	19%
Disaster	47%	27%

Their newspaper section readership is quite limited. For eight out of the fifteen sections, they rank thirteenth or fourteenth. The only newspaper sections having a higher percentage of this segment's members as frequent readers than those in the Athletic and Social Activities segment are:

	Athletic and Social Activities Segment	Indoor Games and Social Activities Segment
World news	17%	27%
Gardening	2%	8%
Cooking	5%	25%
Social news	16%	20%
Business	5%	11%

Though the present segment's *overall* radio usage is much lower than that for the former one, the people in this segment rank somewhat higher on radio drama, religious programs, classical music programs, and instrumental background music.

The overall usage pattern for books, movies, newspapers, and radio for persons in this segment is:

- More intellectually and culturally oriented than that for either of the other two Youth Concentration segments.
- Less oriented toward fantasy and escapist material.
- More directed toward adult role concerns, such as cooking and gardening, as well as toward business.

This pattern is quite consistent with the description of their interests and needs offered in Chapter 4.

Mixed

NEWS AND INFORMATION

Overall. Members of this segment are among the top four with respect to their usage of all types of newspapers. Their usage ranges from a high of 71% above average for financial newspapers to 14% above average for local weeklies. With re-

spect to books, movies, and radio, their usage is average or
below the average for the entire population.

Content. Given the interests of people in this segment, together with their overall pattern of high newspaper usage, it
comes as no surprise that the newspaper sections on which this
segment ranks high allow them to keep informed on a diversity
of subjects. They rank first on all the news-related content areas
(world, national, local, editorial, as well as business) except
social news, on which they rank fifth.

The same interest in general information may account for
their high ranking reading of historical novels, travel books, and
biographical books, as well as movies that are biographical,
historical, or adventure-related.

DETACHED

Overall. Those in the Detached segment are extremely light
users of media. Their usage of every type is below the population average. They rank among the lowest three segments with
regard to their usage of:

(1) National weeklies—12% of average
(2) Books—49% of average for the entire population
(3) Sunday supplements—57% of average
(4) Local weeklies—74% of average

Their highest ranking media are radio and Sunday papers, on
which they rank eighth and ninth respectively.

Content. On only one of the content categories across all
four media do they rank above seventh place, and that is for
black programming.

COSMOPOLITAN SELF-ENRICHMENT

Overall. The membership of this segment is above average in
its usage, never ranking below sixth place, for all of the media
included in this chapter. For books and financial newspapers,
on which they rank first, their relative usage is the highest for
any medium or segment in the study, namely 138% and 167%
greater than average respectively. They also rank first in readership of Sunday supplements and third with respect to Sunday
papers.

Content. For nine of thirteen book categories, people in this segment rank among the top three segments. These nine categories are, with one exception, all nonfiction. The three categories on which they rank the lowest are all types of fiction.

Their usage of films includes material that is high in intellectual content, biographies, documentaries, historical or adventure films, and music, opera, or dance films. In addition, they are the second heaviest viewers of love and romance films.

Their general profile of newspaper usage is oriented to its role as a source of information about entertainment, travel, news, and business.

The radio usage profile of this segment shows its members' appreciation of music in quite diverse formats from classical to rhythm and blues.

HIGHLY DIVERSIFIED

Overall. This segment's members are above average on movies, local weekly newspapers, national weeklies, and radio. Their lowest relative rates of usage are for books and Sunday papers.

Content. Radio appears to be their principal medium for covering their relatively broad range of interests. This segment's members rank among the top four segments on all nineteen of the radio content categories. In general, this segment uses verbal as opposed to printed media to a greater extent than other segments. The printed medium on which they rank highest emphasizes one's immediate surroundings (local newspapers). Even the high ranking content usage categories for newspapers are largely focused on local interests, social news and real estate sections. They also rank relatively high in their usage of financial newspapers.

Their movie viewing is influenced by the fact that a high percentage of the adults in this segment are in households with children present. The mix of movie types on which they rank high ranges from horror to documentaries to religious films. This pattern appears to reflect the seeking of mutually satisfying entertainment for both children and adults in the same manner as their television viewing behavior.

CONCLUSIONS

Thumbnail sketches of the book, movie, newspaper, and radio usage patterns by interest segment are provided in Exhibit 7.1. The general pattern of variation in media usage across segments is partly associated with, and interpretable in light of, segment variation in patterns of interests, needs, and demographic characteristics. By and large, the findings appear to validate the previous interpretations of fourteen interest segments.

Exhibit 7.1

Book, Movie, Newspaper, and Radio Usage
Interest Segmentation Characterization

A. *Adult Male Concentration*

Mechanics and Outdoor Life
> Heavy users of movies and radio, "how to" books, farm and country radio programs. Heavy on escape-related books and movies such as science fiction and horror.'Also heavy readers of newspaper comics.

Money and Nature's Products
> Generally below-average media usage. Daily papers only above-average type. Above-average newspaper readership for real estate, business, and travel. Attracted to types of books and movies in which strong male personalities are in positions of power or control.

Family and Community Centered
> Above-average usage of all newspaper types. Below average on book, movie, and radio usage. Broad subject matter coverage focuses on news in newspapers and on radio. Religious subject matter also ranks high.

B. *Adult Female Concentration*

Elderly Concerns
> Moderate to light users of all four "other" media. Relatively highest rates for Sunday, daily, and local papers. Religious, news, and advertising content all somewhat above average.

Arts and Cultural Activities
> Heavy users of books, Sunday papers and supplements, and daily papers. Generally high intellectual content such as historical novels,

Exhibit 7.1 (Continued)

musicals, operas, or dance movies. Newspapers focus on news sections and entertainment listings section.

Home and Community Centered
Moderate usage of most media. Above average only on Sunday, daily, and local papers. Content is home- and community-related, such as cooking, gardening, social news, entertainment, as well as children's movies and religion.

Family Integrated Activities
Heavy on radio and readership of Sunday supplements. Focus of content is family-related activities, including children's movies, and relationships, such as personal advice newspaper section and psychology self-help books.

C. *Youth Concentration*

Competitive Sports and Science/Engineering
Heavy users of movies. Books and movie content are escapist-oriented, such as science fiction books and horror movies. Highest usage rate for sports in newspapers and on radio. Radio used for broad range of content, with special emphasis on different types of music.

Athletic and Social Activities
Heavy usage of movies and radio, while relatively light for all types of newspapers. Escapist content for books and movies similar to previous segment, but oriented more to love, romance, and children's movies. Radio listening mainly music.

Indoor Games and Social Activities
Heavy on books and movies. Somewhat more intellectual, less escapist than other Youth Concentration segments. Somewhat high readership of biographies, religious books, world news, and business newspaper content, as well as somewhat lighter viewing of horror, science fiction types of movies.

D. *Mixed*

News and Information
Heavy usage of all types of newspapers. Focus on all news sections of newspapers.

Detached
Extremely light users of books, movies, and newspapers.

Exhibit 7.1 (Continued)

Cosmopolitan Self-Enrichment

Moderate to heavy usage of all media, especially books and financial newspapers. Focus on all types of nonfiction books. High
intellectual content in films such as biographies and documentaries.
Newspapers used as source of information related to entertainment
as well as news, travel, and business. Broad range of music in radio
listening.

Highly Diversified

Above-average usage of movies, local weekly papers, and radio.
Radio used as principal vehicle for covering broad range of interests. Newspaper content centers on local concerns, such as real
estate and social news. Movie content reflects impact of children
and probably a process of accommodation to interests of other
family members.

NOTE

1. Four separate fourteen-way multiple discriminant analyses were performed as
part of the process of evaluating the extent of overall segment differences with
respect to types of books, movies, newspaper, sections, and radio programs. Each
discriminant analysis used as independent variables the type measures associated with
one of these four media. The following are the percentage of respondents correctly
classified for each of the four analyses: books—19%, movies—23%, newspaper sections—22%, and radio programs—25%. In each of the four analyses, one would expect
7% correct classification with a random assignment to the fourteen segments or 10%
correct classification if all were assigned to the modal segment. The overall pattern of
the between segment differences for each of the four media was tested using the
Wilk's Lambda statistics. Based on the appropriate F-ratio approximation, the results
for all four analyses were significant at the .005 level.

Part Three
Special Studies

8

Public Television

INTRODUCTION

The growth of the commercial television industry has been phenomenal from the end of World War II to the present. Public broadcasting, as it is constituted today, evolved from the recommendations of the 1967 report of a private commission (Carnegie Commission, 1967) formed to examine noncommercial, educational television, which was at that time an infant industry supported by the federal government, private foundations, educational and other nonprofit institutions, and contributions from the public. Like its commercial counterpart, public television has grown rapidly; in the face of an adolescent identity crisis, a second Carnegie Commission was recently convened to provide guidance for the movement toward adulthood of both public television and radio (Carnegie Commission, 1979).

The Commission's report indicates that the number of public television stations has grown from 114 in 1965 to 280 in 1978. Its signals are now viewable in 80% of the nation's homes, and 46 million households view public television at least once a month.

As we move into the 1980s, public television is under considerable pressure from both citizen groups and legislators to broaden its audience reach without sacrificing its commitment to excellence.

> Many public groups, once staunch supporters of public broadcasting against the blandness and vulgarity of commercial broadcasting, began to express disappointment about the record of public broadcasting on programming for minorities and women, public participation in station governance, equal employment opportunity, clandestine commercialism via corporate underwriting, and the use of so many British imports [Carnegie Commission, 1979: 24].

Public television has done its best work in creatively developing outstanding programs for children and in broadcasting quality programs that appear to serve the intellectually and culturally elite adult populations of the country. To be more responsive to the general population and to broaden its base of financial support, it may be necessary to find ways of appealing to audiences that are currently viewing little or no public television. At the same time, it must maintain those structural, editorial, and quality standards that differentiate it from commercial broadcasting. While these tasks pose a formidable challenge, there is evidence that the potential for success is high.

It has been demonstrated that while many children enjoy watching cartoons and reruns of old situation comedies and adventure shows, they can also be attracted to such quality programs as *Sesame Street, Mister Rogers,* and *Electric Company.* With a comparable commitment on the part of public broadcasting, combined with an understanding of audience needs and interests, virtually any well-defined audience segment could be attracted to the television screen. While produced and broadcast commercially (at considerable expense), the broad-based appeals of *Roots* and *Roots II* demonstrated that television audiences can be lured away from the typical network offerings even during prime time.

Because public television has different objectives from commercial television, its program content and its strategy are necessarily different as well. Critical to both industries, however, is the need for an in-depth understanding of their potential audiences as a basis for determining how to attract them. This need is especially important for public television, as it has generally directed its programming toward smaller, more narrowly defined audience segments than has commercial television. A thorough discussion of this need is offered by Morrisett (1976).

We believe that our segmentation scheme, based on leisure interests and activities, can provide public television stations with data that will be useful in achieving their goals, however they may be formulated and modified over the next decade. Consequently, this chapter is devoted to a discussion of public television viewing, programming preferences, attitudes toward funding, and related issues.

Now that the reader has become thoroughly acquainted with each of the fourteen interest segments through their media behavior, this chapter is organized around the issues related to public television rather than around the segments themselves.

FREQUENCY OF PUBLIC TELEVISION VIEWING

The data in this and subsequent sections are based on self-reported viewing behavior. In this context, it is important to note that while the distinction between public and commercial broadcasting is clear to members of those industries, it is not nearly so clear to their audiences. Many people still confuse public television with the pre-1967 educational television network from which it evolved. Some believe that all UHF stations are public, while others believe that all public broadcasting stations are on UHF channels, with UHF containing a mix of commercial and public broadcasters.

In an effort to minimize ambiguity, we introduced this section of the questionnaire with the following statement: "By Public Television we mean stations which have no commercials for products or services, such as those shown on commercial television."

While we recognize that some confusion between commercial and public television remained present during the interview, our analytic focus is almost exclusively on the *relative* comparisons among audience segments rather than in obtaining accurate estimates of absolute levels of viewing.

Demographic Segment Comparisons

The data in Table 8.1 report the frequency of viewing public television analyzed by selected demographic characteristics.

Almost half the population claim that they never watch public television. However, this figure must take into account the fact that in response to another question, 26% said that there is no public television station in their area. A total of 26% watch once a week or more, with virtually no differences between adult males and females in their viewing. Public television viewing increases somewhat with income, while among minority groups, the elderly are relatively infrequent viewers, and Blacks are somewhat above average. These results are generally consistent with those reported by the Carnegie Commission (Carnegie Commission, 1979: 339), even though the Commission's figures are derived from Nielsen data, using a totally different method of data collection from ours.

Interest Segment Comparisons

Table 8.2 presents an analysis of public television viewing frequency by the fourteen interest segments.

Consistent with their interest patterns and the types of adult programming available on public television, the two segments that are by far the heaviest viewers are the Arts and Cultural Activities segment and the Cosmopolitan Self-Enrichment segment. Half or more of the members of each segment report that they watch public television once a week or more. The percentages of infrequent viewers or nonviewers are extremely low in both segments compared with the remaining population.

The News and Information, Highly Diversified, and Family Integrated Activities segments are also above-average viewers.

The Elderly Concerns and Detached segments are notably low in their viewing of public television, even though the former were shown in Chapter 5 to have the highest in-home availability index among the fourteen segments and to rank third in television exposure. Clearly, the Elderly Concerns segment is selectively electing not to watch public television.

TABLE 8.1 Frequency of Watching Public TV Programs by Selected Demographic Characteristics

| | Total Population % | Adult Women % | Adult Men % | Income | | | Elderly % | Minorities | |
				$7,999 or Less %	$8,000 to $17,499 %	$17,500 or More %		Blacks %	Hispanics %
Every day	7	8	6	7	9	6	5	13	6
One to six times per week	19	18	20	14	18	25	18	18	20
Once or twice a month	10	10	10	6	8	16	7	5	7
A few times a year	10	9	10	6	8	14	4	10	15
Once a year	2	2	3	1	2	4	1	1	1
Don't know	5	5	5	6	5	5	6	8	6
Never	47	48	47	60	50	31	58	46	45

175

TABLE 8.2 Frequency of Viewing Public TV Programs by Interest Segment

	Entire Population	Adult Male Concentration				Adult Female Concentration				Youth Concentration			Mixed		
		Mechanics and Outdoor Life	Money and Nature's Products	Family and Community Centered	Elderly Concerns	Arts and Cultural Activities	Home and Community Centered	Family Integrated Activities	Competitive Sports and Science/Engineering	Athletic and Social Activities	Indoor Games and Social Activities	News and Information	Detached	Cosmopolitan Self-Enrichment	Highly Diversified
Every day	7	4	3	2	3	14	10	11	5	12	9	7	5	8	6
One to six times per week	19	17	12	10	10	39	13	16	13	13	11	24	11	42	24
Once or twice a month	10	12	7	10	4	12	12	13	13	6	5	8	3	20	8
Few times a year	10	8	10	12	7	8	10	9	7	15	8	11	11	12	8
Once a year	2	3	4	–	1	–	2	5	6	2	2	1	–	2	4
Don't know	5	6	5	4	5	3	5	3	8	8	7	4	9	1	5
Never	47	49	59	60	70	25	49	42	49	44	57	43	62	15	45

PROGRAMS VIEWED

Among the 149 programs or program categories included in the survey were 22 programs shown on public television. This section presents the viewing data for these 22 programs. Because the audience for public broadcasting tends to be very small, with the percentages viewing any particular program during a four-week period often less than 1%, these data are presented by showing each segment's share of that total audience. The data are displayed in Table 8.3. The figures were derived by taking the total number of times each program was viewed during the four-week period preceding the interview and determining the percentage of viewings attributable to the individuals in each segment.

Except for children's programs and a few others, the Arts and Cultural Activities segment has the largest audience share of most public broadcasting programs. Their share, however, ranges from a low of 1% for *Mister Rogers* to a remarkably high 51% for various operas, with shares exceeding 40% for *Dickens of London, Upstairs, Downstairs, Great Performances,* and *Evening at the Symphony.* This segment clearly constitutes the primary audience for the classical arts.

The Cosmopolitan Self-Enrichment segment members, as indicated earlier, also tend to be heavy viewers of public broadcasting, and they are highly discriminating with shares ranging from 2% for *In Pursuit of Liberty* to 31% for *Once Upon a Classic.* Their intellectual and cultural interests appear to be somewhat more narrowly focused on literature than those of the previous segment and are much less likely to include various musical performances. Members of the Cosmopolitan Self-Enrichment segment, however, are among the more frequent viewers of children's programs in contrast with the Arts and Cultural Activities segment, who are infrequent viewers of this type of program.

The Highly Diversified segment, with the highest percentage of Blacks, has the largest audience share of *Black Perspective on the News* and *The French Chef.* This segment also tends to be relatively heavy in their viewing of numerous other public television programs. They rank third, for example, in watching

TABLE 8.3 Segment Shares of Public Television Programs by Interest Segment

	Entire Population %	Adult Male Concentration				Adult Female Concentration				Youth Concentration			Mixed		
		Mechanics and Outdoor Life %	Money and Nature's Products %	Family and Community Centered %	Elderly Concerns %	Arts and Cultural Activities %	Home and Community Centered %	Family Integrated Activities %	Competitive Sports and Science/Engineering %	Athletic and Social Activities %	Indoor Games and Social Activities %	News and Information %	Detached %	Cosmopolitan Self-Enrichment %	Highly Diversified %
Age of Uncertainty	100.0	2.4			10.2	21.1	—	8.0	16.8	—	1.1	15.1	1.9	11.3	12.1
Nova	100.0	2.8	3.5	2.0	7.1	22.0	7.6	15.3	5.7	.4	.3	2.9	5.4	16.6	8.3
Dickens of London	100.0	2.3	3.0	.3	1.0	47.8	6.5	—	.6	1.6	1.6	2.3	3.1	27.1	3.0
Visions	100.0	.1	—	.1	.9	34.6	8.8	.5	.7	1.2	3.5	13.3	9.5	16.4	10.6
Upstairs, Downstairs	100.0	2.4	5.0	9.0	10.8	41.4	1.7	—	.2	.2	1.6	1.5	4.1	15.2	6.3
In Pursuit of Liberty	100.0	.2	—	3.8	3.3	15.8	10.0	12.9	—	—	1.6	32.8	3.3	2.2	14.2
Great Performances	100.0	.7	7.0	1.8	7.3	41.4	1.4	.7	—	.3	2.1	7.9	2.1	15.9	11.5
The Best of Families	100.0	3.2	3.5	—	8.4	19.8	.4	11.0	1.0	.1	5.2	16.8	8.5	8.6	13.6
Masterpiece Theater	100.0	3.5	5.1	5.8	7.5	32.5	5.4	11.4	3.3	.3	3.0	3.7	2.2	11.9	4.6
Once Upon a Classic	100.0	2.8	3.2	2.1	.3	17.5	.2	18.9	1.4	3.0	1.0	2.9	4.6	31.4	10.5
Evening at the Symphony	100.0	5.7	7.5	1.1	7.4	40.9	6.0	4.2	.3	—	1.5	2.2	4.0	15.9	3.1
Opera (Varies)	100.0	.2	4.1	—	5.0	51.3	7.4	7.9	—	.1	1.9	.8	3.6	9.2	8.5
Evening at Pops	100.0	4.6	3.8	2.9	4.9	33.5	4.9	4.6	1.0	—	1.8	6.4	6.3	19.4	6.0
Washington Week in Review	100.0	3.0	16.6	6.2	5.7	22.6	10.3	1.8	.5	—	.1	14.3	4.5	6.0	8.3
Wall Street Week	100.0	7.6	9.6	7.8	—	32.6	7.7	—	—	—	.7	19.6	4.0	5.3	5.2
Black Perspective on the News	100.0	3.1	.8	3.3	10.1	9.3	9.0	2.7	1.7	1.0	2.6	13.9	10.3	5.3	27.0
MacNeil/Lehrer Report	100.0	.2	3.0	3.5	1.3	27.1	6.8	—	—	—	.3	24.3	3.1	18.2	12.3
Woman	100.0	1.0	3.0	5.3	30.0	4.9	3.3	8.7	—	—	1.5	7.2	19.1	2.8	13.2
Sesame Street	100.0	1.8	1.1	1.5	1.2	5.2	9.3	33.2	3.3	4.7	2.6	4.0	3.6	16.5	12.1
Mister Rogers	100.0	.1	—	.7	—	1.0	8.8	47.3	6.3	7.2	1.0	—	2.1	16.1	9.4
Electric Company	100.0	4.0	.5	1.5	.8	5.0	8.7	33.8	4.7	5.0	2.0	4.1	3.4	14.4	12.0
The French Chef	100.0	—	3.9	3.3	2.7	12.6	9.3	7.4	3.7	1.8	2.3	4.2	10.9	17.5	20.4

178

In Pursuit of Liberty, The Best of Families, Great Performances, operas, and the three children's programs.

The News and Information segment reports the largest audience share among all segments (33%) for *In Pursuit of Liberty* and the second largest share for the *MacNeil/Lehrer Report, Black Perspective on the News, Wall Street Week,* and *The Best of Families.* Their viewing is concentrated more on those programs that are high in informational content as opposed to those emphasizing musical or literary artistry.

The other segment relatively heavy in viewing of public television is the Family Integrated Activities segment. They have, by far, the largest audience shares of *Sesame Street* (33%), *Mister Rogers* (47%), and *Electric Company* (34%), undoubtedly as a result of watching these programs with their children. For adult-oriented programs, they rank much lower on average, although they are second in share for *Once Upon A Classic* and third for *Nova* and *Masterpiece Theater.* They are extremely low in their viewing of news and information programs on public television.

The remaining segments tend to be infrequent viewers of programs on public broadcasting. However, there are occasional exceptions to this pattern that tend to confirm the relationship between interest patterns and viewing behavior and suggest opportunities for public broadcasting to broaden its viewing audience if it chooses to do so.

Members of the Money and Nature's Products segment, for example, rank second in their share of *Washington Week in Review* (17%) and third on *Wall Street Week* (10%). The Elderly Concerns segment has, by far, the largest share of *Woman* (30%) and ranks third in the viewing of *Upstairs, Downstairs* (11%). The youth segments are uniformly light viewers of public television, yet the Competitive Sports and Science/Engineering segment reports a 17% share for *Age of Uncertainty,* making it the second largest viewing segment. Even the Detached segment ranked second on one program, *Woman,* with a 19% share.

These results indicate that public television is not seen as homogeneous by television audiences. Just as they do with commercial television, and perhaps even more so, people appear to select from the offerings available those programs that are consistent with their own interests and needs. While there are large differences in the frequency of public television viewing across interest segments, there are also extremely large differences in viewing across program types within each segment.

INTEREST IN PROGRAM TYPES

Respondents were presented with a list of nine types of programs that might be shown on public television and were asked to rate their degree of interest in viewing each of them on a four-point rating scale ranging from "very interested" (4) to "not at all interested" (1).

Demographic Segment Comparisons

The mean values of these ratings for several groups are shown in Table 8.4.

The most favored program types for public television are educational, news, special interests, and local events and issues. In general, the range of interests seems relatively narrow, and the level is not high. Not even the highest rated program type achieved an average of "somewhat interested."

Demographic differences are extremely small, although Blacks and Hispanics show above-average interests in "programs appealing to certain kinds of people," presumably programs directed toward ethnic minorities such as themselves.

We also classified respondents into frequent, occasional, or nonviewers of public television based on their self-reported viewing behavior. Frequent viewers were defined as those who watch public television programs once a week or more often; occasional viewers watch once a year or more, and nonviewers said either that they never watch public television or they don't know if they do. While the data in Table 8.4 indicate that the more frequently one views public television, the greater is one's interest in all program types, the *patterns* of interest are not markedly different across these three subgroups.

TABLE 8.4 Interest in Public Television Program Types*

	Total Population	Adult Women	Adult Men	Income $7,999 or Less	Income $8,000 to $17,499	Income $17,500 or More	Minorities Elderly	Minorities Blacks	Minorities Hispanics	Frequency of PTV Viewing Frequent	Frequency of PTV Viewing Occasional	Frequency of PTV Viewing Undetermined or Never
Cultural programs	2.0	2.2	1.8	2.0	1.9	2.2	2.1	1.9	2.0	2.6	2.2	1.7
Programs similar to those on commercial TV	2.2	2.2	2.1	2.2	2.2	2.1	2.1	2.2	2.3	2.0	2.3	2.2
Music only programs	2.1	2.2	2.0	2.1	2.0	2.1	2.1	2.1	2.2	2.3	2.2	1.9
Programs appealing to certain kinds of people	1.9	2.0	1.7	2.0	1.9	1.8	1.8	2.5	2.4	2.1	2.0	1.7
Programs about local events and issues	2.4	2.5	2.4	2.5	2.4	2.4	2.6	2.5	2.3	2.6	2.5	2.3
News programs	2.5	2.5	2.5	2.6	2.5	2.5	2.8	2.6	2.5	2.7	2.5	2.4
Programs about special interests	2.4	2.5	2.3	2.3	2.4	2.6	2.4	2.2	2.2	2.7	2.7	2.2
Educational programs	2.6	2.7	2.5	2.5	2.7	2.7	2.5	2.7	2.6	3.0	2.9	2.3
Children's programs	2.3	2.5	2.2	2.2	2.4	2.4	1.9	2.6	2.4	2.6	2.5	2.1

*Mean scale values: 4 = very interested, 3 = somewhat interested, 2 = not very interested, 1 = not at all interested.

Interest Segment Comparisons

Unlike the demographic differences discussed above, public television program type preferences differ markedly across the interest segments as shown in Table 8.5.

The Arts and Cultural Activities segment and the Cosmopolitan Self-Enrichment segment, the heaviest viewers of public television, indicate their strongest preferences are for educational and cultural programs. Since a large amount of programming on public television falls into these categories, these two segments are apparently relatively satisfied with what is available, and this accounts for their viewing behavior. It is notable that except for the Highly Diversified segment, none of the remaining segments expresses an above-average interest in cultural programs. While the definition of what is meant by cultural programs is undoubtedly ambiguous, the appeal of the concept is limited to a strong interest on the part of a relatively small subgroup of the population.

Among the second tier of above-average public television viewers are the Highly Diversified, News and Information, and Family Integrated Activities segments.

The Highly Diversified segment exhibits greatest interest in children's programs and in other types that are heavy in news and informational content, including programs "appealing to certain kinds of people." While they are slightly above average in their ratings of all program types for public television, they appear less interested in cultural and artistic programming (e.g., music) than in other types. Given the distinctively low socio-economic status of this group, they appear to be interested in using public television as a vehicle for self-education.

The News and Information segment shows greatest interest in educational programs, news programs, and programs about local events and issues. These preferences are consistent with their interest patterns and with their viewing preferences for commercial television as well.

The Family Integrated Activities segment is most interested in educational and children's programs and programs about special interests.

TABLE 8.5 Interest in Public TV Program Types[*]

	Entire Population	Adult Male Concentration			Adult Female Concentration				Youth Concentration				Mixed		
		Mechanics and Outdoor Life	Money and Nature's Products	Family and Community Centered	Elderly Concerns	Arts and Cultural Activities	Home and Community Centered	Family Integrated Activities	Competitive Sports and Science/Engineering	Athletic and Social Activities	Indoor Games and Social Activities	News and Information	Detached	Cosmopolitan Self-Enrichment	Highly Diversified
Cultural programs	2.0	1.5	1.6	1.8	1.9	3.2	1.8	2.0	1.6	1.6	1.8	1.9	1.6	3.0	2.2
Programs similar to those on commercial TV	2.2	2.3	2.2	2.1	2.2	2.0	2.1	2.2	2.3	2.4	2.1	2.2	1.8	1.8	2.4
Music only programs	2.1	1.8	1.8	2.0	2.2	2.5	2.1	2.0	1.9	1.7	2.0	2.1	1.7	2.5	2.2
Programs appealing to certain kinds of people	1.9	1.6	1.6	1.7	1.9	2.0	1.8	1.9	1.6	2.0	1.8	1.8	1.6	2.3	2.3
Programs about local events and issues	2.4	2.1	2.5	2.5	2.7	2.8	2.4	2.4	2.1	2.1	2.0	2.8	2.0	2.6	2.7
News programs	2.5	2.2	2.8	2.6	2.9	2.9	2.5	2.4	2.2	1.8	2.1	2.8	2.0	2.5	2.8
Programs about special interests	2.4	2.1	2.4	2.4	2.3	2.7	2.4	2.7	2.2	2.4	2.4	2.6	1.9	2.8	2.7
Educational programs	2.6	2.3	2.2	2.8	2.3	3.1	2.6	3.0	2.2	2.3	2.5	2.9	2.0	3.2	2.9
Children's programs	2.3	2.0	1.8	2.4	1.9	2.6	2.3	2.8	1.8	2.2	2.5	2.5	1.9	2.7	2.8

[*] Mean scale values: 4 = very interested, 3 = somewhat interested, 2 = not very interested, 1 = not at all interested.

The overall interest in having programs on public television like those on commercial television is not very high. People seem to recognize that public television should offer programming distinct from what is otherwise available.

Most of the interest segments, including those that are relatively light viewers of public television, indicate higher than average interest in one or more program types. Members of the Elderly Concerns segment, for example, the least frequent viewers of public television, report a high interest in news programs and in programs about local events and issues. Thus, they could be lured into the public broadcasting audience by public broadcasting's commitment to offer programs to match these interests and create awareness of their existence among members of this segment.

REACTION TO NEW PROGRAM CONCEPTS

In one portion of the interview, respondents were presented with printed descriptions of eight new program concepts and were asked to rate their interest on a four-point scale ranging from "extremely interested" (4) to "not at all interested" (1). The concepts are shown in Exhibit 8.1. These were selected to represent a diversity of appeals in the hope that they would elicit differential reactions among the interest segments. In particular, we hoped to discover that people would favor program concepts consistent with their patterns of interests and activities. Not only would this reinforce the validity of the segmentation approach, but it might offer promise for the use of new program concepts as an early screening device for evaluating the potential of new programs to expand the base of public television viewers.

At the time the survey was being conducted, none of the eight program concepts had been produced and broadcast.

Interest Segment Comparisons

The data in Table 8.6 present the reactions to the eight concepts. The top number in each cell is the mean interest rating and the bottom number is the percentage of people who

Exhibit 8.1

New Program Concepts for Public Television

Just Plain Country

"Music City, U.S.A.," "City of ten thousand pickers," or "Music capital of the world. . . ." Call it what you will, Nashville, Tennessee, is the home of the Grand Ole Opry and a wealth of talent which has supplied the world with country music. This program takes advantage of this abundance of Nashville talent to appeal to television's blue-collar viewers whose language is spoken in every country song, the fans who fill the auditoriums around the country when the bus carrying their favorite star pulls into town.

Mother's Little Network

Mother's Little Network (MLN) offers something unique—a comedy born, bred, and rooted in America. Posing as an up-and-coming family-owned broadcasting company, MLN hits the air every week with its own brand of video humor—a series of fast-paced sketches, animations, parodies, and personalities, with a format owing nothing to anyone or anything, including the meaning of its title.

MLN restores a freshness and regularity to your TV viewing. All new punchlines! All new accents! All new breaches of regional and national standards of good taste!

Sportlight

Sportlight gives viewers—in a regular, weekly, ninety-minute format of live or edited coverage—the chance to see and follow a variety of first-rate competitive amateur athletic events not to be found elsewhere on American television.

On-air hosts are top journalists or well-known participants in the field, men and women who speak colorfully and incisively on the event and the issues that surround it, e.g., Bud Collins, Arthur Ashe, Donald Dell, Kem Prince, Judy Dixon, and others, who go into the background of each sport and give instructional tips where appropriate.

Your Retirement Dollar

Your Retirement Dollar is a series of thirteen half-hour programs based on the syndicated newspaper column, "Your Retirement Dollar," by Peter Weaver, who serves as the program's host and chief expert.

The series covers a variety of topics of interest and concern to the retired, and those approaching retirement, in the areas of family finances, buying habits, good values, safe types of investments, personal pension plans,

Exhibit 8.1 (Continued)

money management on a reduced income, retirement job opportunities, and so on. Two guest experts assist Mr. Weaver in further exploring subject areas. The series contains on-location footage demonstrating many of the traps facing the elderly in areas of nutrition, personal health, nursing homes, personal loans, and legal aid.

Hollywood Television Theatre: Habit

Habit is an originally created serial for *Hollywood Television Theatre*. Based upon a true story, *Habit* explores the human condition from a uniquely sensitive view.

It is based on a profound social change which occurred as a result of the precedent-breaking Vatican Council II, and the individual struggle and change that came to a number of extraordinary women who suggested they should receive a small stipend for teaching; choose their own form of government; shift their energies from church-related to social, economic, intellectual, and spiritual needs of the family of man; and choose their own clothing to wear when working outside the College of the Immaculate Heart.

An uproar ensued, and this series tells the story in personal terms by focusing on the emotional struggles of four or five individual nuns.

The Fertile Crescent

A thirteen-part series on the history and culture of the Near East, demonstrating the accuracy of the term "Cradle of Civilization" by examining the enormous cultural contributions of the Near East to Western civilization.

It was filmed at important archaeological sites and monuments, reconstructions, and sites of custom and ritual. Also shown is the art, much of it now preserved in national museums in the Near East, in the British Museum and the Louvre, and in such fabled cities of the Near East as Baghdad, Damascus, Cairo, Jerusalem. It is safe to say that viewers will see moving sights of glory they have never beheld before.

What in the World

What in the World is a panel game show which entertains and educates by using the artifacts and treasures of the Smithsonian Institution (Museum) as its subject. The format is deceptively simple: engage two panels of three people each in a friendly, witty debate over the identity of an object from the Smithsonian.

Exhibit 8.1 (Continued)

The basic object of the game is for one panel to stump the other by weaving curious but true descriptions and stories about the object—two not fitting and one fitting the object per round—so there is a pitting of wills, wit, and intellect in the process.

Woman's Place

What does being a woman mean today? What are the special problems that our age of change thrusts into women's lives? Considering the shifts in the patterns of women's lives attending their new awakening (with responses ranging from radical feminism to Total Womanhood), what is *Woman's Place*—as it was, as it is, as it may become?

This series of thirteen hour-long TV programs attempts to answer these and many other questions as it presents a picture of the multiple activities and the flexible strength to be found among women who come from many backgrounds and diverse views.

indicated that they were either "extremely interested" or "quite interested."

Across the entire population, the mean ratings for the new program concepts ranged from a low of 2.1 (*Hollywood Television Theatre*) to a high of 2.5 (*Your Retirement Dollar*), with the corresponding percentages of people expressing interest ranging from 33% to 49% respectively. Both within and across the interest segments, however, the reactions to these concepts were dramatically more variable.

The Arts and Cultural Activities segment tends to express above-average interest in most of the concepts, but members are especially high in their ratings of *The Fertile Crescent, Your Retirement Dollar, What in the World,* and *Hollywood Television Theatre*. These programs, with the exception of *Your Retirement Dollar,* are laden with historical content. All appear to be intellectually enriching and serious in their purpose and presentation. The program concepts that embody lighter forms of entertainment attracted less interest from this segment.

The Cosmopolitan Self-Enrichment segment was the only other segment rating *The Fertile Crescent* relatively high. They also showed well above average interest in *Woman's Place,* showing at least as much interest as any of the four segments

TABLE 8.6 Evaluations of Eight New Program Concepts for Public Television by Interest Segment*

	Entire Population	Adult Male Concentration				Adult Female Concentration			Youth Concentration				Mixed		
		Outdoor Life and Mechanics and	Money and Nature's Products	Family and Community Centered	Elderly Concerns	Arts and Cultural Activities	Home and Community Centered	Family Integrated Activities	Competitive Sports and Science/Engineering	Athletic and Social Activities	Indoor Games and Social Activities	News and Information	Detached	Cosmopolitan Self-Enrichment	Highly Diversified
Just Plain Country	2.3	2.3	2.5	2.4	2.5	2.2	2.4	2.3	2.0	1.9	2.0	2.5	2.2	1.9	2.4
	40%	42%	58%	50%	51%	32%	46%	38%	32%	20%	29%	53%	36%	26%	43%
Mother's Little Network	2.2	2.2	1.9	2.2	2.1	2.1	2.4	2.3	2.2	2.2	2.1	2.3	1.8	2.2	2.4
	36	35	21	36	40	33	44	43	36	35	34	44	20	36	43
Sportlight	2.3	2.2	2.4	2.6	2.0	2.4	2.1	2.0	3.1	2.4	2.1	2.8	2.0	2.3	2.7
	44	37	51	52	29	47	40	32	78	41	30	61	28	46	61
Your Retirement Dollar	2.5	2.2	2.9	2.7	2.8	2.8	2.6	2.6	1.9	1.7	2.0	3.1	2.0	2.3	2.6
	49	33	72	57	66	62	55	55	20	11	32	75	34	43	57
Hollywood Television Theatre	2.1	1.9	1.9	1.8	1.9	2.5	2.0	2.2	1.9	2.3	2.2	2.2	1.9	2.3	2.5
	33	17	28	16	28	51	27	38	23	41	34	37	25	36	48
The Fertile Crescent	2.3	2.1	2.3	2.4	2.2	3.1	2.0	2.2	2.0	2.0	1.8	2.5	1.8	3.0	2.5
	45	36	40	47	47	80	28	38	27	27	25	59	24	77	56
What in the World	2.2	2.1	2.1	2.2	2.1	2.6	2.1	2.4	2.3	2.2	2.2	2.2	1.9	2.4	2.6
	41	36	34	36	40	56	29	46	42	37	35	41	28	46	58
Woman's Place	2.2	1.6	1.8	2.0	2.0	2.4	2.2	2.6	1.6	2.5	2.2	2.3	1.7	2.5	2.7
	37	11	22	24	40	50	38	55	9	51	43	42	17	57	56

*Top number in cell is mean interest rating: 4 = extremely interested, 3 = quite interested, 2 = not very interested, 1 = not at all interested. Bottom number is percentage rating 4 or 3.

with adult female concentrations. Like the Arts and Cultural Activities segment, these people are least interested in light entertainment programming.

The Highly Diversified segment offered above-average ratings for every one of the eight new program concepts. They, too, showed less interest in *Just Plain Country* and *Mother's Little Network,* with uniformly high ratings for all the rest.

The News and Information segment expressed a higher level of interest in *Your Retirement Dollar* than did any other segment and also rated *Sportlight* very high. The other concepts elicited considerably less interest from them and resulted in ratings close to the population averages.

The highest interest for the Family Integrated Activities segment was elicited by *Your Retirement Dollar* and *Woman's Place.* Other ratings were close to the population averages.

Several of the interest segments who normally watch little public television indicated relatively high levels of interest in one or more of the new program concepts.

The Money and Nature's Products segment, for example, had a mean rating of 2.9 for *Your Retirement Dollar,* with 72% saying they would be extremely or quite interested in watching such a program. Similarly, 58% were interested in *Just Plain Country.* The Family and Community Centered segment showed relatively strong interest in *Your Retirement Dollar, Sportlight,* and *Just Plain Country.* The Elderly Concerns segment, extremely light viewers of public television, rated *Your Retirement Dollar* high (mean of 2.8 and 66% expressing high interest), along with *Just Plain Country.* Among the youth concentration segments, those in the Competitive Sports and Science/Engineering segment rated *Sportlight* higher than did any other segment, with 78% expressing interest. The Athletic and Social Activities segment rated *Woman's Place* well above average.

Of course, not all of the people expressing interest in a program concept would watch it if it were implemented and put on the air. Clearly, the execution of a program concept is vital to its ability to attract and retain an audience—and even the manner of concept execution may be segmented in its appeal. Furthermore, interested potential viewers must be aware that a program is being broadcast, and they must be available to watch it (though this will become less important as home videotaping continues to grow).

Nevertheless, the differential appeal of alternative program concepts does reflect the relative *potential* for attracting audiences from the various interest segments. A concept that elicits high levels of interest has more potential, given comparable execution values, than one that elicits lower levels of interest. Similarly, other things being equal, a segment that exhibits greater interest in viewing a program based on the concept description has a greater potential to produce an audience for the program.

We believe that the diversity of ratings obtained for each new program concept across interest segments and across concepts within segments indicates that this segmentation scheme has considerable promise as a tool for integrating the early screening of new concepts into overall programming strategies for attracting target audiences. While the concepts tested in this study were oriented toward public broadcasting, there is no reason to believe that a comparably heterogeneous set of concepts for commercial broadcasting would have produced any less diversity of response.

FINANCIAL SUPPORT FOR PUBLIC TELEVISION

The history of public broadcasting has been punctuated with debate on the appropriate mix of alternative sources of funding. This issue has been important for two reasons: (1) Adequate funding is necessary to the continued existence of public broadcasting, and (2) the sources of funding have an impact on its character as an institution and its ability to retain editorial and artistic control over its own programming. A comprehensive analysis of these issues is offered in the recent Carnegie Commission report (Carnegie Commission, 1979), along with recommendations for dealing with them.

Because of the critical importance of funding, we included a series of questions to measure the public's attitudes toward alternative sources of financing.

Table 8.7 presents data on the responses to two questions. The first asked whether the respondent had ever supported his or her local public television station with a donation, and the second asked which one of the following sources of funding the respondent would like to see as the major source of funding for public television:

- Use of federal taxes to fund public TV.
- State government funding of public TV.
- Local community funds for public TV.
- Television set tax—a tax placed on each new TV set purchased. Revenue from this tax would be used to support public TV.
- Commercial time sold between public TV programs to support public TV.
- Income tax checkoff—every individual would be given an option to designate a small portion of his or her income tax payment to be used for the support of public TV.

As shown in Table 8.7, only 11% of the population claim to have ever supported their local public television station with a donation. The incidence of donations is related to frequency of viewing, but even among the most frequent viewers, only 27% report donations. Differences are negligible among minorities, who report almost the same incidence as the population in general.

By far, the most preferred source of funding is commercials shown between programs, followed by an income tax checkoff. Differences among the remaining sources were small, except that there is little public support for a tax on television sets, which is probably seen as the most direct means of obtaining money from viewers.

Frequent viewers of public television are much less likely to favor the use of commercials and are more positively disposed toward an income tax checkoff.

Blacks and Hispanics also indicate less of a preference for commercials than the population in general and are more favorable toward the use of federal taxes and state funds.

TABLE 8.7 Preferred Sources of Funding for Public Television

	Total Population %	Frequency of PTV Viewing			Elderly %	Minorities	
		Frequent %	Occasional %	Undetermined or Never %		Blacks %	Hispanics %
Ever supported local PTV station with a donation	11	27	11	2	10	9	9
Federal taxes	13	14	15	12	12	20	22
State government	10	12	13	8	9	14	18
Local community	11	15	10	10	9	8	13
TV set tax	6	8	6	5	6	5	8
Networks taxed	12	13	11	12	13	13	14
Commercials	30	17	31	36	30	22	19
Income tax checkoff	17	24	14	14	15	14	8

CONCLUSIONS

It appears that public television will continue to receive pressure from a variety of sources to broaden its appeal to a larger portion of the total population. These pressures will emanate not only from those special interest groups who seek programming consistent with their own interests, but also from the need to attract contributions from a larger number of viewers to finance its own growth.

The problem of attracting current nonviewers of public television, while maintaining a commitment to excellence in programming, is not a simple one to solve. How can public television present programming to appeal to women, given the diversity of interests we have already seen in this group? Similar differences exist within such subpopulations as the elderly, Blacks, Hispanics, and other groups.

Given this situation, we believe that our interest-based audience segmentation scheme provides an extremely useful conceptual tool for analyzing and developing solutions to the problem of attracting more viewers to public television.

First and foremost, we believe that by examining the interests, needs, and other characteristics of each of the fourteen segments, a mix of programs could be developed to have a broad reach. This does not mean that any single program need have a broad appeal—that is a necessary component for commercial broadcasts—but that among the total mix of programs available on public television during the course of a week, each of the interest segments could find several attractive offerings.

Second, by studying the demographic characteristics and other media behavior of each interest segment, it is possible to develop efficient strategies for reaching target interest segments to inform them of the existence of programs they will want to view and to let them know when they will be broadcast.

Third, we believe there is an additional benefit in approaching the audience problem in this way, as it is inherently less politicized. Since women and minority groups are dispersed across the fourteen interest segments, their needs will in fact be served if programs are available to attract most of the interest segments.

Because programs on public television can be successful with much smaller audiences than programs broadcast commercially, developing a comprehensive strategy to appeal to a broader audience with a diverse mix of program types is actually easier for public than for commercial television programmers. The former can offer individual programs designed to appeal to only one or two segments, as long as the total array of programs covers all or most of the population segments. The latter needs to attract the maximum audience possible for each program broadcast, in an effort to obtain more money for the commercials that accompany it, since the cost for commercial time is pegged to the size of the viewing audience.

NOTE

1. The concepts used in the survey were selected from a larger number of concepts graciously made available to the authors by the Corporation for Public Broadcasting and the Public Broadcasting Service.

REFERENCES

Carnegie Commission (1967) Public Television: A Program for Action. New York: Harper & Row.
——— (1979) A Public Trust: The Report of the Carnegie Commission on the Future of Public Broadcasting. New York: Bantam.
MORRISSETT, L. N. (1976) "Prescription for public broadcasting," in D. Cater and M. J. Nyhan (eds.) The Future of Public Broadcasting. New York: Praeger.

9

The Television Viewing Context

INTRODUCTION

Throughout the preceding chapters, the discussion of television has focused upon the relationship between interests, needs, and demographics on the one hand and audience decisions as to what is watched on the other.

The purpose of the analyses reported in this chapter is to go "behind" these decisions and to examine the context in which they were made by the members of each segment. The results address the following questions for each interest segment:

(1) To what extent are the members of the television audience sufficiently involved in viewing:

    (a) To plan ahead what is to be watched?

    (b) To be disappointed if they were to miss an episode of a program?

    (c) To pay sole attention to what they are viewing as opposed to doing something else while watching?

(2) To what degree do television viewers watch by themselves rather than with other people?

(3) How much influence do various audience members have on the decision as to what is watched?

In spite of the fact that answers to these questions may help to further our understanding of viewing behavior, virtually no attention has been given to them in past research. Though our interest segmentation scheme was developed for the sole purpose of understanding why different programs are watched, we thought that the scheme also might be helpful in understanding the context in which television is used.

For each of the 149 programs or program categories for which respondents reported their viewing behavior, they were also asked a series of questions to measure 3 aspects of the context in which the viewing took place: (1) the extent to which they are involved with the program, (2) whether they usually watch it alone or with others, and (3) the degree to which they influence the choice of what is being viewed.

A series of indices were developed to measure these aspects, with each designed to represent the average behavior of the viewers in each segment across all programs viewed. For example, one index of television involvement was designed to measure the extent to which the people in a segment usually planned in advance to watch the programs they reported viewing. The following example illustrates how this index, called Advance Planning, was calculated. Suppose two persons were the only members of a segment. Furthermore, suppose their program viewing behavior was as reported below:

	Person	
	1	2
Number of programs and/or program categories they reported viewing	50	10
Of these, the number for which each person indicated that they "usually plan in advance to watch"	10	10

The Advance Planning index for this segment is 33.3%. It is computed by taking the total number of programs for which the members of the segment planned in advance to watch (10 + 10 = 20) and dividing by the total number of programs viewed (50 + 10 = 60). It is a self-weighted average, where the weight for each respondent is proportionate to the number of programs that respondent watched. Seven indices, including Advance Planning, were computed in a manner similar to that for Advance Planning; that is, each is based on answers added up across programs and the people in each segment.

Table 9.1 reports the indices. To facilitate comparisons, the ratio of the average score for the people in a segment to the average for the entire population is reported. For example, the Advance Planning score of 114% for those in the Elderly Concerns segment indicates that the percentage of all programs watched, for which they planned in advance to watch, is 14% above the average for the entire population (55.4%). Cosmopolitan Self-Enrichment segment members, on the other hand, are 61% of average on their Advance Planning score.

The definitions of each of the indices, listed on the left-hand side of Table 9.1, are provided in turn as each index is discussed.

TELEVISION INVOLVEMENT

Three indices of television involvement were developed. Each is discussed in turn.

Advance Planning

Respondents were asked, for each of the programs they reported watching, if they "usually plan in advance to watch this program." *Advance Planning* is the percentage of programs watched that are reported as involving such planning.

Across the entire television audience over half (55.4%) of the television programs watched involved a degree of Advance Planning.

The members of four segments are more than 10% above average on Advance Planning. They are:

(1) Detached, 18% above average
(2) Elderly Concerns, 14% above average
(3) Highly Diversified, 14% above average
(4) News and Information, 10% above average

TABLE 9.1 Television Viewing Context Indices by Interest Segment

	Entire Population	Adult Male Concentration			Adult Female Concentration				Youth Concentration				Mixed		
		Mechanics and Outdoor Life	Money and Nature's Products	Family and Community Centered	Elderly Concerns	Arts and Cultural Activities	Home and Community Centered	Family Integrated Activities	Competitive Sports and Science/Engineering	Athletic and Social Activities	Indoor Games and Social Activities	News and Information	Detached	Cosmopolitan Self-Enrichment	Highly Diversified
Involvement															
Advance Planning	55.4	94	99	96	114	98	100	93	102	97	107	110	118	61	114
Episode Disappointment	10.3	70	76	83	146	83	108	68	90	83	148	119	101	28	183
Undivided Attention	64.6	103	111	110	117	98	87	85	108	106	98	106	113	63	107
Viewing Alone	28.9	82	87	75	172	134	85	83	92	80	85	117	112	96	74
Decision-Making															
Overall Influence	60.7	104	100	99	121	112	87	87	111	96	88	109	105	92	89
Influence in the Presence of Adults	52.3	114	104	107	108	102	91	84	115	99	96	95	104	91	95
Influence in the Presence of Children	44.0	99	77	115	88	95	76	80	130	110	100	125	98	98	109

Only one segment has members who are less than 90% of average on Advance Planning, namely those in the Cosmopolitan Self-Enrichment segment, who are only 61% of average.

Advance Planning is positively associated with the amount of television viewing engaged in by persons in a segment. Three of the four segments that are among the highest in Advance Planning are also the three highest in total television viewing, as reported in Chapter 5:

(1) News and Information, 34% above average in television viewing
(2) Highly Diversified, 20% above average in television viewing
(3) Elderly Concerns, 14% above average in television viewing

Consistent with this pattern, people in the Cosmopolitan Self-Enrichment segment, who engage in the least amount of Advance Planning, are also the lightest television viewers (only 75% of average).

For people in some segments, the correspondence between levels of television viewing and Advance Planning is reinforced by the nature of the needs television appears to satisfy. For example:

(1) *Elderly Concerns.* The same needs for coping with loneliness and maintaining a sense of social integration that lead people in this segment to use television as a vehicle for developing surrogate friendships may also lead to more Advance Planning regarding what they watch. Friends are seldom developed, let alone maintained, on the basis of one exposure.

(2) *Highly Diversified.* The people in this segment use television as a vehicle for bringing members of the family together, as well as for educational purposes. These functions may necessitate an above-average degree of Advance Planning.

(3) *News and Information.* In Chapter 5 we indicated that individuals in this segment appear to use television as a vehicle to become knowledgeable in order to make themselves more socially stimulating and better able to converse with others. The conversation value for most specific topics has a "short shelf life." Day-to-day conversa-

tion is driven in large part by whatever recent events have occurred that are of general interest in one's circle of acquaintances. Hence, members of the News and Information segment may be high on Advance Planning to ensure a continuity in the flow of information in order to stay "current."

(4) *Cosmopolitan Self-Enrichment.* Those in this segment are exceptionally light users of television and heavy users of print media (especially books). They tend to selectively use the media they find to be informative and intellectually stimulating. We would hypothesize that, except in rare circumstances, the people in this segment do not feel that television performs these functions for them. Yet their viewing is highly selective, as indicated by the programs they do watch. This apparent anomaly can be resolved by recognizing that Advance Planning may be seen to involve more of a commitment to watch than the people in this segment are willing to admit to. When they do watch television, they choose their programs carefully, but their commitment to viewing appears to be limited.

In the case of people in the Detached segment, we can find no rationale in the needs satisfied by television for their above-average Advance Planning index. If anything, it is totally inconsistent with their low level of involvement in virtually all other types of activities examined in this study.

Episode Disappointment

For each program watched, respondents were asked to rate the extent to which they would be disappointed if they missed an episode, using a four-point scale ranging from "not at all" to "extremely." Episode disappointment is the percentage of programs for which respondents reported they would be "extremely" disappointed if they missed an episode.

Though over half of programs viewed are defined as involving Advance Planning, only 10.3% of programs viewed are described by viewers as ones for which they would be extremely disappointed if they missed an episode.

There are four segments whose members score 10% or more above average on Episode Disappointment. They are:

(1) Highly Diversified, 83% above average
(2) Indoor Games and Social Activities, 48% above average
(3) Elderly Concerns, 46% above average
(4) News and Information, 19% above average

Members of three of these segments also scored 10% or more above average on Advance Planning. Members of the Indoor Games and Social Activities segment are the only ones who did not.

In our judgment, the same reasons that account for the high scores on Advance Planning for the three segments also account for their correspondingly high scores on Episode Disappointment.

The people in the Indoor Games and Social Activities segment are also somewhat above average on Advance Planning (7%), ranking fifth out of the fourteen segments. We believe that the principal reason they score high on both Advance Planning and Episode Disappointment is that, as they are typically in an early stage of the life cycle (close to establishing or having just established their own home), their opportunities for engaging in other away-from-home activities are more restricted than for individuals in a number of the other segments. Their greater involvement in television may be the result of a temporary constraint on alternative activities, over and above whatever interest they may have in the program per se. They watch a lot of television, and it appears to be an important activity for them.

There are eight segments scoring 90% of average or less. They are:

(1) Cosmopolitan Self-Enrichment, 28% of average
(2) Family Integrated Activities, 68% of average
(3) Mechanics and Outdoor Life, 70% of average
(4) Money and Nature's Products, 76% of average
(5) Family and Community Centered, 83% of average
(6) Arts and Cultural Activities, 83% of average
(7) Athletic and Social Activities, 83% of average
(8) Competitive Sports and Science/Engineering, 90% of average

Most viewers of television do not have the need for the continuity of exposure that the four high scoring segments have. Lacking any functional requirements driving continuity of exposure, they are not especially concerned about missing an episode of whatever programs or series they watch.

Undivided Attention

Undivided Attention is defined as the percentage of programs watched for which respondents indicated "I give it my full attention," when asked whether they usually give the program full attention or do other things while watching.

For almost two-thirds of programs viewed (64.6%), respondents indicate that when they watch, they give the program their full attention.

Members of the Elderly Concerns segment score higher on Undivided Attention (17% above average) than does any other segment. Second are those in the Detached segment, who are 13% above average. A major reason for the undivided attention of both these segments may be their narrower range of interests than most of the other segments. In addition, the Elderly Concerns segment members are less likely to be distracted by the presence of others, since many live alone or with only one other person. This interpretation is consistent with the fact that the only other two segments whose members are 10% or more above average are the Money and Nature's Products segment (11%) and the Family and Community Centered segment (10%). Members of both these groups also have a narrower range of interests than do most other segments.

The lowest scoring segment on Undivided Attention is the Cosmopolitan Self-Enrichment segment, who score 63% of average. That is, they are much more apt to be engaged in some other activity while watching television. The intellectually up-scaled nature, as well as the wide range, of their interests probably contributes to their low score. Two other segments whose members score low on Undivided Attention are the Home and Community Activities and the Family Integrated Activities segments. In both cases, the predominantly married, adult women in them score high on the need for family ties. Viewing with other family members may be part of a pattern of behavior that helps to satisfy their needs. This, in turn, causes their attention to be more frequently split between the television set and other family-related activities.

VIEWING ALONE

One index was computed to measure this aspect of the television viewing context. It is defined as the percentage of programs watched that the respondent reported as usually watching alone.

A relatively small percentage of television viewing is done by oneself (28.9%). By far, most program viewing is done in the presence of others.

As one would expect, the highest scoring persons on Viewing Alone are those in the Elderly Concerns segment, who are 72% above average. Those in three other segments are 10% or more above average. They are:

(1) *Arts and Cultural Activities,* 34% above average. For individuals in this segment, it is likely that the reason for their viewing alone is the upscaled intellectual content of their interests and viewing preferences which, we suspect, are less apt to be shared with other members of the family than are the preferences of persons in most other segments. They tend to watch programs with a narrow base of audience appeal.

(2) *News and Information,* 17% above average. Two factors contribute to the relatively high percentage of programs viewed alone by the members of this segment:
   (a) They have a high percentage of retirees compared to the entire population (23% versus 15%). Hence, they are more apt to be home alone during the day.
   (b) They watch more television than people in any other segment. This extreme behavior is less apt to be shared by other household members, especially young children and teenagers.

(3) *Detached*, 12% above average. The people in this segment also have higher percentages than the entire population of both retirees (22% versus 15%) and Widowers (15% versus 8%). As in the case of the Elderly Concerns segment, these characteristics contribute to their above-average tendency to view alone.

Most of the other ten segments predominantly watch television in the presence of others.

High scores on Viewing Alone appear to be the result of one or more special circumstances. These include (1) being retired or widowed, (2) watching programs with a narrow audience appeal, and (3) watching television to an extreme not shared by other household members. In the absence of these elements, the people in most other segments tend to be involved in considerably more joint viewing activity.

The segment whose members most frequently view programs with others is the Highly Diversified segment. This is the segment for which we hypothesized that television viewing is very much a family affair.

TELEVISION PROGRAM
DECISION-MAKING INFLUENCE

Three indices are used to measure decision-making influence. They measure:

(1) The usual tendency for people in a segment to choose the programs they watch
(2) The usual tendency for people in a segment to choose what is watched when adults are also viewing
(3) The usual tendency for people in a segment to choose what is watched when children are also viewing

Overall Influence

For each program watched, respondents were asked who usually decides to watch. Decision-making influence is the percentage of programs watched for which respondents reported themselves as usually deciding to watch (60.7% for the entire population).

There are only three segments that score more than 10% above average. They are:

(1) Elderly Concerns, 21% above average
(2) Arts and Cultural Activities, 12% above average
(3) Competitive Sports and Science/Engineering, 11% above average

For the first two of these, their Overall Influence is directly associated with their above-average score on Viewing Alone. Given our definition of Overall Influence, a high Viewing Alone score will tend to be associated with a high Overall Influence score.

The high Overall Influence score for individuals in the Competitive Sports and Science/Engineering segment is more interesting, as they did not score above average on Viewing Alone. Their high Overall Influence score appears to reflect a tendency of adolescent males to get their own way in program selection. This is discussed in more detail as we analyze decision-making influence in the next two sections.

Of the four segments whose members score 90% or less than average for the entire population, all are more apt to be in viewing situations with others present; consequently, they are less likely on the average to dictate the program selected.

Influence in the Presence of Adults

In this context, influence with respect to decision-making is meaningful in situations where others are present and have the opportunity to participate in the decision-making process. Hence, for the purpose of measuring influence, information from each respondent about *who usually decides to watch* a given program needs to be combined with data on *who else usually watches it.* This index measures the respondent's decision-making influence in viewing situations involving adults.

> Influence with Adults Present is defined as the percentage of programs watched where other adults are usually present, for which the respondent indicated that he or she usually decides what to watch (52.3% for the entire population).

Members of only two segments score 10% or more above

average when it comes to exerting their influence in the presence of adults:

(1) Competitive Sports and Science/Engineering, 15% above average
(2) Mechanics and Outdoor Life, 14% above average

The orientation of the first segment's interests in competitive
activities and the need to achieve independence are both factors
that we would expect to be associated with the above-average
influence of this group of predominantly adolescent males.

The above-average influence of the members of the Mechanics and Outdoor Life segment may be due to their relative lack
of needs that are tied to relationships with other people. If
interpersonal relationships were more important to them, they
might be more willing to compromise when it comes to choosing what is to be watched.

Individuals in only one segment scored less than 90% of the
average for the entire population, those in the Family Integrated Activities segment (84% of average). The predominantly
adult females in this segment have a high need for family ties,
combined with the use of television as a means for bringing
both adults and children in the household together. To accomplish this, the people in this segment appear willing to relinquish
set control.

Influence in the Presence of Children

This index measures the respondent's influence in situations where
children are reported as usually being present. The definition is the
same as the one for adults present, except that it is based on
programs watched, where the "others who usually watch" are
children (44.0%).

Individuals in five segments are above average on their influence score in the presence of children:

(1) Competitive Sports and Science/Engineering, 30% above average
(2) News and Information, 25% above average
(3) Family and Community Centered, 15% above average
(4) Athletic and Social Activities, 10% above average
(5) Highly Diversified, 9% above average

For the people in the first of these five segments, their striving for independence most likely accounts for their above-average score on influence for viewing situations where children are present, as well as for situations involving adults.

Many of the programs viewed by the News and Information segment have little appeal for children. It is not surprising that when children do watch these programs, it is the adult who has been most influential in dictating the program selection.

The members of the Family and Community Centered segment have a low rate of watching television alone and appear to watch often in the presence of children. As indicated in Chapter 5, they tend to have a strong religious orientation and to favor programs that are least offensive. Apparently, their convictions lead them to exert relatively strong controls over what programs their children watch as well (at least when they are together).

Members of the Athletic and Social Activities segment have low needs for family ties and high needs to escape from the problems of home life. They may be less yielding to younger children in the family, as it is one area of family life where they have more opportunity to control.

As indicated in Chapters 4 and 5, members of the Highly Diversified segment have strong needs for intellectual stimulation and growth and use television as a vehicle for satisfying these needs both for themselves and for other members of their families. Their tendency to exert above-average control over program selection when viewing with children is quite consistent with this pattern.

At the low end of the Influence in the Presence of Children index are four segments whose members score 90% of average or less:

(1) Money and Nature's Products, 77% of average
(2) Home and Community Centered, 76% of average
(3) Family Integrated Activities, 80% of average
(4) Elderly Concerns, 88% of average

For persons in the Money and Nature's Products and the Elderly Concerns segment, their below-average Influence in the Presence of Children may be in part a function of the fact that their children are older and by implication more difficult to control. Also, the people in these two adult segments have the highest average ages (53 and 61 years) of any of the fourteen segments. While we did not ask whether or not a respondent was a grandparent, or how often their grandchildren were present in their homes, it is likely that these two segments entertain grandchildren more than the other segments do. As grandparents, they may be more indulgent in catering to children's program preferences.

For the Family Integrated Activities segment, the desire for family participation that led to their below-average score for Influence in the Presence of Adults is most likely the main reason for their below-average score for Influence in the Presence of Children.

Lastly, members of the Home and Community Centered segment may be below average due to a combination of their high need for family ties and their interest orientation, which is relatively narrow. As indicated in Chapter 4, these people tend to assume the role of homemaker in a very narrow, traditional manner. In this role, they tend to be oriented toward pleasing others in the family and are probably somewhat passive in asserting their own preferences. They are below average in their influence whenever others are present, but even more with children than with adults.

CONCLUDING COMMENTS

From the outset of this study, it was our objective to understand the reasons underlying the choices audience members make about what programs to watch. It is gratifying to find that the interest-based segmentation scheme developed for that purpose also is of some use in understanding the involvement, individual viewing, and decision-making influence aspects of the context in which television is watched. Clearly, these issues have major implications for improving programming strategies and possibly for the selection of advertising vehicles that will be most effective in attracting viewers' attention to commercial messages.

We hope that the results reported in this chapter will encourage persons in both academia and industry to investigate more intensively the context in which television is viewed.

Part Four
Conclusion

10

Interest and Demographic Audience Segments: A Comparison

A FRAMEWORK FOR COMPARISON

The most often used bases for segmenting audiences for television, as well as the other media, are demographic characteristics, especially sex and age. In the case of television, one set of audience segments frequently used by media measurement services is the following:

(1) Adult males, age 18-34
(2) Adult males, age 35-49
(3) Adult males, age 50 and over
(4) Adult females, age 18-34
(5) Adult females, age 35-49
(6) Adult females, age 50 and over
(7) Teenage males, age 13-17
(8) Teenage females, age 13-17

This chapter provides some comparisons between our interest-based segmentation of audiences and this more traditional demographic-based approach. These comparisons address two sets of questions:

(1) What is the correspondence between a person's membership in a particular interest segment and his or her demographic segment membership? Are the two classification systems redundant? Does the interest segmentation highlight individual differences useful in

understanding media behavior that are not taken into account by
traditional demographic means of audience classification?

(2) How much variation in television viewing behavior across individuals is accounted for by these eight traditional demographic
segments? By our interest segmentation? What is the net addition
to "explaining" variation in television viewing behavior of adding
our interest segmentation to the demographic system? Stated
another way, what does the interest-based segmentation contribute
to accounting for differences in television usage?

Answering these questions will help to evaluate the usefulness
of our interest-based segmentation scheme relative to the more
traditional demographic approach to understanding audience
media behavior.

In general, the less redundant our interest-based segmentation
and the higher the levels of explained variation in media behavior associated with it relative to demographic segmentation, the
stronger the argument for its use, at least as a complement to
traditional demographic segmentation.

In addition to these two criteria (degree of redundancy and
relative variance explained), a third criterion is of paramount
importance: that is, the relative usefulness of interest versus
demographic segmentation in understanding the "whys" of
audience behavior. In effect, all the earlier chapters reporting
our findings argue the case for interest segmentation being at
least as useful, in our opinion more useful, than demographic
data when it comes to the "whys" of audience behavior. This is
true if for no other reason than because with demographics one
has to make inferences about audience interests, while our
segmentation system deals directly with them. As we have
shown, this leads to an ability to understand in rather graphic
terms many of the reasons for individual differences in media
usage.

This chapter focuses exclusively on the interrelationship between the two segmentation schemes and their association with
television viewing, since the diagnostic issue has been treated
throughout the preceding chapters.

Finally, the comparisons between demographic-based and
interest-based segmentation schemes reported here are quite
limited. They serve only to compare one of the more frequently

used demographic schemes to our interest-based classification system. Readers interested in pursuing a more intensive analysis comparing the two or in pursuing demographic segmentation in and of itself are encouraged to do so. The entire data base used in this study is in the public domain and readily accessible.[1] We hope that others will be stimulated by our efforts to pursue alternative analyses on what we believe to be an unusually rich and comprehensive set of data.

DEMOGRAPHIC AND INTEREST SEGMENT INTERRELATIONSHIP

Table 10.1 reports the percentage of males and females in various age categories belonging to each of the fourteen interest segments. For example, as indicated in the second column of the table, 16.6% of the adult males in the population are members of the Mechanics and Outdoor Life segment, while fewer than 1% are members of the Indoor Games and Social Activities segment.

One measure of the degree of association or overlap between the two sets of segments is the maximum percentage of each demographic segment's members who are members of a single interest segment. These percentages are all circled in Table 10.1. As demonstrated in previous chapters, there is clearly a relationship between a person's age and sex and interest segment membership. Nonetheless, that relationship is relatively modest in that:

(1) Even for teenage males, who have the greatest concentration in any one interest segment, only 50.7% of them belong to it, namely, the Competitive Sports and Science/Engineering segment. Hence, fully 49.3% of male teenagers fall into the other thirteen interest segments.

(2) The second greatest concentration is for teenage females, 34.6% of whom are members of the Athletic and Social Activities segment, with the remaining 65.4% classified into one of the other interest segments.

TABLE 10.1 Age and Sex Distribution by Interest Segment

Segment	Entire Population %	Adults Males %	Adults Females %	Teenagers Males %	Teenagers Females %	Adult Males by Age 18–34 %	Adult Males by Age 35–49 %	Adult Males by Age 50 & Over %	Adult Females by Age 18–34 %	Adult Females by Age 35–49 %	Adult Females by Age 50 & Over %
Adult Male Concentration											
Mechanics and Outdoor Life	8.3	16.6	0.7	19.6	1.2	26.0	16.3	4.5	0.9	0.2	0.5
Money and Nature's Products	6.2	10.1	2.7	2.2	0.7	4.1	8.4	22.1	0.6	2.0	6.0
Family and Community Centered	6.4	11.1	2.1	2.8	0.2	6.0	18.4	15.3	1.0	3.2	3.3
Total	20.9	37.8	5.5	24.6	2.1	36.1	43.1	41.9	2.5	5.4	9.8
Adult Female Concentration											
Elderly Concerns	8.0	4.9	10.9	0.1	2.4	1.6	3.2	12.6	2.2	5.2	25.9
Arts and Cultural Activities	8.7	5.8	11.4	1.7	1.4	5.1	7.0	7.7	11.1	15.8	12.4
Home and Community Centered	7.8	2.6	12.5	2.2	5.2	1.9	1.0	4.8	8.7	22.2	13.3
Family Integrated Activities	9.9	2.7	16.5	1.2	6.4	3.9	2.7	2.1	30.1	14.5	8.2
Total	34.4	16.0	51.3	5.2	15.4	12.5	13.9	27.2	52.1	57.7	59.8
Youth Concentration											
Competitive Sports and Science/Engineering	6.5	13.1	0.6	50.7	3.2	10.6	6.1	2.2	0.2	0.5	—
Athletic and Social Activities	4.2	1.5	6.7	3.1	34.6	2.5	0.5	0.2	6.0	1.4	—
Indoor Games and Social Activities	4.0	0.7	7.0	4.4	25.2	0.2	—	—	8.8	2.8	1.0
Total	14.7	15.3	14.3	58.2	63.0	13.2	6.6	2.4	15.0	4.7	1.0
Mixed											
News and Information	5.4	6.4	4.4	—	1.0	4.5	8.5	10.5	4.4	6.3	4.7
Detached	8.6	9.6	7.8	5.1	7.0	8.0	10.5	13.1	5.5	7.5	10.5
Cosmopolitan Self-Enrichment	7.9	6.8	8.9	0.6	3.9	13.2	7.7	1.7	9.9	11.4	8.3
Highly Diversified	8.0	8.2	7.8	6.3	7.7	12.4	9.8	3.2	10.5	6.9	5.8
Total	29.9	31.0	28.9	12.0	19.6	38.1	36.5	28.5	30.3	32.1	28.3

Table 10.2 summarizes the figures for each of the demographic segments defined at the outset of this chapter, along with the name of the interest segment which accounts for the greatest proportion of its members. As stated previously, teenage males have the greatest degree of overlap, with 50.7% of them belonging to one interest segment and 49.3% excluded from it. None of the adult male or female demographic segments approaches this degree of overlap with a single interest segment. For the six adult demographic segments, the highest concentrations in interest segments range from 30.7% to 18.4%.

This lack of overlap is not simply a by-product of choosing an extreme criterion. Including the two interest segments with the highest concentrations, rather than just the highest one, yields 58.2% to 65.3% of the demographic segment members being classified into the remaining twelve interest segments.

We conclude that the fourteen interest segments classify individual audience members into quite different categories than one would find in a traditional demographic (age/sex)

TABLE 10.2 Demographic/Interest Segment Overlap Summary

Demographic Segments	Highest Percentage Interest Segments	Included %	Excluded %
1. Adult Males, 18–34	Mechanics and Outdoor Life	26.0	74.0
2. Adult Males, 35–49	Family and Community Centered	18.4	81.6
3. Adult Males, 50 and Over	Money and Nature's Products	22.1	77.9
4. Adult Females, 18–34	Family Integrated Activities	30.7	69.3
5. Adult Females, 35–49	Home and Community Centered	22.2	77.8
6. Adult Females, 50 and Over	Elderly Concerns	25.9	74.1
7. Teenage Males, 13–17	Competitive Sports and Science Engineering	50.7	49.3
8. Teenage Females, 13–17	Athletic and Social Activities	34.6	65.4

analysis of the viewing audience. At best, there is only a modest degree of interrelationship (overlap) between the two classification systems.[2]

EXPLAINING TELEVISION VIEWING BEHAVIOR

In order to measure the degree of variation in television viewing behavior across individuals that is associated with each of the two segmentation schemes, three multiple regression analyses were run for each of the nineteen types of television programs discussed in Chapter 5.

For each set of three regressions, the dependent variable was the number of times a respondent reported watching the programs included in a given program type. For example, the Adventure category includes six programs. The dependent variable for all three of the Adventure regressions was the total number of times in the last four weeks each respondent reported viewing any of the six programs.

The independent variables in each of the three regressions are the same across all nineteen program types. They are dummy variables representing:

(1) The eight sex/age demographic segments
(2) The fourteen interest segments
(3) Both the age/sex demographic segments and the interest segments[3]

Table 10.3 reports the coefficient of multiple determination for each of the 57 multiple regressions (19 program types times 3 different runs for each type). These coefficients measure the percentage of variance in individual program type viewing behavior accounted for by each of the three respective sets of independent variables. The results are as follows:

(1) Both the demographic segment and the interest segment regressions account for an identical, but nonetheless relatively small percentage of the variation in program type television viewing behavior. Across all nineteen of the program types:

   (a) The mean percentage of variance in viewing behavior accounted for by the eight sex/age segments is 5.4%, with a low

TABLE 10.3 Coefficients of Determination[a] by Television Program Type and Segmentation Scheme

| | Segmentation Scheme[b] | | | Combined Minus Demographics[c] (3) – (1) % | Combined Divided by Demographics (3) ÷ (1) x 100 |
	Demographic (1) %	Interests (2) %	Combined (3) %		
Adventure	3.4	7.8	10.1	6.4	297
Children's Programs	8.0	3.3	9.3	1.3	116
Crime Drama	0.8	5.0	5.7	4.9	713
Documentary	0.2	0.7	1.2	1.0	600
Dramas	5.1	3.9	7.6	2.5	149
Game Shows	3.2	4.1	5.8	2.6	181
Movies	2.4	2.5	4.4	2.0	183
Musical Performances	3.8	6.7	8.7	4.9	229
News/Commentary	6.9	8.1	11.4	4.5	165
News Shows – Daily	15.8	11.8	19.0	3.2	120
Science Fiction	5.4	3.6	7.2	1.8	133
Situation Comedy	6.4	6.4	9.3	2.9	145
Soap Operas	12.8	7.1	15.4	2.6	120
Specials	0.7	2.0	2.3	1.6	329
Sports	11.6	10.1	17.0	5.4	147
Talk Shows	6.1	4.7	7.9	1.8	130
Theatrical Performances	0.3	4.6	4.4	4.1	1467
Variety Shows	3.0	4.6	6.6	3.6	220
Others	6.2	6.4	9.1	2.9	147
Mean	5.4	5.4	8.5	3.1	155

a. All coefficients of determination reported in this table are adjusted for degrees of freedom.
b. All of the F-ratios associated with these regressions are significant at the .005 level.
c. All of the F-ratios used to evaluate the net addition to explained variance by adding the interest segment variables to the demographics are significant at the .01 level.

217

of 0.2% for Documentaries to a high of 15.8% for Daily News Shows.

(b) The mean percentage of variance in viewing behavior associated with the fourteen interest segments is identical to that for the demographics, namely, 5.4% ranging from 0.7% for Documentaries to 11.8% for Daily News Shows.

(2) When both segmentation schemes are used in combination, the average percentage of variance in viewing behavior accounted for is 8.5%, ranging from 1.2% for Documentaries to a high of 19.0% for Daily News Shows. Hence, adding the interest segmentation scheme to the demographic one already in frequent use results in an increase of explained variance of 3.1 percentage points, or 55% over and above that accounted for by the demographics alone.

CONCLUSIONS

Our interest segmentation scheme plays a complementary role to the more traditional age/sex approach to audience segmentation. There is only a relatively modest degree of overlap in segment membership between the two. The interest segmentation scheme accounts for differences in program type television viewing behavior as well as the demographic scheme does; using the two approaches in combination provides a substantial percentage increase in the ability to account for viewing behavior.

Neither segmentation scheme separately nor both of them in combination, however, explain a very high percentage of the variation in viewing behavior.[4]

NOTES

1. See Chapter 11 for information as to how data can be obtained.

2. This conclusion is a subjective evaluation of the redundancy or degree of association between the two classification systems. Clearly, any standard statistical test of their independence would result in the conclusion that the two systems are not statistically independent.

3. Due to the problem of multicollinearity, the actual number of variables in each of the three types of regressions is one less than the number of categories in each of

the segmentation schemes involved. Hence, it is seven for the demographic regressions, thirteen for the interest segment regressions, and twenty for the combined runs.

4. The findings reported in this chapter are consistent with those reported elsewhere, indicating that the coefficients of determination for almost any aspect of individual behavior using variables such as demographics or other general interest measures as predictors are typically quite low (Frank, 1968 and Frank et al., 1971).

REFERENCES

FRANK, R. E. (1968) "Market segmentation research: findings and implications," in F. M. Bass et al. (eds.) Applications of the Sciences in Marketing Management. New York: John Wiley.
--- J. C. BECKNELL, and J. D. CLOKEY (1971) "Television program types." Journal of Marketing Research 8 (May): 204-211.

11

Interpretation, Validity, and Utilization

INTRODUCTION

The purpose of this chapter is to place our findings in a somewhat broader context in terms of three issues: their *interpretability*, their *validity*, and their *utility* in relation to policy formulation and research. Our discussion of future research is focused on opportunities relating directly to the interest segmentation scheme and the other data used in this investigation. We have chosen not to provide a comprehensive agenda for future television research, as this has been done recently and well elsewhere by Katz (1977) and Comstock and Lindsey (1975).

The following discussion addresses these questions:

(1) *Interpretability*. Is the structure of the interest segments cohesive and interpretable? Given only the data on interests, needs, demographic and socioeconomic characteristics, do the segments "make sense" individually and collectively? Does the segmentation structure provide a well-focused conceptual framework for describing television audiences?

(2) *Validity*. Are there systematic and interpretable relationships among the interest segments in their behavior regarding:

   (a) Television viewing?
   (b) Media usage other than television (magazines, books, movies, newspapers, and radio)?
   (c) The television decision-making process?

(3) *Utility*. Can the results of this study contribute to television network or station program policy and strategy formulation, as well as to the development, evaluation, and promotion of specific programs? Might our findings be used in a similar manner by other media organizations such as television or movie production companies? Book, magazine, and newspaper publishers? Radio networks or stations? To what subject matter, other than media, might our interest segmentation scheme be applied? How might the interest segmentation scheme developed in this study be "transferred" so that other investigators might be able to use it as the basis for pursuing their own research interests?

In contrast to previous chapters that summarized what we have learned about media behavior, the present discussion focuses principally on how this information might be used to advantage by people in a wide range of institutional settings.

INTERPRETABILITY

Substantial portions of the preceding chapters have centered upon interpreting the nature of the people in each of the fourteen segments. In so doing, we have tried to provide a sufficiently detailed description of each segment's members so that their character would be reasonably transparent. The process through which the reader has been taken is somewhat akin to the painting of a portrait. At first, it is not obvious to the observer who is to be depicted on the canvas. However, at some point along the way, one has a revelation. All of a sudden, the subject of the portrait is apparent, accompanied by the recognition that the emerging parts could have fit no other whole. So it is with the interpretation of the character of the members of the fourteen segments. It is not uncommon for readers to say: "I know someone like that." Members of the Mechanics and Outdoor Life, the Arts and Cultural Activities, and Highly Diversified segments, as well as those of the other eleven, come alive as real individuals. As audience types, there is an apparent, indeed obvious, correspondence between the characterizations of the fourteen segments and the people with whom we associate in everyday life.

We recognize, of course, that any attempt to classify or categorize individuals is necessarily restrictive. When we reduce a large population to a fourteen-segment typology, or classification scheme, the richness of the very real individual differences among us is lost.

Each segment description represents an average of millions of people, and, in reality, no one individual is likely to fit the average description of any single segment perfectly. We all contain certain elements of many segments, but at the same time we fit some segments better than others. Hopefully, our structure is sufficiently detailed and accurate to be acceptable as a reasonable categorization of the interest and need profiles of the American population.

VALIDITY

Our objective at the start of this investigation was to develop an interest segmentation scheme that would be a valid indicator of differences in television viewing behavior. It was something of an afterthought that led us to include data on other media—and we did so only because we thought the data might help us better understand the interest segments.

The validity of the segmentation structure developed in this study can be assessed in a number of ways. One is to examine its internal consistency and the interpretations of the segments themselves. We feel, as indicated in the previous section, that the "face validity" of the segmentation scheme is apparent and needs no further elaboration at this point.

More important in the validation process is demonstrating that segments identified and characterized in terms of their patterns of interests and needs do in fact differ in their behavior—behavior not utilized in the development of the segmentation scheme itself. We had hypothesized that certain types of behavior would be related to interests and needs in much the same manner that social scientists relate behavior to attitudes. Evidence of this linkage would provide a kind of external validity to the measurement process that would reinforce our faith in the segmentation as a valid and useful conceptual framework for analyzing the population as a whole.

In fact, as our findings have indicated, not only is the interest segmentation scheme useful in identifying and interpreting differences in television-related behavior, but differences in behavior regarding other media as well, including books, magazines, movies, newspapers, and radio.

Exhibit 11.1 reports in a relatively concise format the thumbnail sketches of each segment's media behavior. These are the same thumbnail sketches provided at the end of Chapters 5 through 7 reporting the principal findings regarding media behavior. They are reported again at this juncture as a convenience to the reader to serve as a relatively brief overall summary of our findings across all the media.

After reading the results reported in this study, these statements regarding validity may seem obvious to some. However, at the time the study was originally proposed, the thought that an interest segmentation scheme might be strongly associated with differences in television viewing behavior, let alone other media behavior, was met with reactions ranging from considerable skepticism to outright rejection.

Our findings show consistent, statistically significant and interpretable differences in every aspect of media behavior investigated.

UTILITY

This study was designed primarily to understand the uses of television from the point of view of its audience. We will, therefore, discuss first in some detail the potential usefulness of our findings to the television networks and stations. We will then extend our comments to other media organizations as well as to organizations marketing certain other consumer products and services.

Exhibit 11.1

Overall Media Behavior
Interest Segment Characteristics

A. *Adult Male Concentration*

Mechanics and Outdoor Life
> *Television.* Below-average television exposure and in-home availability. Relatively high on escape/fantasy-related adventure, science fiction, crime, movies. Low on programming containing intellectual content. Quite low on sports programming, especially for a predominantly male segment. *Magazine.* Heavy users of men's, outdoor, automotive, mechanics, and miscellaneous (*Modern Photography*). Magazine readership concentrated on entertainment and recreation, especially on personal interests and hobbies. *Books, Movies, Newspapers, and Radio (Other Media).* Heavy users of movies and radio, "how to" books, farm and country radio programs. Heavy on escape-related books and movies such as science fiction and horror. Also heavy readers of newspaper comics.

Money and Nature's Products
> *Television.* Average viewing level. Attracted to programming associated with one or more of the following four elements: outdoor nature-related activities; need for social contact, support, and respect; interest in money/business; need to be knowledgeable about events and trends in the world around them. Support of traditional American virtues. *Magazines.* Below-average overall magazine readership. Only type on which they are above fifth is outdoor. Next in line are automotive, mechanics, and business/finance. *Other Media.* Generally below-average media usage. Daily papers only above-average type. Above-average newspaper readership for real estate, business, and travel. Attracted to types of books and movies in which strong male personalities are in positions of power or control.

Family and Community Centered
> *Television.* Below-average television viewers, with family and com-

Exhibit 11.1 (Continued)

munity activities competing for time. Religious convictions may
limit use of television. Program types favored tend to be least
offensive—religious, sports, news. *Magazines.* Below-average readership of magazines. Third on outdoor. Fourth on sports, automotive, mechanics, and business/finance. Breadth and level of
interests not well matched to magazines. Better suited to local,
daily newspapers. *Other Media.* Above-average usage of all newspaper types. Below average on book, movie, and radio usage. Broad
subject matter coverage focuses on news in newspapers and on
radio. Religious subject matter also ranks high.

B.   *Adult Female Concentration*

Elderly Concerns

Television. Above-average viewers. Highest in-home availability.
Needs for vicarious participation, social integration, and acceptance
appear to be common denominators of above-average viewing behavior. Favored program types—dramas, game shows, soap operas,
religious programming, as well as news, talk shows, and variety
shows. Typical programs—*The Waltons,* Merv Griffin, Lawrence
Welk. *Magazines.* Lightest of all magazine users. Slightly higher
levels of usage among women-oriented magazines, romance. Magazine choices seem, in general, to help them cope with loneliness.
Other Media. Moderate to light users of all four "other" media.
Relatively highest rates for Sunday, daily, and local papers. Religious, news, and advertising content all somewhat above average.

Arts and Cultural Activities

Television. Average viewing level. Selective viewers satisfying informational needs and seeking to broaden intellectual and cultural
horizons. Extremely high on theatrical performances, musical performances, documentaries, news/commentary. *Magazine.* Above-
average readership. Heavy on select, business/finance, and news.
Lower relative to other adult female segments on women's services
and home service/home. *Other Media.* Heavy users of books, Sunday papers and supplements, and daily papers. Generally high
intellectual content such as historical novels, musicals, operas, or
dance movies. Newspapers focus on news sections and entertainment listings section.

Home and Community Centered

Television. Slightly below-average overall viewing. Focus on family
relations. Favored program types—soap operas, religious. *Magazines.* Average overall readership. Heavy on women's services,

Exhibit 11.1 (Continued)

home services/home. Narrow subject matter focus of reading tends to be related to home activities. *Other Media.* Moderate usage of most media. About average only on Sunday, daily, and local papers. Content is home and community related, such as cooking, gardening, social news, and entertainment, as well as children's movies and religion.

Family Integrated Activities

Television. Slightly above-average viewing rate. Focus on family entertainment and child development. Program types—children's programs, dramas, and movies. Exceptionally high on educational children's programs such as *Sesame Street, Mister Rogers.* Dramas tend to be nonviolent with family content. Also true of programs in other categories—*Once Upon a Classic, All My Children, Family Feud.* Television used as a means to bring together adults and children for shared viewing experiences. *Magazines.* Heavy users. Rank first on women's services and home service/home. Broad home/family readership is reflected in their ranking first on eleven of the sixteen magazines in these categories. *Other Media.* Heavy on radio and readership of Sunday supplements. Focus of content is family-related activities including children's movies and relationships, such as personal advice newspaper section and psychology self-help books.

C. *Youth Concentration*

Competitive Sports and Science/Engineering

Television. Average level of viewing. Heavy viewers of programs and program types with male personalities, especially young men who are admired because of their physical and/or social prowess. Watch programs that mock authority figures. Low on programming that is intellectually upscaled or abstract, copes with problems that do not yield to immediate solutions, or features female personalities in assertive roles. Generally avoid traditional authority relationships that appear to threaten their need to establish personal independence. *Magazines.* Intermediate overall readership. First on sports, automotive, and mechanics. Also high on men's and miscellaneous (*National Lampoon*). *Other Media.* Heavy users of movies. Books and movie content are escapist-oriented, such as science fiction books and horror movies. Highest usage rate for sports in newspapers and on radio. Radio used for broad range of content, with special emphasis on different types of music.

Exhibit 11.1 (Continued)

Athletic and Social Activities

Television. Well below average television viewers. Lowest level of in-home availability. Heavy viewers of escape programming and programming involving male-female relationships in nonfamily, light-hearted contexts. Need to get away from problems of home life. *Magazines.* Intermediate usage. Along with Indoor Games and Social Activities segment, heavy on women's services, romance, and fashion. Somewhat more usage than the female youth segment on outdoor, automotive, and mechanics. *Other Media.* Heavy usage of movies and radio while relatively light for all types of newspapers. Escapist content for books and movies similar to previous segment, but more oriented to love, romance, and children's movies. Radio listening mainly music.

Indoor Games and Social Activities

Television. Well above average viewers of television. Low on informational or cultural program types. Above average on virtually all others. Overall profile reflects combination of youth and young homemaker oriented programming. Both roles coexist in segment. Television a major source of entertainment for this segment. *Magazines.* Above-average readership. Along with Athletic and Social Activities segment, heavy on women's services, romance, and fashion. Somewhat more usage than the other segment of men's, home service/home, general, and Black publications. *Other Media.* Heavy on books and movies. Somewhat more intellectual, less escapist than other Youth Concentration segments. Somewhat high readership of biographies, religious books, world news, and business newspaper content, as well as viewing of horror, science fiction types of movies.

D. *Mixed*

News and Information

Television. Highest of any segment in overall television viewing. Second highest on television share of in-home time. Favor news, talk shows, variety shows, documentaries, movies, sports. Good cannon fodder for day-to-day casual conversation. Need to be socially stimulating and conversant with many subjects. *Magazines.* Slightly below-average overall readership. Heavy on news and general. *Other Media.* Heavy usage of all types of newspapers. Focus on all news sections of newspapers.

Exhibit 11.1 (Continued)

Detached

Television. Below-average viewing. Less intellectually demanding, somewhat escape-oriented. Crime dramas, movies, science fiction, soap operas are high for the segment, but not compared to others. *Magazines.* Second lightest overall readership. Below population average on fourteen out of fifteen types. Highest ranking types are Black and mechanics. *Other Media.* Extremely light users of books, movies, and newspapers.

Cosmopolitan Self-Enrichment

Television. Lightest television viewing segment. Highly literate, print-oriented persons. Television viewing is highly selective. Program types/programs favored that resemble print preferences. Theatrical performances (*Once Upon a Classic, Dickens of London*), news shows, talk shows, documentaries. Avoid escape, general entertainment-oriented program types such as adventure and crime drama. *Magazine.* Heavy overall readership, especially select, news, business/finance, sports, miscellaneous. Next in line are men's magazines. *Other Media.* Moderate to heavy usage of all media, especially books and financial newspapers. Focus on all types of nonfiction books. High intellectual content regarding films such as biographies and documentaries. Newspapers used as source of information related to entertainment, as well as news, travel, and business. Broad range of music in radio listening.

Highly Diversified

Television. Second highest viewing segment. Highest share of in-home time watching television. Average or above average on eighteen of nineteen program types. General family fare viewing reflects diversity of family member interests. Highest scoring types— adventure, crime drama, movies, musical performances (*Soul Train, Music Hall America*). Also high on children's programs (cartoons), science fiction, specials, religion. *Magazines.* Heaviest overall readership. Rank sixth or higher on all fifteen types of magazines, especially Black. *Other Media.* Above-average usage of movies, local weekly papers, and radio. Radio used as principal vehicle for covering broad range of interests. Newspaper content centers on local concerns such as real estate and social news. Movie content reflects impact of children and probably a process of accommodation to interests of other family members.

Television Networks and Stations

There are at least five areas involving network or station programming policy and strategy where we believe findings from this investigation may be of use:

(1) Determination and evaluation of network/station audience attraction policies.

(2) Development of new program series concepts.

(3) Promotion of new and existing programs.

(4) Program scheduling decisions.

(5) Evaluation of stations and programs.

AUDIENCE ATTRACTION POLICIES

Implicit in the concept of market segmentation research and its practice is a conviction that the audience composition for a television network, station, or program need not, and indeed should not, be the result of pure happenstance. The positioning of television in general, and of particular stations and programs, is one of the most important policy decisions facing both commercial and public television. In the context of this discussion, by positioning, we mean the conscious and deliberate selection of certain population segments as target audiences, combined with a strategy and implementation designed to attract them.

Toward this end, population segments have been traditionally defined using demographic and socioeconomic characteristics as the dominant frame of reference. Placing the primary emphasis on demographic and socioeconomic characteristics in developing a segmentation scheme to be used by management as a tool for determining its positioning strategy has a major limitation, however. While such measures are helpful in determining *who* should be appealed to, they provide little guidance in determining *what,* by way of general programming strategy or individual programs, is likely to appeal to those segments. Knowledge of the interests and needs of target segments, combined with their demographic and socioeconomic characteristics, should be maximally helpful to management in determining not only who to appeal to, but how to appeal to them.

In practice, demographic and socioeconomic data are somewhat helpful in answering the "what" and "how" questions, because such data are, to some extent, correlated with interests and needs. But why settle for what are at best rough indicators of interests and needs, especially if coherent segments based on direct measures can be identified and shown to be associated with differential television viewing and other media behavior?

In summary, our argument is threefold:

(1) The positioning of commercial and public television in general (as well as individual stations and programs) can be and should be the result of an explicit, planned process.

(2) The choice of the mix of programs to be given development priorities should begin with definitions of the specific audience segment(s) to which that mix is intended to appeal.

(3) For the aforementioned purposes, an interest-based segmentation scheme (supplemented by demographic and socioeconomic measures) is considerably more appropriate than one defined solely by demographic and socioeconomic descriptors. Surely such descriptions as those characterizing the Family Integrated Activities, the Money and Nature's Products, and the Cosmopolitan Self-Enrichment segment members comprise far richer inputs to understanding what will appeal to them than do descriptions based primarily on sex, age, income, education, and so on.

In this context, the usefulness of our investigation is not to provide recommendations as to what segment or segments should be pursued, but rather to ensure that the specific frame of reference used to define the target segments is a provocative and stimulating one—one that will be useful to those with programming responsibilities in implementing *whatever* policy or strategy decisions are adopted. The frame of reference implicit in the interest segmentation scheme we have developed can be a useful tool whether one wishes to develop a market for an opera or a soap opera.

DEVELOPING NEW PROGRAM SERIES

Directly related to the potential utility of our interest-based segmentation scheme as a framework for programming strategy is its use as an input to the creative process employed in generating new program or program series concepts, and in the execution of these concepts. We believe that a process of new program development utilizing this type of data as input will have a greater likelihood of success than one without it.

We envision two levels of application. The first assumes that this information is sufficiently provocative that persons involved with the process of generating ideas for new programs and program series will find it of use as one source (though not the sole source) of such ideas. As one becomes familiar with our fourteen portraits, one cannot help but speculate as to what new types of programming might appeal to each segment or to combinations of them.

In addition to serving as one more input for generating new program ideas, this research can be useful in evaluating existing program concepts, choosing which ones to develop, and helping to refine the details.

Often in the course of making these decisions, some form of consumer research is conducted to evaluate alternative program concepts or executions (e.g., use of different actors in a given role, different settings, and so on). Studies such as these are frequently done on relatively modest budgets and under tight time constraints. For our interest segmentation scheme to be maximally useful in this context, one should be able to apply it easily and inexpensively. Then it could be used as a tool for evaluating any aspect of television programming of interest, regardless of whether or not that particular aspect was examined in the project reported in this volume.

To accomplish this, one needs a "short form" questionnaire and scoring procedure that could be added to whatever data are already being utilized. The short form questionnaire and scoring procedure can be used in *any* study to classify respondents efficiently into the interest segments developed in this research.

We look upon this capability as an important way to leverage the interest segmentation we have developed so that it can be useful to others in evaluating new program concepts or executions.

We have developed such a short form questionnaire and scoring procedure for precisely this purpose. It is described in Appendix H.

These same procedures can also be used by researchers interested in a much broader range of problems than those associated with program development. These other areas of application are discussed in the following three sections.

PROGRAM PROMOTION

Assume that one has a program or program series to be promoted and that target audience segments have also been identified. The problem now is to be sure that the segments are aware of the program and its scheduled time slot for viewing.

There are two distinct contributions that the present type of research can make toward solving this problem. The first is to identify the media most likely to be currently used by the target segment(s). These media then become primary candidates to be used for placing announcements or advertisements about the program or series. Second, where budgets permit the placement of television commercials or magazine ads, the segment descriptions can also be used by copywriters (as is done for many other products and services) as a basis for determining effective appeals for attracting the interest of members of the target segment(s).

PROGRAM SCHEDULING

Though it has not been our principal concern, this research may also contribute to program scheduling decisions. The mix of segments available for viewing is obviously not constant across time of day or day of week. The proportion of persons available for watching by segment can help determine when programs with differing target audiences should be aired.

Finally, this type of analysis may help to determine what programs are best to show in competition with the program offerings of competing stations. By knowing what segment(s) other networks or stations are likely to attract, one can better determine what offerings would have the best chance of succeeding in the competitive environment for any given time period.

STATION AND PROGRAM EVALUATION

Ideally, the interest segmentation scheme we have developed would be available to any and all investigators wishing to pursue research, whether to evaluate a particular station's audience characteristics or the appeal of various program concepts under consideration for future development and broadcasting.

The short form questionnaire and scoring procedure previously discussed in this chapter provides a means of using our segmentation scheme for this class of problems as well.

ALTERNATIVE DATA ANALYSES

We recognize that some potential users of this information may not be comfortable with the specific structure (the fourteen segments) we have developed using this data. With this in mind, we are also making the entire data base available to anyone who wishes to analyze it using other approaches.[1]

Other Media

The determination and evaluation of audience attraction policies, the developing of new program (product) concepts, the promotion of new and existing programs (products), and the evaluation of existing programs (products) are problems common to all media organizations. With relatively minor modification, our comments on these issues in relation to television are equally appropriate for program or movie production companies, book, magazine, and newspaper publishers, as well as radio networks and stations.

For example, like television networks, magazine publishers are faced with the problem of determining what segment or segments they wish to attract, based on the magazines or mix of magazines they currently publish or plan to publish. As we have shown, our interest-based segmentation structure is also useful for understanding this type of media behavior. It should come as no surprise that these same uses and our discussion of them regarding television are applicable to other media as well.

In contrast, our discussion of scheduling is not generally applicable to media other than television and radio.

Classes of Leisure-Related Products and Services

In our judgment, there are three classes of products and services that are apt to have audiences or customers whose behavior might be better understood if examined in relation to the interest segmentation scheme we have developed:

(1) Leisure products and services such as tennis rackets, camping equipment, athletic clothing, and so on.

(2) Public as well as private recreational facilities such as national parks, bowling alleys, golf clubs, tennis clubs, and so on.

(3) Classical arts related products and services such as live theater, symphonies, operas, ballets, museums, and so on.

The utility of our findings for products and services in these three categories parallels closely our discussion of television with respect to the determination and evaluation of audience (customer) attraction policies, the development of new programs (products and services), and the promotion of new and existing programs (products and services).

Agencies and Advertisers

The interest-based segmentation structure can also be useful to advertisers and their agencies in arriving at decisions regarding advertising content. Many advertising agencies and their clients routinely use segmentation research based on customer attitudes, perceptions, or preferences toward the product category and toward brands as a basis for developing and testing new advertisements.

236

For some of these agencies and advertisers, knowledge of the interest segments principally attracted to a given advertising vehicle (e.g., program, magazine, or newspaper) may provide another basis for determining what creative treatments are likely to be most effective.

This is apt to be especially true if there is some correspondence between customer segment membership in our interest segmentation scheme and membership in whatever segmentation scheme is used by the agency and its client. The correspondence of these two segmentation schemes can be measured by adding our short form questionnaire to a client's segmentation research questionnaire, using our scoring procedure to assign respondents to interest segments, and then comparing their interest segment membership with their membership in whatever scheme is traditionally used by the client.

CONCLUDING COMMENTS

The interest-based segmentation structure we have developed may be thought of as a new product. We hope that this book, the short form questionnaire and scoring procedure, and the public availability of the data base will create awareness of this product and will encourage others to use it.

While we have tried to point to potential uses in television, radio, and other media as well as in the marketing of consumer products and services, there are undoubtedly applications we have not foreseen. We hope we have been able to stimulate interest in some new ways of looking at television audiences that complement some of the more traditional approaches used during the relatively brief history of this industry.

We do not view this study as a completed permanent structure. Rather it is designed to serve as a foundation on which others, as well as we, can build, altering it, extending it, and adapting it to serve the needs of its users.

NOTE

1. A complete data tape and detailed documentation, along with copies of the questionnaire, can be obtained at a current (1980) cost of $275.00 by writing to:

Marshall G. Greenberg
National Analysts
400 Market Street
Philadelphia, PA 19106

Availability and cost are subject to change in future years.

REFERENCES

COMSTOCK, G. and G. LINDSEY (1975) Television and Human Behavior: The Research Horizon, Future and Present. Santa Monica, CA: Rand Corporation.
KATZ, E. (1977) Social Research on Broadcasting: Proposals for Further Development. London: British Broadcasting Corporation.

Appendices

Appendix A

QUESTIONNAIRE

SEGMENT #: _____ D.U. #_____

NATIONAL ANALYSTS   Study #1-923
A Division of Booz, Allen & Hamilton Inc.   Fall, 1977

SPECIAL INTERESTS STUDY
PART 1A

WRITE YOUR NAME HERE: _____

INSTRUCTIONS FOR COMPLETING PART 1

On the green pages that follow, you will find a list of items describing leisure interest and activities. We would like to know how interested you are in each of these.

Please tell us how interested you are in each by circling the one number from 1 to 4 which shows how you feel. Your answers should refer to each item regardless of whether your general interest is in doing it, watching it, learning about it or whatever.

EXAMPLES:

1. If you are not at all interested in badminton, you would answer like this:

	Not at All *Interested*	*Not Very* *Interested*	*Very* *Interested*	*Extremely* *Interested*
Badminton	①	2	3	4

2. However, if you are extremely interested in looking at architecture, you would answer like this:

	Not at All *Interested*	*Not Very* *Interested*	*Very* *Interested*	*Extremely* *Interested*
Architecture	1	2	3	④

(NOW PLEASE TURN THE PAGE AND BEGIN.)

PART 1A – YOUR INTERESTS

Please indicate how interested you are in each of the items listed below.
Circle one number from 1 to 4 for each.

	Not at All Interested	Not Very Interested	Very Interested	Extremely Interested
Antiques	1	2	3	4
Auto repair	1	2	3	4
Auto racing	1	2	3	4
Backpacking	1	2	3	4
Ballet	1	2	3	4
Baseball	1	2	3	4
Basketball	1	2	3	4
Being a wine connoisseur	1	2	3	4
Bicycling	1	2	3	4
Billiards/pool	1	2	3	4
Board games (Backgammon, Scrabble, Monopoly, etc.)	1	2	3	4
Boating (rowing, canoeing, sailing, etc.)	1	2	3	4
Bowling	1	2	3	4
Boxing	1	2	3	4
Camping	1	2	3	4
Ceramics/pottery	1	2	3	4
Charities and civic associations	1	2	3	4
Chess/checkers	1	2	3	4
Child related activities (PTA, Scouts, etc.)	1	2	3	4
CB radio	1	2	3	4
Classical music	1	2	3	4
Coin or stamp collecting	1	2	3	4
Community social functions	1	2	3	4
Crossword/jigsaw puzzles	1	2	3	4
Dancing (discotheque, ballroom, etc.)	1	2	3	4
Dining out	1	2	3	4
Driving/motoring	1	2	3	4

PART 1A – YOUR INTERESTS (Cont)

	Not at All Interested	Not Very Interested	Very Interested	Extremely Interested
Entertainment at home	1	2	3	4
Fishing	1	2	3	4
Football	1	2	3	4
Gardening	1	2	3	4
Golf	1	2	3	4
Gourmet cooking	1	2	3	4
Hiking	1	2	3	4
Hockey	1	2	3	4
House cleaning	1	2	3	4
Horse racing	1	2	3	4
Household management	1	2	3	4
Household pets	1	2	3	4
Hunting	1	2	3	4
Ice skating	1	2	3	4
Indoor plants	1	2	3	4
Interior decorating	1	2	3	4
Jogging	1	2	3	4
Judo/karate	1	2	3	4
Literature	1	2	3	4
Live theater (plays, musicals, etc.)	1	2	3	4
Local cultural activities	1	2	3	4
Maintenance and repairs of the home	1	2	3	4
Meal preparation	1	2	3	4
Model building (cars, ships, etc.)	1	2	3	4
Modern dance	1	2	3	4
Motorcycles	1	2	3	4
Movies (cinema)	1	2	3	4
Needlework (needlepoint, knitting, etc.)	1	2	3	4
Opera	1	2	3	4
Paintings	1	2	3	4

PART 1A – YOUR INTERESTS (Cont)

	Not at All Interested	Not Very Interested	Very Interested	Extremely Interested
Party games (Charades, Password, etc.)	1	2	3	4
Photography	1	2	3	4
Playing a musical instrument	1	2	3	4
Playing cards (rummy, bridge, etc.)	1	2	3	4
Poetry	1	2	3	4
Popular music (jazz, folk, rock, country, etc.)	1	2	3	4
Radio	1	2	3	4
Religious organization activities	1	2	3	4
Sculpture	1	2	3	4
Sewing (making clothes, drapes, etc.)	1	2	3	4
Shopping	1	2	3	4
Snow skiing	1	2	3	4
Soccer	1	2	3	4
Squash/handball	1	2	3	4
Swimming	1	2	3	4
Table tennis/ping pong	1	2	3	4
Television	1	2	3	4
Tennis	1	2	3	4
Travel/sightseeing	1	2	3	4
Visiting friends	1	2	3	4
Volleyball	1	2	3	4
Water skiing	1	2	3	4
Woodworking	1	2	3	4

PART 1B — YOUR INTEREST IN SUBJECTS

The following pages contain a list of various subjects that you may or may not be interested in. Please consider your degree of interest in each subject regardless of your specific opinion (either pro or con) or the nature of your involvement.

Tell us how interested you are in each subject by circling the number from 1 to 4 which shows how you feel.

EXAMPLE:

If you are very interested in the subject of rising costs of higher education, you would answer like this:

	Not at All Interested	Not Very Interested	Very Interested	Extremely Interested
Rising costs of higher education	1	2	③	4

PLEASE TURN TO THE NEXT PAGE AND BEGIN.

PART 1B – YOUR INTEREST IN SUBJECTS

Please indicate how interested you are in each of the items listed below. Circle one number from 1 to 4 for each.

	Not at All Interested	Not Very Interested	Very Interested	Extremely Interested
Abortion vs. right-to-life issues	1	2	3	4
Advertising and marketing	1	2	3	4
Aging and retirement	1	2	3	4
Air transportation (planes, jets, etc.)	1	2	3	4
Agriculture and farming	1	2	3	4
Arms race	1	2	3	4
Balance of trade	1	2	3	4
Capital punishment of criminals	1	2	3	4
Career guidance	1	2	3	4
Causes and prevention of crime	1	2	3	4
Chemistry	1	2	3	4
Child rearing methods	1	2	3	4
Community issues	1	2	3	4
Conflict in the Middle East	1	2	3	4
Conservation/ecology	1	2	3	4
Consumerism	1	2	3	4
Divorce in the U.S.	1	2	3	4
Education and schools	1	2	3	4
Election campaigns (funding, organizing, supporting, etc.)	1	2	3	4
Electronics	1	2	3	4
Engineering	1	2	3	4
Foreign languages	1	2	3	4
Foreign policy	1	2	3	4
Geology	1	2	3	4
Health and nutrition	1	2	3	4
How and when to use a lawyer	1	2	3	4
Labor unions in the U.S.	1	2	3	4

PART 1B – YOUR INTERESTS (Cont)

	Not at All Interested	Not Very Interested	Very Interested	Extremely Interested
Legal processes in U.S. courts	1	2	3	4
Local history	1	2	3	4
Managing a business	1	2	3	4
Managing money (finance, taxes, etc.)	1	2	3	4
Mathematics	1	2	3	4
Medical sciences (anatomy, physiology, etc.)	1	2	3	4
Mental illness and its treatment	1	2	3	4
Morality in politics	1	2	3	4
National economy	1	2	3	4
National unemployment	1	2	3	4
Natural history (birds, fish, wildlife, etc.)	1	2	3	4
Nuclear energy	1	2	3	4
Preventive medicine	1	2	3	4
Problems of drug abuse	1	2	3	4
Psychology	1	2	3	4
Railroads	1	2	3	4
Real estate investment	1	2	3	4
Religion	1	2	3	4
Rights of minority groups	1	2	3	4
Sex education	1	2	3	4
Sexual attitudes and behavior	1	2	3	4
Social etiquette	1	2	3	4
Social security system	1	2	3	4
Sources and uses of energy	1	2	3	4
Space travel	1	2	3	4
State issues	1	2	3	4
Tax laws	1	2	3	4
The occult	1	2	3	4
The stock market	1	2	3	4
Welfare system	1	2	3	4
Wills and estate planning	1	2	3	4
Women's rights/roles	1	2	3	4

SEGMENT #: _____ D.U. # _____

NATIONAL ANALYSTS   Study #1-923
A Division of Booz, Allen and Hamilton Inc.   Fall, 1977

SPECIAL INTERESTS STUDY
PART 2

WRITE YOUR NAME HERE: _____

INSTRUCTIONS FOR COMPLETING PART 2

So far you have told us about the different leisure interests and activities
and subjects you are interested in. We would now like to find out why
you are interested in these.

The next part of the questionnaire asks you about your reasons for being
interested in the various lesiure interests, activities and subjects, that you
indicated in PARTS 1A and 1B.

On the pink pages which follow, you will find a list of reasons which may
or may not be important to you. For each one, please indicate how
important it is to you by circling the number from 1 to 4 which best
shows how you feel.

(PLEASE TURN THE PAGE AND BEGIN.)

PART 2 — The following list contains a number of reasons for being interested in items from Part 1. Please indicate how important each of these reasons is to you by circling the one number from 1 to 4 which best shows how you feel.

		Not at All Important	Not Very Important	Very Important	Extremely Important
1.	To understand myself better	1	2	3	4
2.	To lift my spirits	1	2	3	4
3.	To feel I am using my time in the best way possible	1	2	3	4
4.	To overcome loneliness	1	2	3	4
5.	To be more like people I respect	1	2	3	4
6.	To develop good taste	1	2	3	4
7.	To spend time with my family	1	2	3	4
8.	To kill time	1	2	3	4
9.	To learn more about what is going on in the world	1	2	3	4
10.	To be entertained	1	2	3	4
11.	To help other people	1	2	3	4
12.	To forget my problems for awhile	1	2	3	4
13.	To learn about new things to do	1	2	3	4
14.	To experience again events and places I enjoyed in the past	1	2	3	4
15.	To feel I am important to other people	1	2	3	4
16.	To find that my ideas are often shared by others	1	2	3	4
17.	To be physically active	1	2	3	4
18.	To feel good about life in general	1	2	3	4
19.	To do things which I am familiar with	1	2	3	4
20.	To meet new people	1	2	3	4
21.	To have peace of mind	1	2	3	4
22.	To get away from the pressures of work	1	2	3	4
23.	To further improve my skills and abilities	1	2	3	4
24.	To help develop strong family ties	1	2	3	4

PART 2 – (Cont)

		Not at All Important	Not Very Important	Very Important	Extremely Important
25.	To be alone with my thoughts	1	2	3	4
26.	To participate in discussion with my friends	1	2	3	4
27.	To be interesting and stimulating to other people	1	2	3	4
28.	To have a sense of direction and purpose in life	1	2	3	4
29.	To have interesting experiences which I can tell others about	1	2	3	4
30.	To escape from the reality of everyday life	1	2	3	4
31.	To get a feeling of adventure and excitement	1	2	3	4
32.	To feel unique, different from other people	1	2	3	4
33.	To be like other people	1	2	3	4
34.	To better understand why people behave the way they do	1	2	3	4
35.	To get the most out of the daily experiences that life has to offer	1	2	3	4
36.	To feel independent, free from the authority of others	1	2	3	4
37.	To understand how other people think	1	2	3	4
38.	To do things which are different from what I'm used to	1	2	3	4
39.	To feel creative	1	2	3	4
40.	To be more of a leader	1	2	3	4
41.	To impress people	1	2	3	4
42.	To compete against others	1	2	3	4
43.	To really excel in some area of my life	1	2	3	4
44.	To learn about new places to see	1	2	3	4
45.	To feel closer to my family	1	2	3	4
46.	To know that other people have the same problems I have	1	2	3	4
47.	To spend time with friends	1	2	3	4

PART 2 – (Cont)

	Not at All Important	Not Very Important	Very Important	Extremely Important
48. To do unique things	1	2	3	4
49. To help me imagine other ways of living my life	1	2	3	4
50. To feel more physically attractive	1	2	3	4
51. To get away from the pressures and responsibilities of my home life	1	2	3	4
52. To have more influence on other people	1	2	3	4
53. To be more in control of my own life	1	2	3	4
54. To learn new thoughts and ideas	1	2	3	4
55. To feel more important than I really am	1	2	3	4
56. To find out more about how things work	1	2	3	4
57. To free myself from traditional roles	1	2	3	4
58. To relax	1	2	3	4
59. To get a better idea of how I want to live my life when I get older	1	2	3	4

O relates to infl y MM or ddy

RESPONDENT #: _____   SEGMENT #: _____   D.U. # _____

NATIONAL ANALYSTS   Study #1-923
A Division of Booz, Allen & Hamilton Inc.   Fall, 1977

SPECIAL INTERESTS STUDY

PART 3
Head(s) of Household

WRITE YOUR NAME HERE: _____

INSTRUCTIONS FOR COMPLETING PART 3

This next part deals with the programs you watch on TV. The list does not contain every program shown on TV, but we have tried to include as many programs as possible.

As you will see when you turn the page, the questions are all on the top of the page. Circle the appropriate code of your answer for each question.

The programs are listed by day and time shown. These days and times may not correspond to the days and times certain programs are shown in your area. Just answer the questions pertaining to the program, regardless of the program's scheduling in your area.

Note in Question A: If you did not watch the specific television program in the past four weeks, circle "No" and go on to the next program.

Part 3: Television Viewing

		A — Did you watch this program in the past four weeks? CIRCLE ONE — IF NO GO TO NEXT PROGRAM / IF YES CONTINUE ANSWERING Q's B THRU G	B — How many times did you watch this program in the past four weeks? CIRCLE NUMBER OF TIMES	C — Who usually decides to watch this program? 1-I do 2-My spouse does 3-Some other adult does 4-My children do 5-Other. CIRCLE ONLY ONE NUMBER	D — Who else usually watches this program with you? 1-No one else 2-My spouse 3-Some other adult 4-My children 5-Other. YOU MAY CIRCLE MORE THAN ONE NUMBER IF THIS APPLIES	E — Do you usually give this program your full attention or are you doing other things while watching it? 1-I give it my full attention 2-I do other things while watching it. CIRCLE ONLY ONE NUMBER	F — Do you usually plan in advance to watch this program? CIRCLE CODE FOR EITHER YES OR NO (Yes / No)	G — If you missed an episode of this program, how disappointed would you be? 1-Not at all 2-Somewhat 3-Very 4-Extremely. CIRCLE ONLY ONE NUMBER

I. NIGHTTIME PROGRAMS

SUNDAY
7:00 PM – 9:00 PM

#	Program	A	B	C	D	E	F (Yes / No)	G
01	Nancy Drew/Hardy Boys Mystery Show	No / Yes	1 2 3 4 5+	1 2 3 4 5	1 2 3 4 5	1 2	1 / 2	1 2 3 4
02	Sixty Minutes	No / Yes	1 2 3 4 5+	1 2 3 4 5	1 2 3 4 5	1 2	1 / 2	1 2 3 4
03	The Wonderful World of Disney	No / Yes	1 2 3 4 5+	1 2 3 4 5	1 2 3 4 5	1 2	1 / 2	1 2 3 4
04	Evening at Symphony	No / Yes	1 2 3 4 5+	1 2 3 4 5	1 2 3 4 5	1 2	1 / 2	1 2 3 4
05	Rhoda	No / Yes	1 2 3 4 5+	1 2 3 4 5	1 2 3 4 5	1 2	1 / 2	1 2 3 4
06	On Our Own	No / Yes	1 2 3 4 5+	1 2 3 4 5	1 2 3 4 5	1 2	1 / 2	1 2 3 4
07	Six Million Dollar Man	No / Yes	1 2 3 4 5+	1 2 3 4 5	1 2 3 4 5	1 2	1 / 2	1 2 3 4

Part 3: Television Viewing (Continued)

		A	B	C	D	E	F		G
		Did you watch this program in the past four weeks? CIRCLE ONE — IF NO GO TO NEXT PROGRAM / IF YES CONTINUE ANSWERING Q's B THRU G	How many times did you watch this program in the past four weeks? CIRCLE NUMBER OF TIMES	Who usually decides to watch this program? 1-I do 2-My spouse does 3-Some other adult does 4-My children do 5-Other CIRCLE ONLY ONE NUMBER	Who else usually watches this program with you? 1-No one else 2-My spouse 3-Some other adult 4-My children 5-Other YOU MAY CIRCLE MORE THAN ONE NUMBER IF THIS APPLIES	Do you usually give this program your full attention or are you doing other things while watching it? 1-I give it my full attention 2-I do other things while watching it CIRCLE ONLY ONE NUMBER	Do you usually plan in advance to watch this program? CIRCLE CODE FOR EITHER YES OR NO		If you missed an episode of this program, how disappointed would you be? 1-Not at all 2-Somewhat 3-Very 4-Extremely CIRCLE ONLY ONE NUMBER
							Yes	No	
9:00 PM – 11:00 PM									
All in the Family	08	No Yes	1 2 3 4 5+	1 2 3 4 5	1 2 3 4 5	1 2	1	2	1 2 3 4
Alice	09	No Yes	1 2 3 4 5+	1 2 3 4 5	1 2 3 4 5	1 2	1	2	1 2 3 4
Kojak	10	No Yes	1 2 3 4 5+	1 2 3 4 5	1 2 3 4 5	1 2	1	2	1 2 3 4
Sunday Night Movie	11	No Yes	1 2 3 4 5+	1 2 3 4 5	1 2 3 4 5	1 2	1	2	1 2 3 4
Dickens of London	12	No Yes	1 2 3 4 5+	1 2 3 4 5	1 2 3 4 5	1 2	1	2	1 2 3 4
Visions	13	No Yes	1 2 3 4 5+	1 2 3 4 5	1 2 3 4 5	1 2	1	2	1 2 3 4
The Big Event (Varies)		No Yes	1 2 3 4 5+	1 2 3 4 5	1 2 3 4 5	1 2	1	2	1 2 3 4
MONDAY **8:00 PM – 9:00 PM**									
The San Pedro Beach Bums	01	No Yes	1 2 3 4 5+	1 2 3 4 5	1 2 3 4 5	1 2	1	2	1 2 3 4
Upstairs, Downstairs	02	No Yes	1 2 3 4 5+	1 2 3 4 5	1 2 3 4 5	1 2	1	2	1 2 3 4
Young Dan'l Boone	03	No Yes	1 2 3 4 5+	1 2 3 4 5	1 2 3 4 5	1 2	1	2	1 2 3 4
Little House on the Prairie	04	No Yes	1 2 3 4 5+	1 2 3 4 5	1 2 3 4 5	1 2	1	2	1 2 3 4

9:00 PM – 11:00 PM

Program	No.							
Monday Night Movie	05	No	Yes	1 2 3 4 5+	1 2 3 4 5	1 2 3 4 5	1 2 1 2 3 4	2 1 2 3 4
The Betty White Show	06	No	Yes	1 2 3 4 5+	1 2 3 4 5	1 2 3 4 5	1 2 1 2 3 4	2 1 2 3 4
Maude	07	No	Yes	1 2 3 4 5+	1 2 3 4 5	1 2 3 4 5	1 2 1 2 3 4	2 1 2 3 4
Rafferty	08	No	Yes	1 2 3 4 5+	1 2 3 4 5	1 2 3 4 5	1 2 1 2 3 4	2 1 2 3 4
NFL Football	09	No	Yes	1 2 3 4 5+	1 2 3 4 5	1 2 3 4 5	1 2 1 2 3 4	2 1 2 3 4
Age of Uncertainty	10	No	Yes	1 2 3 4 5+	1 2 3 4 5	1 2 3 4 5	1 2 1 2 3 4	2 1 2 3 4
In Pursuit of Liberty	11	No	Yes	1 2 3 4 5+	1 2 3 4 5	1 2 3 4 5	1 2 1 2 3 4	2 1 2 3 4

TUESDAY
8:00 PM – 9:00 PM

Program	No.							
The Richard Pryor Show	12	No	Yes	1 2 3 4 5+	1 2 3 4 5	1 2 3 4 5	1 2 1 2 3 4	2 1 2 3 4
The Fitzpatricks	13	No	Yes	1 2 3 4 5+	1 2 3 4 5	1 2 3 4 5	1 2 1 2 3 4	2 1 2 3 4
Happy Days	14	No	Yes	1 2 3 4 5+	1 2 3 4 5	1 2 3 4 5	1 2 1 2 3 4	2 1 2 3 4
Laverne & Shirley	15	No	Yes	1 2 3 4 5+	1 2 3 4 5	1 2 3 4 5	1 2 1 2 3 4	2 1 2 3 4

9:00 PM – 10:00 PM

Program	No.							
Three's Company	01	No	Yes	1 2 3 4 5+	1 2 3 4 5	1 2 3 4 5	1 2 1 2 3 4	2 1 2 3 4
Soap	02	No	Yes	1 2 3 4 5+	1 2 3 4 5	1 2 3 4 5	1 2 1 2 3 4	2 1 2 3 4
MASH	03	No	Yes	1 2 3 4 5+	1 2 3 4 5	1 2 3 4 5	1 2 1 2 3 4	2 1 2 3 4
One Day at a Time	04	No	Yes	1 2 3 4 5+	1 2 3 4 5	1 2 3 4 5	1 2 1 2 3 4	2 1 2 3 4
Mulligan's Stew	05	No	Yes	1 2 3 4 5+	1 2 3 4 5	1 2 3 4 5	1 2 1 2 3 4	2 1 2 3 4
Opera (varies)	06	No	Yes	1 2 3 4 5+	1 2 3 4 5	1 2 3 4 5	1 2 1 2 3 4	2 1 2 3 4

10:00 PM – 11:00 PM

Program	No.							
Lou Grant	07	No	Yes	1 2 3 4 5+	1 2 3 4 5	1 2 3 4 5	1 2 1 2 3 4	2 1 2 3 4
Family	08	No	Yes	1 2 3 4 5+	1 2 3 4 5	1 2 3 4 5	1 2 1 2 3 4	2 1 2 3 4
Police Woman	09	No	Yes	1 2 3 4 5+	1 2 3 4 5	1 2 3 4 5	1 2 1 2 3 4	2 1 2 3 4

WEDNESDAY
8:00 PM – 9:00 PM

Program	No.							
Nova	10	No	Yes	1 2 3 4 5+	1 2 3 4 5	1 2 3 4 5	1 2 1	2 1 2 3 4

Part 3: Television Viewing (Continued)

		A — Did you watch this program in the past four weeks? CIRCLE ONE. IF NO GO TO NEXT PROGRAM. IF YES CONTINUE ANSWERING Q's B THRU G	B — How many times did you watch this program in the past four weeks? CIRCLE NUMBER OF TIMES	C — Who usually decides to watch this program? 1-I do 2-My spouse does 3-Some other adult does 4-My children do 5-Other. CIRCLE ONLY ONE NUMBER	D — Who else usually watches this program with you? 1-No one else 2-My spouse 3-Some other adult 4-My children 5-Other. YOU MAY CIRCLE MORE THAN ONE NUMBER IF THIS APPLIES	E — Do you usually give this program your full attention or are you doing other things while watching it? 1-I give it my full attention 2-I do other things while watching it. CIRCLE ONLY ONE NUMBER	F — Do you usually plan in advance to watch this program? CIRCLE CODE FOR EITHER YES OR NO	G — If you missed an episode of this program, how disappointed would you be? 1-Not at all 2-Somewhat 3-Very 4-Extremely. CIRCLE ONLY ONE NUMBER
The Life and Times of							Yes / No	
Grizzly Adams	11	Yes / No	1 2 3 4 5+	1 2 3 4 5	1 2 3 4 5	1 2	1 / 2	1 2 3 4
Eight is Enough	12	Yes / No	1 2 3 4 5+	1 2 3 4 5	1 2 3 4 5	1 2	1 / 2	1 2 3 4
Good Times	13	Yes / No	1 2 3 4 5+	1 2 3 4 5	1 2 3 4 5	1 2	1 / 2	1 2 3 4
Busting Loose	14	Yes / No	1 2 3 4 5+	1 2 3 4 5	1 2 3 4 5	1 2	1 / 2	1 2 3 4
9:00 PM – 11:00 PM								
Wednesday Night Movie	01	Yes / No	1 2 3 4 5+	1 2 3 4 5	1 2 3 4 5	1 2	1 / 2	1 2 3 4
Great Performances	02	Yes / No	1 2 3 4 5+	1 2 3 4 5	1 2 3 4 5	1 2	1 / 2	1 2 3 4
Oregon Trail	03	Yes / No	1 2 3 4 5+	1 2 3 4 5	1 2 3 4 5	1 2	1 / 2	1 2 3 4
Big Hawaii	04	Yes / No	1 2 3 4 5+	1 2 3 4 5	1 2 3 4 5	1 2	1 / 2	1 2 3 4
Charlie's Angels	05	Yes / No	1 2 3 4 5+	1 2 3 4 5	1 2 3 4 5	1 2	1 / 2	1 2 3 4
Baretta	06	Yes / No	1 2 3 4 5+	1 2 3 4 5	1 2 3 4 5	1 2	1 / 2	1 2 3 4

THURSDAY
8:00 PM – 9:00 PM

Program	No.	Yes	No								
The Waltons	07	Yes	No	1 2 3 4 5+	1 2 3 4 5	1	1 2 3 4 5	1	2	1 2 3 4
Welcome Back, Kotter	08	Yes	No	1 2 3 4 5+	1 2 3 4 5	1	1 2 3 4 5	1	2	1 2 3 4
What's Happening!	09	Yes	No	1 2 3 4 5+	1 2 3 4 5	1	1 2 3 4 5	1	2	1 2 3 4
Chips	10	Yes	No	1 2 3 4 5+	1 2 3 4 5	1	1 2 3 4 5	1	2	1 2 3 4

9:00 PM – 10:00 PM

Program	No.	Yes	No								
Barney Miller	11	Yes	No	1 2 3 4 5+	1 2 3 4 5	1	1 2 3 4 5	1	2	1 2 3 4
Carter Country	12	Yes	No	1 2 3 4 5+	1 2 3 4 5	1	1 2 3 4 5	1	2	1 2 3 4
The Man from Atlantis	13	Yes	No	1 2 3 4 5+	1 2 3 4 5	1	1 2 3 4 5	1	2	1 2 3 4
Hawaii Five-O	14	Yes	No	1 2 3 4 5+	1 2 3 4 5	1	1 2 3 4 5	1	2	1 2 3 4
The Best of Families	15	Yes	No	1 2 3 4 5+	1 2 3 4 5	1	1 2 3 4 5	1	2	1 2 3 4

10:00 PM – 11:00 PM

Program	No.	Yes	No								
Redd Foxx	01	Yes	No	1 2 3 4 5+	1 2 3 4 5	1	1 2 3 4 5	1	2	1 2 3 4
Masterpiece Theater	02	Yes	No	1 2 3 4 5+	1 2 3 4 5	1	1 2 3 4 5	1	2	1 2 3 4
Barnaby Jones	03	Yes	No	1 2 3 4 5+	1 2 3 4 5	1	1 2 3 4 5	1	2	1 2 3 4
Rosetti and Ryan	04	Yes	No	1 2 3 4 5+	1 2 3 4 5	1	1 2 3 4 5	1	2	1 2 3 4

FRIDAY
8:00 PM – 9:00 PM

Program	No.	Yes	No								
Washington in Review	05	Yes	No	1 2 3 4 5+	1 2 3 4 5	1	1 2 3 4 5	1	2	1 2 3 4
Wall Street Week	06	Yes	No	1 2 3 4 5+	1 2 3 4 5	1	1 2 3 4 5	1	2	1 2 3 4
The New Adventures of Wonder Woman	07	Yes	No	1 2 3 4 5+	1 2 3 4 5	1	1 2 3 4 5	1	2	1 2 3 4
Donnie & Marie	08	Yes	No	1 2 3 4 5+	1 2 3 4 5	1	1 2 3 4 5	1	2	1 2 3 4
Sanford Arms	09	Yes	No	1 2 3 4 5+	1 2 3 4 5	1	1 2 3 4 5	1	2	1 2 3 4
Chico and the Man	10	Yes	No	1 2 3 4 5+	1 2 3 4 5	1	1 2 3 4 5	1	2	1 2 3 4

9:00 PM – 11:00 PM

Program	No.	Yes	No								
Friday Night Movie	11	Yes	No	1 2 3 4 5+	1 2 3 4 5	1	1 2 3 4 5	1	2	1 2 3 4
Logan's Run	12	Yes	No	1 2 3 4 5+	1 2 3 4 5	1	1 2 3 4 5	1	2	1 2 3 4
Switch	13	Yes	No	1 2 3 4 5+	1 2 3 4 5	1	1 2 3 4 5	1	2	1 2 3 4

257

Part 3: Television Viewing (Continued)

Program		A — Did you watch this program in the past four weeks? CIRCLE ONE (IF NO GO TO NEXT PROGRAM / IF YES CONTINUE ANSWERING Q's B THRU G)	B — How many times did you watch this program in the past four weeks? CIRCLE NUMBER OF TIMES	C — Who usually decides to watch this program? (1-I do; 2-My spouse does; 3-Some other adult does; 4-My children do; 5-Other) CIRCLE ONLY ONE NUMBER	D — Who else usually watches this program with you? (1-No one else; 2-My spouse; 3-Some other adult; 4-My children; 5-Other) YOU MAY CIRCLE MORE THAN ONE NUMBER IF THIS APPLIES	E — Do you usually give this program your full attention or are you doing other things while watching it? (1-I give it my full attention; 2-I do other things while watching it) CIRCLE ONLY ONE NUMBER	F — Do you usually plan in advance to watch this program? CIRCLE CODE FOR EITHER YES OR NO	G — If you missed an episode of this program, how disappointed would you be? (1-Not at all; 2-Somewhat; 3-Very; 4-Extremely) CIRCLE ONLY ONE NUMBER
14	The Rockford Files	Yes / No	1 2 3 4 5+	1 2 3 4 5	1 2 3 4 5	1 2	Yes 1 / No 2	1 2 3 4
15	Quincy	Yes / No	1 2 3 4 5+	1 2 3 4 5	1 2 3 4 5	1 2	Yes 1 / No 2	1 2 3 4
16	Evening at Pop's	Yes / No	1 2 3 4 5+	1 2 3 4 5	1 2 3 4 5	1 2	Yes 1 / No 2	1 2 3 4
17	Black Perspective on the News	Yes / No	1 2 3 4 5+	1 2 3 4 5	1 2 3 4 5	1 2	Yes 1 / No 2	1 2 3 4
	SATURDAY 8:00 PM – 9:00 PM							
01	Bob Newhart	Yes / No	1 2 3 4 5+	1 2 3 4 5	1 2 3 4 5	1 2	Yes 1 / No 2	1 2 3 4
02	We've Got Each Other	Yes / No	1 2 3 4 5+	1 2 3 4 5	1 2 3 4 5	1 2	Yes 1 / No 2	1 2 3 4
03	The Bionic Woman	Yes / No	1 2 3 4 5+	1 2 3 4 5	1 2 3 4 5	1 2	Yes 1 / No 2	1 2 3 4
04	Fish	Yes / No	1 2 3 4 5+	1 2 3 4 5	1 2 3 4 5	1 2	Yes 1 / No 2	1 2 3 4
05	Operation Petticoat	Yes / No	1 2 3 4 5+	1 2 3 4 5	1 2 3 4 5	1 2	Yes 1 / No 2	1 2 3 4
	9:00 PM – 11:00 PM							
06	Starsky & Hutch	Yes / No	1 2 3 4 5+	1 2 3 4 5	1 2 3 4 5	1 2	Yes 1 / No 2	1 2 3 4

Code	Program	No	Yes	Rating scales
07	The Jeffersons	No	Yes	1 2 3 4 · 1 · 2 · 1 2 3 4 5 · 1 2 3 4 · 1 2 3 4 5 · 1 · 2 · 1 2 3 4 5 · 1 2 3 4 · 2 3 4
08	Tony Randall	No	Yes	1 2 3 4 · 1 · 2 · 1 2 3 4 5 · 1 2 3 4 · 1 2 3 4 5 · 1 · 2 · 1 2 3 4 5 · 1 2 3 4 · 2 3 4
09	Saturday Night Movie	No	Yes	1 2 3 4 · 1 · 2 · 1 2 3 4 5 · 1 2 3 4 · 1 2 3 4 5 · 1 · 2 · 1 2 3 4 5 · 1 2 3 4 · 2 3 4
10	The Love Boat	No	Yes	1 2 3 4 · 1 · 2 · 1 2 3 4 5 · 1 2 3 4 · 1 2 3 4 5 · 1 · 2 · 1 2 3 4 5 · 1 2 3 4 · 2 3 4
11	The Carol Burnett Show	No	Yes	1 2 3 4 · 1 · 2 · 1 2 3 4 5 · 1 2 3 4 · 1 2 3 4 5 · 1 · 2 · 1 2 3 4 5 · 1 2 3 4 · 2 3 4

LATE NIGHT

MONDAY TO FRIDAY 11:30 PM – 1:00 AM

Code	Program	No	Yes	Rating scales
12	Fernwood 2 Night	No	Yes	1 2 3 4 · 1 · 2 · 1 2 3 4 5 · 1 2 3 4 · 1 2 3 4 5 · 1 · 2 · 1 2 3 4 5 · 1 2 3 4 · 2 3 4
13	Johnny Carson	No	Yes	1 2 3 4 · 1 · 2 · 1 2 3 4 5 · 1 2 3 4 · 1 2 3 4 5 · 1 · 2 · 1 2 3 4 5 · 1 2 3 4 · 2 3 4
14	Late Night Movies	No	Yes	1 2 3 4 · 1 · 2 · 1 2 3 4 5 · 1 2 3 4 · 1 2 3 4 5 · 1 · 2 · 1 2 3 4 5 · 1 2 3 4 · 2 3 4

II. DAYTIME PROGRAMS

MORNING

MONDAY TO FRIDAY 7:00 AM – 10:00 AM

Code	Program	No	Yes	Rating scales
01	Today	No	Yes	1 2 3 4 5+ · 1 · 2 · 1 2 3 4 5 · 1 2 3 4 · 1 2 3 4 5 · 1 · 2 · 1 2 3 4 5 · 1 2 3 4 · 2 3 4
02	Good Morning America	No	Yes	1 2 3 4 5+ · 1 · 2 · 1 2 3 4 5 · 1 2 3 4 · 1 2 3 4 5 · 1 · 2 · 1 2 3 4 5 · 1 2 3 4 · 2 3 4
03	Captain Kangaroo	No	Yes	1 2 3 4 5+ · 1 · 2 · 1 2 3 4 5 · 1 2 3 4 · 1 2 3 4 5 · 1 · 2 · 1 2 3 4 5 · 1 2 3 4 · 2 3 4
04	Captain Noah	No	Yes	1 2 3 4 5+ · 1 · 2 · 1 2 3 4 5 · 1 2 3 4 · 1 2 3 4 5 · 1 · 2 · 1 2 3 4 5 · 1 2 3 4 · 2 3 4
05	Phil Donahue	No	Yes	1 2 3 4 5+ · 1 · 2 · 1 2 3 4 5 · 1 2 3 4 · 1 2 3 4 5 · 1 · 2 · 1 2 3 4 5 · 1 2 3 4 · 2 3 4
06	Joel A. Spivak	No	Yes	1 2 3 4 5+ · 1 · 2 · 1 2 3 4 5 · 1 2 3 4 · 1 2 3 4 5 · 1 · 2 · 1 2 3 4 5 · 1 2 3 4 · 2 3 4
07	Sesame Street	No	Yes	1 2 3 4 5+ · 1 · 2 · 1 2 3 4 5 · 1 2 3 4 · 1 2 3 4 5 · 1 · 2 · 1 2 3 4 5 · 1 2 3 4 · 2 3 4

10:00 AM – 12 NOON

Code	Program	No	Yes	Rating scales
08	Mister Rogers	No	Yes	1 2 3 4 5+ · 1 · 2 · 1 2 3 4 5 · 1 2 3 4 · 1 2 3 4 5 · 1 · 2 · 1 2 3 4 5 · 1 2 3 4 · 2 3 4
09	Dialing for Dollars	No	Yes	1 2 3 4 5+ · 1 · 2 · 1 2 3 4 5 · 1 2 3 4 · 1 2 3 4 5 · 1 · 2 · 1 2 3 4 5 · 1 2 3 4 · 2 3 4
10	Hollywood Squares	No	Yes	1 2 3 4 5+ · 1 · 2 · 1 2 3 4 5 · 1 2 3 4 · 1 2 3 4 5 · 1 · 2 · 1 2 3 4 5 · 1 2 3 4 · 2 3 4
11	The Price is Right	No	Yes	1 2 3 4 5+ · 1 · 2 · 1 2 3 4 5 · 1 2 3 4 · 1 2 3 4 5 · 1 · 2 · 1 2 3 4 5 · 1 2 3 4 · 2 3 4
12	Electric Company	No	Yes	1 2 3 4 5+ · 1 · 2 · 1 2 3 4 5 · 1 2 3 4 · 1 2 3 4 5 · 1 · 2 · 1 2 3 4 5 · 1 2 3 4 · 2 3 4
13	Wheel of Fortune	No	Yes	1 2 3 4 5+ · 1 · 2 · 1 2 3 4 5 · 1 2 3 4 · 1 2 3 4 5 · 1 · 2 · 1 2 3 4 5 · 1 2 3 4 · 2 3 4
14	Family Feud	No	Yes	1 2 3 4 5+ · 1 · 2 · 1 2 3 4 5 · 1 2 3 4 · 1 2 3 4 5 · 1 · 2 · 1 2 3 4 5 · 1 2 3 4 · 2 3 4

Part 3: Television Viewing (Continued)

	A — Did you watch this program in the past four weeks? CIRCLE ONE (IF NO GO TO NEXT PROGRAM / IF YES CONTINUE ANSWERING Q's B THRU G)	B — How many times did you watch this program in the past four weeks? CIRCLE NUMBER OF TIMES	C — Who usually decides to watch this program? 1-I do, 2-My spouse does, 3-Some other adult does, 4-My children do, 5-Other. CIRCLE ONLY ONE NUMBER	D — Who else usually watches this program with you? 1-No one else, 2-My spouse, 3-Some other adult, 4-My children, 5-Other. YOU MAY CIRCLE MORE THAN ONE NUMBER IF THIS APPLIES	E — Do you usually give this program your full attention or are you doing other things while watching it? 1-I give it my full attention, 2-I do other things while watching it. CIRCLE ONLY ONE NUMBER	F — Do you usually plan in advance to watch this program? CIRCLE CODE FOR EITHER YES OR NO. Yes / No	G — If you missed an episode of this program, how disappointed would you be? 1-Not at all, 2-Somewhat, 3-Very, 4-Extremely. CIRCLE ONLY ONE NUMBER
15 Love of Life	No Yes	1 2 3 4 5+	1 2 3 4 5	1 2 3 4 5	1 2	1 2	1 2 3 4
16 It's Anybody's Guess	No Yes	1 2 3 4 5+	1 2 3 4 5	1 2 3 4 5	1 2	1 2	1 2 3 4
AFTERNOON 12:00 NOON – 2:00 PM							
01 The French Chef	No Yes	1 2 3 4 5+	1 2 3 4 5	1 2 3 4 5	1 2	1 2	1 2 3 4
02 The Young and the Restless	No Yes	1 2 3 4 5+	1 2 3 4 5	1 2 3 4 5	1 2	1 2	1 2 3 4
03 Search for Tomorrow	No Yes	1 2 3 4 5+	1 2 3 4 5	1 2 3 4 5	1 2	1 2	1 2 3 4
04 Woman	No Yes	1 2 3 4 5+	1 2 3 4 5	1 2 3 4 5	1 2	1 2	1 2 3 4
05 All My Children	No Yes	1 2 3 4 5+	1 2 3 4 5	1 2 3 4 5	1 2	1 2	1 2 3 4
06 Gong Show	No Yes	1 2 3 4 5+	1 2 3 4 5	1 2 3 4 5	1 2	1 2	1 2 3 4
07 Tattletales	No Yes	1 2 3 4 5+	1 2 3 4 5	1 2 3 4 5	1 2	1 2	1 2 3 4
08 Days of Our Lives	No Yes	1 2 3 4 5+	1 2 3 4 5	1 2 3 4 5	1 2	1 2	1 2 3 4
09 As the World Turns	No Yes	1 2 3 4 5+	1 2 3 4 5	1 2 3 4 5	1 2	1 2	1 2 3 4

2:00 PM – 5:30 PM

Program	Code	Yes	No									
$20,000 Pyramid	10	Yes	No	1 2 3 4 5+	1 2 3 4 5	1	2 3 4 5	1 2 3 4 5	1	2 3 4	2	1 2 3 4
The Doctors	11	Yes	No	1 2 3 4 5+	1 2 3 4 5	1	2 3 4 5	1 2 3 4 5	1	2 3 4	2	1 2 3 4
One Life to Live	12	Yes	No	1 2 3 4 5+	1 2 3 4 5	1	2 3 4 5	1 2 3 4 5	1	2 3 4	2	1 2 3 4
The Guiding Light	13	Yes	No	1 2 3 4 5+	1 2 3 4 5	1	2 3 4 5	1 2 3 4 5	1	2 3 4	2	1 2 3 4
Another World	14	Yes	No	1 2 3 4 5+	1 2 3 4 5	1	2 3 4 5	1 2 3 4 5	1	2 3 4	2	1 2 3 4
General Hospital	15	Yes	No	1 2 3 4 5+	1 2 3 4 5	1	2 3 4 5	1 2 3 4 5	1	2 3 4	2	1 2 3 4
Match Game '77	16	Yes	No	1 2 3 4 5+	1 2 3 4 5	1	2 3 4 5	1 2 3 4 5	1	2 3 4	2	1 2 3 4
Mike Douglas	17	Yes	No	1 2 3 4 5+	1 2 3 4 5	1	2 3 4 5	1 2 3 4 5	1	2 3 4	2	1 2 3 4
Dinah	18	Yes	No	1 2 3 4 5+	1 2 3 4 5	1	2 3 4 5	1 2 3 4 5	1	2 3 4	2	1 2 3 4
Merv Griffin Show	19	Yes	No	1 2 3 4 5+	1 2 3 4 5	1	2 3 4 5	1 2 3 4 5	1	2 3 4	2	1 2 3 4

EVENING

5:30 PM – 8:00 PM

Program	Code	Yes	No									
Local News (any station)	01	Yes	No	1 2 3 4 5+	1 2 3 4 5	1	2 3 4 5	1 2 3 4 5	1	2 3 4	2	1 2 3 4
National Network News (ABC, CBS, NBC)	02	Yes	No	1 2 3 4 5+	1 2 3 4 5	1	2 3 4 5	1 2 3 4 5	1	2 3 4	2	1 2 3 4
Evening Magazine	03	Yes	No	1 2 3 4 5+	1 2 3 4 5	1	2 3 4 5	1 2 3 4 5	1	2 3 4	2	1 2 3 4
MacNeil/Lehrer Report	04	Yes	No	1 2 3 4 5+	1 2 3 4 5	1	2 3 4 5	1 2 3 4 5	1	2 3 4	2	1 2 3 4

III. WEEKEND PROGRAMS

SATURDAY

Program	Code	Yes	No									
Children's Cartoons	05	Yes	No	1 2 3 4 5+	1 2 3 4 5	1	2 3 4 5	1 2 3 4 5	1	2 3 4	2	1 2 3 4
American Bandstand	06	Yes	No	1 2 3 4 5+	1 2 3 4 5	1	2 3 4 5	1 2 3 4 5	1	2 3 4	2	1 2 3 4
Wide World of Sports	07	Yes	No	1 2 3 4 5+	1 2 3 4 5	1	2 3 4 5	1 2 3 4 5	1	2 3 4	2	1 2 3 4
Lawrence Welk	08	Yes	No	1 2 3 4 5+	1 2 3 4 5	1	2 3 4 5	1 2 3 4 5	1	2 3 4	2	1 2 3 4
Last of the Wild	09	Yes	No	1 2 3 4 5+	1 2 3 4 5	1	2 3 4 5	1 2 3 4 5	1	2 3 4	2	1 2 3 4
Saturday Night Live	10	Yes	No	1 2 3 4 5+	1 2 3 4 5	1	2 3 4 5	1 2 3 4 5	1	2 3 4	2	1 2 3 4
Soul Train	11	Yes	No	1 2 3 4 5+	1 2 3 4 5	1	2 3 4 5	1 2 3 4 5	1	2 3 4	2	1 2 3 4

SUNDAY

Program	Code	Yes	No									
Any Religious Program(s)	12	Yes	No	1 2 3 4 5+	1 2 3 4 5	1	2 3 4 5	1 2 3 4 5	1	2 3 4	2	1 2 3 4
Face the Nation	13	Yes	No	1 2 3 4 5+	1 2 3 4 5	1	2 3 4 5	1 2 3 4 5	1	2 3 4	2	1 2 3 4

Part 3: Television Viewing (Continued)		A — Did you watch this program in the past four weeks? CIRCLE ONE. IF NO GO TO NEXT PROGRAM. IF YES CONTINUE ANSWERING Q's B THRU G	B — How many times did you watch this program in the past four weeks? CIRCLE NUMBER OF TIMES	C — Who usually decides to watch this program? 1-I do 2-My spouse does 3-Some other adult does 4-My children do 5-Other CIRCLE ONLY ONE NUMBER	D — Who else usually watches this program with you? 1-No one else 2-My spouse 3-Some other adult 4-My children 5-Other YOU MAY CIRCLE MORE THAN ONE NUMBER IF THIS APPLIES	E — Do you usually give this program your full attention or are you doing other things while watching it? 1-I give it my full attention 2-I do other things while watching it CIRCLE ONLY ONE NUMBER	F — Do you usually plan in advance to watch this program? CIRCLE CODE FOR EITHER YES OR NO (Yes / No)	G — If you missed an episode of this program, how disappointed would you be? 1-Not at all 2-Somewhat 3-Very 4-Extremely CIRCLE ONLY ONE NUMBER
Meet the Press	14	No Yes	1 2 3 4 5+	1 2 3 4 5	1 2 3 4 5	1 2	Yes 1 No 2	1 2 3 4
Once Upon a Classic	15	No Yes	1 2 3 4 5+	1 2 3 4 5	1 2 3 4 5	1 2	Yes 1 No 2	1 2 3 4
Music Hall of America	16	No Yes	1 2 3 4 5+	1 2 3 4 5	1 2 3 4 5	1 2	Yes 1 No 2	1 2 3 4
Andy Williams	17	No Yes	1 2 3 4 5+	1 2 3 4 5	1 2 3 4 5	1 2	Yes 1 No 2	1 2 3 4
IV. OTHER PROGRAMS								
SPORTS								
Football	01	No Yes	1 2 3 4 5+	1 2 3 4 5	1 2 3 4 5	1 2	Yes 1 No 2	1 2 3 4
Basketball	02	No Yes	1 2 3 4 5+	1 2 3 4 5	1 2 3 4 5	1 2	Yes 1 No 2	1 2 3 4
Hockey	03	No Yes	1 2 3 4 5+	1 2 3 4 5	1 2 3 4 5	1 2	Yes 1 No 2	1 2 3 4
Baseball	04	No Yes	1 2 3 4 5+	1 2 3 4 5	1 2 3 4 5	1 2	Yes 1 No 2	1 2 3 4
Other	05	No Yes	1 2 3 4 5+	1 2 3 4 5	1 2 3 4 5	1 2	Yes 1 No 2	1 2 3 4
Any Spanish Programs	06	No Yes	1 2 3 4 5+	1 2 3 4 5	1 2 3 4 5	1 2	Yes 1 No 2	1 2 3 4
SPECIALS								
Washington: Behind Closed Doors	07	No Yes	1 2 3 4 5+	1 2 3 4 5	1 2 3 4 5	1 2	Yes 1 No 2	1 2 3 4
The Trial of Lee Harvey Oswald	08	No Yes	1 2 3 4 5+	1 2 3 4 5	1 2 3 4 5	1 2	Yes 1 No 2	1 2 3 4
Kill Me If You Can (The Caryl Chessman Story)	09	No Yes	1 2 3 4 5+	1 2 3 4 5	1 2 3 4 5	1 2	Yes 1 No 2	1 2 3 4

NATIONAL ANALYSTS
A Division of Booz, Allen & Hamilton Inc.

Study #1-923
Fall, 1977

SPECIAL INTERESTS STUDY

PART 3

Children

INSTRUCTIONS FOR COMPLETING PART 3

This next part deals with the programs you watch on TV.

As you will see when you turn the page, the questions are all on the top of the page. Circle the appropriate code of your answer for each question.

The programs are listed by day and time shown. These days and times may not correspond to the days and times certain programs are shown in your area. Just answer the questions pertaining to the program, regardless of the program's scheduling in your area.

Note in Question A: If you did not watch the specific television program in the past four weeks, circle "No" and go on to the next program.

Part 3: Television Viewing

	A Did you watch this program in the past four weeks? CIRCLE ONE — IF NO GO TO NEXT PROGRAM — IF YES CONTINUE ANSWERING Q's B THRU G	B How many times did you watch this program in the past four weeks? CIRCLE NUMBER OF TIMES	C Who usually decides to watch this program? 1-I do 2-My father does 3-My mother does 4-My brother or sister does 5-Some other adult does CIRCLE ONLY ONE NUMBER	D Who else usually watches this program with you? 1-No one else 2-My father 3-My mother 4-My brother or sister 5-Some other adult does YOU MAY CIRCLE MORE THAN ONE NUMBER IF THIS APPLIES	E Do you usually give this program your full attention or are you usually doing other things while watching it? 1-I give it my full attention 2-I do other things while watching it CIRCLE ONLY ONE NUMBER	F Do you usually plan in advance to watch this program? CIRCLE EITHER YES OR NO (Yes / No)	G If you missed an episode of this program, how disappointed would you be? 1-Not at all 2-Somewhat 3-Very 4-Extremely CIRCLE ONLY ONE NUMBER

I. NIGHTTIME PROGRAMS

SUNDAY
7:00 PM – 9:00 PM

Program	A	B	C	D	E	F (Yes / No)	G
Nancy Drew/Hardy Boys Mystery Show	No Yes	1 2 3 4	1 2 3 4 5	1 2 3 4 5	1 2	1 2	1 2 3 4
Sixty Minutes	No Yes	1 2 3 4	1 2 3 4 5	1 2 3 4 5	1 2	1 2	1 2 3 4
The Wonderful World of Disney	No Yes	1 2 3 4	1 2 3 4 5	1 2 3 4 5	1 2	1 2	1 2 3 4
Evening at Symphony	No Yes	1 2 3 4	1 2 3 4 5	1 2 3 4 5	1 2	1 2	1 2 3 4
Rhoda	No Yes	1 2 3 4	1 2 3 4 5	1 2 3 4 5	1 2	1 2	1 2 3 4
On Our Own	No Yes	1 2 3 4	1 2 3 4 5	1 2 3 4 5	1 2	1 2	1 2 3 4
Six Million Dollar Man	No Yes	1 2 3 4	1 2 3 4 5	1 2 3 4 5	1 2	1 2	1 2 3 4

9:00 PM – 11:00 PM

All in the Family	No	Yes	1 2 3 4	1 2 3 4	1 2 3 4 5	1	1 2 3 4 5	1 2 3 4	1	2	1 2 3 4
Alice	No	Yes	1 2 3 4	1 2 3 4	1 2 3 4 5	1	1 2 3 4 5	1 2 3 4	1	2	1 2 3 4
Kojak	No	Yes	1 2 3 4	1 2 3 4	1 2 3 4 5	1	1 2 3 4 5	1 2 3 4	1	2	1 2 3 4
Sunday Night Movie	No	Yes	1 2 3 4	1 2 3 4	1 2 3 4 5	1	1 2 3 4 5	1 2 3 4	1	2	1 2 3 4
Dickens of London	No	Yes	1 2 3 4	1 2 3 4	1 2 3 4 5	1	1 2 3 4 5	1 2 3 4	1	2	1 2 3 4
Visions	No	Yes	1 2 3 4	1 2 3 4	1 2 3 4 5	1	1 2 3 4 5	1 2 3 4	1	2	1 2 3 4
The Big Event (varies)	No	Yes	1 2 3 4	1 2 3 4	1 2 3 4 5	1	1 2 3 4 5	1 2 3 4	1	2	1 2 3 4

MONDAY
8:00 PM – 9:00 PM

The San Pedro Beach Bums	No	Yes	1 2 3 4	1 2 3 4	1 2 3 4 5	1	1 2 3 4 5	1 2 3 4	1	2	1 2 3 4
Upstairs, Downstairs	No	Yes	1 2 3 4	1 2 3 4	1 2 3 4 5	1	1 2 3 4 5	1 2 3 4	1	2	1 2 3 4
Young Dan'l Boone	No	Yes	1 2 3 4	1 2 3 4	1 2 3 4 5	1	1 2 3 4 5	1 2 3 4	1	2	1 2 3 4
Little House on the Prairie	No	Yes	1 2 3 4	1 2 3 4	1 2 3 4 5	1	1 2 3 4 5	1 2 3 4	1	2	1 2 3 4

9:00 PM – 11:00 PM

Monday Night Movie	No	Yes	1 2 3 4	1 2 3 4	1 2 3 4 5	1	1 2 3 4 5	1 2 3 4	1	2	1 2 3 4
The Betty White Show	No	Yes	1 2 3 4	1 2 3 4	1 2 3 4 5	1	1 2 3 4 5	1 2 3 4	1	2	1 2 3 4
Maude	No	Yes	1 2 3 4	1 2 3 4	1 2 3 4 5	1	1 2 3 4 5	1 2 3 4	1	2	1 2 3 4
Rafferty	No	Yes	1 2 3 4	1 2 3 4	1 2 3 4 5	1	1 2 3 4 5	1 2 3 4	1	2	1 2 3 4
NFL Football	No	Yes	1 2 3 4	1 2 3 4	1 2 3 4 5	1	1 2 3 4 5	1 2 3 4	1	2	1 2 3 4
Age of Uncertainty	No	Yes	1 2 3 4	1 2 3 4	1 2 3 4 5	1	1 2 3 4 5	1 2 3 4	1	2	1 2 3 4
In Pursuit of Liberty	No	Yes	1 2 3 4	1 2 3 4	1 2 3 4 5	1	1 2 3 4 5	1 2 3 4	1	2	1 2 3 4

TUESDAY
8:00 PM – 9:00 PM

The Richard Pryor Show	No	Yes	1 2 3 4	1 2 3 4	1 2 3 4 5	1	1 2 3 4 5	1 2 3 4	1	2	1 2 3 4
The Fitzpatricks	No	Yes	1 2 3 4	1 2 3 4	1 2 3 4 5	1	1 2 3 4 5	1 2 3 4	1	2	1 2 3 4
Happy Days	No	Yes	1 2 3 4	1 2 3 4	1 2 3 4 5	1	1 2 3 4 5	1 2 3 4	1	2	1 2 3 4
Laverne & Shirley	No	Yes	1 2 3 4	1 2 3 4	1 2 3 4 5	1	1 2 3 4 5	1 2 3 4	1	2	1 2 3 4

Part 3: Television Viewing (Continued)

Program	A. Did you watch this program in the past four weeks? CIRCLE ONE (IF NO GO TO NEXT PROGRAM. IF YES CONTINUE ANSWERING Q's B THRU G)	B. How many times did you watch this program in the past four weeks? CIRCLE NUMBER OF TIMES	C. Who usually decides to watch this program? (1-I do, 2-My father does, 3-My mother does, 4-My brother or sister does, 5-Some other adult does) CIRCLE ONLY ONE NUMBER	D. Who else usually watches this program with you? (1-No one else, 2-My father, 3-My mother, 4-My brother or sister, 5-Some other adult does) YOU MAY CIRCLE MORE THAN ONE NUMBER IF THIS APPLIES	E. Do you usually give this program your full attention or are you usually doing other things while watching it? (1-I give it my full attention, 2-I do other things while watching it) CIRCLE ONLY ONE NUMBER	F. Do you usually plan in advance to watch this program? CIRCLE EITHER YES OR NO	G. If you missed an episode of this program, how disappointed would you be? (1-Not at all, 2-Somewhat, 3-Very, 4-Extremely) CIRCLE ONLY ONE NUMBER
9:00 PM – 10:00 PM						Yes No	
Three's Company	No Yes	1 2 3 4	1 2 3 4 5	1 2 3 4 5	1 2	1 2	1 2 3 4
Soap	No Yes	1 2 3 4	1 2 3 4 5	1 2 3 4 5	1 2	1 2	1 2 3 4
MASH	No Yes	1 2 3 4	1 2 3 4 5	1 2 3 4 5	1 2	1 2	1 2 3 4
One Day at a Time	No Yes	1 2 3 4	1 2 3 4 5	1 2 3 4 5	1 2	1 2	1 2 3 4
Mulligan's Stew	No Yes	1 2 3 4	1 2 3 4 5	1 2 3 4 5	1 2	1 2	1 2 3 4
Opera (varies)	No Yes	1 2 3 4	1 2 3 4 5	1 2 3 4 5	1 2	1 2	1 2 3 4
10:00 PM – 11:00 PM							
Lou Grant	No Yes	1 2 3 4	1 2 3 4 5	1 2 3 4 5	1 2	1 2	1 2 3 4
Family	No Yes	1 2 3 4	1 2 3 4 5	1 2 3 4 5	1 2	1 2	1 2 3 4
Police Woman	No Yes	1 2 3 4	1 2 3 4 5	1 2 3 4 5	1 2	1 2	1 2 3 4

WEDNESDAY
8:00 PM – 9:00 PM

Nova	Yes	No	1 2 3 4
The Life and Times of Grizzly Adams	Yes	No	1 2 3 4
Eight Is Enough	Yes	No	1 2 3 4
Good Times	Yes	No	1 2 3 4
Busting Loose	Yes	No	1 2 3 4

9:00 PM – 11:00 PM

Wednesday Night Movie	Yes	No	1 2 3 4
Great Performances	Yes	No	1 2 3 4
Oregon Trail	Yes	No	1 2 3 4
Big Hawaii	Yes	No	1 2 3 4
Charlie's Angels	Yes	No	1 2 3 4
Baretta	Yes	No	1 2 3 4

THURSDAY
8:00 PM – 9:00 PM

The Waltons	Yes	No	1 2 3 4
Welcome Back, Kotter	Yes	No	1 2 3 4
What's Happening!	Yes	No	1 2 3 4
Chips	Yes	No	1 2 3 4

9:00 PM – 10:00 PM

Barney Miller	Yes	No	1 2 3 4
Carter Country	Yes	No	1 2 3 4
The Man from Atlantis	Yes	No	1 2 3 4
Hawaii Five-O	Yes	No	1 2 3 4
Best of Families	Yes	No	1 2 3 4

10:00 PM – 11:00 PM

Redd Foxx	Yes	No	1 2 3 4
Masterpiece Theater	Yes	No	1 2 3 4

	A — Did you watch this program in the past four weeks? CIRCLE ONE. IF NO GO TO NEXT PROGRAM. IF YES CONTINUE ANSWERING Q's B THRU G	B — How many times did you watch this program in the past four weeks? CIRCLE NUMBER OF TIMES	C — Who usually decides to watch this program? 1-I do 2-My father does 3-My mother does 4-My brother or sister does 5-Some other adult does. CIRCLE ONLY ONE NUMBER	D — Who else usually watches this program with you? 1-No one else 2-My father 3-My mother 4-My brother or sister 5-Some other adult does. YOU MAY CIRCLE MORE THAN ONE NUMBER IF THIS APPLIES	E — Do you usually give this program your full attention or are you usually doing other things while watching it? 1-I give it my full attention 2-I do other things while watching it. CIRCLE ONLY ONE NUMBER	F — Do you usually plan in advance to watch this program? CIRCLE EITHER YES OR NO (Yes / No)	G — If you missed an episode of this program, how disappointed would you be? 1-Not at all 2-Somewhat 3-Very 4-Extremely. CIRCLE ONLY ONE NUMBER
Part 3: Television Viewing (Continued)							
Barnaby Jones	No Yes	1 2 3 4	1 2 3 4 5	1 2 3 4 5	1 2	1 2	1 2 3 4
Rosetti and Ryan	No Yes	1 2 3 4	1 2 3 4 5	1 2 3 4 5	1 2	1 2	1 2 3 4
FRIDAY 8:00 PM – 9:00 PM							
Washington in Review	No Yes	1 2 3 4	1 2 3 4 5	1 2 3 4 5	1 2	1 2	1 2 3 4
Wall Street Week	No Yes	1 2 3 4	1 2 3 4 5	1 2 3 4 5	1 2	1 2	1 2 3 4
The New Adventures of Wonder Woman	No Yes	1 2 3 4	1 2 3 4 5	1 2 3 4 5	1 2	1 2	1 2 3 4
Donnie & Marie	No Yes	1 2 3 4	1 2 3 4 5	1 2 3 4 5	1 2	1 2	1 2 3 4
Sanford Arms	No Yes	1 2 3 4	1 2 3 4 5	1 2 3 4 5	1 2	1 2	1 2 3 4
Chico and the Man	No Yes	1 2 3 4	1 2 3 4 5	1 2 3 4 5	1 2	1 2	1 2 3 4
9:00 PM – 11:00 PM							
Friday Night Movie	No Yes	1 2 3 4	1 2 3 4 5	1 2 3 4 5	1 2	1 2	1 2 3 4

Program			Rating scales
SATURDAY 8:00 PM – 9:00 PM			
Logan's Run	Yes	No	1 2 3 4 1 2 3 4 5 1 2 3 4 5 1 2 1 2 1 2 3 4
Switch	Yes	No	1 2 3 4 1 2 3 4 5 1 2 3 4 5 1 2 1 2 1 2 3 4
The Rockford Files	Yes	No	1 2 3 4 1 2 3 4 5 1 2 3 4 5 1 2 1 2 1 2 3 4
Quincy	Yes	No	1 2 3 4 1 2 3 4 5 1 2 3 4 5 1 2 1 2 1 2 3 4
Evening at Pop's	Yes	No	1 2 3 4 1 2 3 4 5 1 2 3 4 5 1 2 1 2 1 2 3 4
Black Perspective on the News	Yes	No	1 2 3 4 1 2 3 4 5 1 2 3 4 5 1 2 1 2 1 2 3 4
SATURDAY 8:00 PM – 9:00 PM			
Bob Newhart	Yes	No	1 2 3 4 1 2 3 4 5 1 2 3 4 5 1 2 1 2 1 2 3 4
We've Got Each Other	Yes	No	1 2 3 4 1 2 3 4 5 1 2 3 4 5 1 2 1 2 1 2 3 4
The Bionic Woman	Yes	No	1 2 3 4 1 2 3 4 5 1 2 3 4 5 1 2 1 2 1 2 3 4
Fish	Yes	No	1 2 3 4 1 2 3 4 5 1 2 3 4 5 1 2 1 2 1 2 3 4
Operation Petticoat	Yes	No	1 2 3 4 1 2 3 4 5 1 2 3 4 5 1 2 1 2 1 2 3 4
Best of Families	Yes	No	1 2 3 4 1 2 3 4 5 1 2 3 4 5 1 2 1 2 1 2 3 4
9:00 PM – 11:00 PM			
Starsky & Hutch	Yes	No	1 2 3 4 1 2 3 4 5 1 2 3 4 5 1 2 1 2 1 2 3 4
The Jeffersons	Yes	No	1 2 3 4 1 2 3 4 5 1 2 3 4 5 1 2 1 2 1 2 3 4
Tony Randall	Yes	No	1 2 3 4 1 2 3 4 5 1 2 3 4 5 1 2 1 2 1 2 3 4
Saturday Night Movie	Yes	No	1 2 3 4 1 2 3 4 5 1 2 3 4 5 1 2 1 2 1 2 3 4
The Love Boat	Yes	No	1 2 3 4 1 2 3 4 5 1 2 3 4 5 1 2 1 2 1 2 3 4
The Carol Burnett Show	Yes	No	1 2 3 4 1 2 3 4 5 1 2 3 4 5 1 2 1 2 1 2 3 4
LATE NIGHT			
MONDAY TO FRIDAY 11:30 PM – 1:00 AM			
Fernwood 2 Night	Yes	No	1 2 3 4 1 2 3 4 5 1 2 3 4 5 1 2 1 2 1 2 3 4
Johnny Carson	Yes	No	1 2 3 4 1 2 3 4 5 1 2 3 4 5 1 2 1 2 1 2 3 4
Late Night Movies	Yes	No	1 2 3 4 1 2 3 4 5 1 2 3 4 5 1 2 1 2 1 2 3 4

	A	B	C	D	E	F		G
Part 3: Television Viewing (Continued)	*Did you watch this program in the past four weeks?* CIRCLE ONE IF NO GO TO NEXT PROGRAM / IF YES CONTINUE ANSWERING Q's B THRU G	*How many times did you watch this program in the past four weeks?* CIRCLE NUMBER OF TIMES	*Who usually decides to watch this program?* 1-I do 2-My father does 3-My mother does 4-My brother or sister does 5-Some other adult does CIRCLE ONLY ONE NUMBER	*Who else usually watches this program with you?* 1-No one else 2-My father 3-My mother 4-My brother or sister 5-Some other adult does YOU MAY CIRCLE MORE THAN ONE NUMBER IF THIS APPLIES	*Do you usually give this program your full attention or are you usually doing other things while watching it?* 1-I give it my full attention 2-I do other things while watching it CIRCLE ONLY ONE NUMBER	*Do you usually plan in advance to watch this program?* CIRCLE EITHER YES OR NO Yes	No	*If you missed an episode of this program, how disappointed would you be?* 1-Not at all 2-Somewhat 3-Very 4-Extremely CIRCLE ONLY ONE NUMBER
II. DAYTIME PROGRAMS								
MORNING								
MONDAY TO FRIDAY								
7:00 AM – 10:00 AM								
Today	No Yes	1 2 3 4	1 2 3 4 5	1 2 3 4 5	1 2	1	2	1 2 3 4
Good Morning America	No Yes	1 2 3 4	1 2 3 4 5	1 2 3 4 5	1 2	1	2	1 2 3 4
Captain Kangaroo	No Yes	1 2 3 4	1 2 3 4 5	1 2 3 4 5	1 2	1	2	1 2 3 4
Captain Noah	No Yes	1 2 3 4	1 2 3 4 5	1 2 3 4 5	1 2	1	2	1 2 3 4
Phil Donahue	No Yes	1 2 3 4	1 2 3 4 5	1 2 3 4 5	1 2	1	2	1 2 3 4
Joel A. Spivak	No Yes	1 2 3 4	1 2 3 4 5	1 2 3 4 5	1 2	1	2	1 2 3 4
Sesame Street	No Yes	1 2 3 4	1 2 3 4 5	1 2 3 4 5	1 2	1	2	1 2 3 4
10:00 AM – 12:00 NOON								
Mister Rogers	No Yes	1 2 3 4	1 2 3 4 5	1 2 3 4 5	1 2	1	2	1 2 3 4
Dialing for Dollars	No Yes	1 2 3 4	1 2 3 4 5	1 2 3 4 5	1 2	1	2	1 2 3 4

AFTERNOON 12:00 NOON – 2:00 PM

Hollywood Squares	No	Yes
The Price is Right	No	Yes
Electric Company	No	Yes
Wheel of Fortune	No	Yes
Family Feud	No	Yes
Love of Life	No	Yes
It's Anybody's Guess	No	Yes

12:00 NOON – 2:00 PM

The French Chef	No	Yes
The Young and the Restless	No	Yes
Search for Tomorrow	No	Yes
Woman	No	Yes
All My Children	No	Yes
Gong Show	No	Yes
Tattletales	No	Yes
Days of Our Lives	No	Yes
As the World Turns	No	Yes

2:00 PM – 5:30 PM

$20,000 Pyramid	No	Yes
The Doctors	No	Yes
One Life to Live	No	Yes
The Guiding Light	No	Yes
Another World	No	Yes
General Hospital	No	Yes
Match Game '77	No	Yes
Mike Douglas	No	Yes
Dinah	No	Yes
Merv Griffin Show	No	Yes

EVENING 5:30 PM – 8:00 PM

Local News (any station)	No	Yes

(Each program row is followed by a series of rating scales, variously numbered 1 2 3 4; 1 2 3 4 5; 1; 1 2.)

Part 3: Television Viewing (Continued)

	A — Did you watch this program in the past four weeks? CIRCLE ONE. IF NO GO TO NEXT PROGRAM. IF YES CONTINUE ANSWERING Q's B THRU G	B — How many times did you watch this program in the past four weeks? CIRCLE NUMBER OF TIMES	C — Who usually decides to watch this program? 1-I do 2-My father does 3-My mother does 4-My brother or sister does 5-Some other adult does CIRCLE ONLY ONE NUMBER	D — Who else usually watches this program with you? 1-No one else 2-My father 3-My mother 4-My brother or sister 5-Some other adult does YOU MAY CIRCLE MORE THAN ONE NUMBER IF THIS APPLIES	E — Do you usually give this program your full attention or are you usually doing other things while watching it? 1-I give it my full attention 2-I do other things while watching it CIRCLE ONLY ONE NUMBER	F — Do you usually plan in advance to watch this program? CIRCLE EITHER YES OR NO (Yes / No)	G — If you missed an episode of this program, how disappointed would you be? 1-Not at all 2-Somewhat 3-Very 4-Extremely CIRCLE ONLY ONE NUMBER
National Network News (ABC, CBS, NBC)	No Yes	1 2 3 4	1 2 3 4 5	1 2 3 4 5	1 2	1 2	1 2 3 4
Evening Magazine	No Yes	1 2 3 4	1 2 3 4 5	1 2 3 4 5	1 2	1 2	1 2 3 4
MacNeil/Lehrer Report	No Yes	1 2 3 4	1 2 3 4 5	1 2 3 4 5	1 2	1 2	1 2 3 4

III. WEEKEND PROGRAMS

SATURDAY

	A	B	C	D	E	F	G
Children's Cartoons	No Yes	1 2 3 4	1 2 3 4 5	1 2 3 4 5	1 2	1 2	1 2 3 4
American Bandstand	No Yes	1 2 3 4	1 2 3 4 5	1 2 3 4 5	1 2	1 2	1 2 3 4
Wide World of Sports	No Yes	1 2 3 4	1 2 3 4 5	1 2 3 4 5	1 2	1 2	1 2 3 4
Lawrence Welk	No Yes	1 2 3 4	1 2 3 4 5	1 2 3 4 5	1 2	1 2	1 2 3 4
Last of the Wild	No Yes	1 2 3 4	1 2 3 4 5	1 2 3 4 5	1 2	1 2	1 2 3 4
Saturday Night Live	No Yes	1 2 3 4	1 2 3 4 5	1 2 3 4 5	1 2	1 2	1 2 3 4
Soul Train	No Yes	1 2 3 4	1 2 3 4 5	1 2 3 4 5	1 2	1 2	1 2 3 4

SUNDAY

Any Religious Program(s)	No	Yes	1 2 3 4	1 2 3 4 5	1 2 3 4 5	1	2 1 2 3 4	1 2 3 4
Face the Nation	No	Yes	1 2 3 4	1 2 3 4 5	1 2 3 4 5	1	2 1 2 3 4	1 2 3 4
Meet the Press	No	Yes	1 2 3 4	1 2 3 4 5	1 2 3 4 5	1	2 1 2 3 4	1 2 3 4
Once Upon a Classic	No	Yes	1 2 3 4	1 2 3 4 5	1 2 3 4 5	1	2 1 2 3 4	1 2 3 4
Music Hall America	No	Yes	1 2 3 4	1 2 3 4 5	1 2 3 4 5	1	2 1 2 3 4	1 2 3 4
Andy Williams	No	Yes	1 2 3 4	1 2 3 4 5	1 2 3 4 5	1	2 1 2 3 4	1 2 3 4

SEGMENT #: _____ D.U. #: _____

NATIONAL ANALYSTS   Study #1-923
A Division of Booz, Allen & Hamilton Inc.   Fall, 1977

SPECIAL INTERESTS STUDY
PART 4

WRITE YOUR NAME HERE: _____

INSTRUCTIONS FOR COMPLETING PART 4

In this part of the questionnaire, we would like you to tell us how often you watch television, how often you listen to the radio and how often you read magazines, newspapers and books.

We also would like to find out what kinds of radio programs you listen to, and what kinds of magazines and books you read, and the types of movies you watch.

(NOW PLEASE TURN THE PAGE AND BEGIN.)

NATIONAL ANALYSTS   Study #1-923
A Division of Booz, Allen & Hamilton Inc.   Fall, 1977

SPECIAL INTERESTS STUDY
PART 4

This part of the questionnaire asks some questions about you. These questions are used to classify your answers with those of other people who are similar to you.

1. During what hours of the day on a "typical" weekday, Saturday and Sunday are you usually at home? In the space below circle the codes of the times of the day that you are usually at home on each "typical" day.

	(CIRCLE ALL THAT APPLY FOR EACH DAY)		
	Typical Weekday	*Typical Saturday*	*Typical Sunday*
Early morning – 6 A.M. to 9 A.M.	1	1	1
Morning – 9 A.M. to Noon	2	2	2
Early afternoon – Noon to 3 P.M.	3	3	3
Late afternoon – 3 P.M. to 5 P.M.	4	4	4
Early evening – 5 P.M. to 7 P.M.	5	5	5
Evening – 7 P.M. to Midnight	6	6	6
Late at night – Midnight to 6 A.M.	7	7	7

2. In the space provided below, please indicate those times during a typical week when you watch television.

	Mon.	Tues.	Wed.	Thur.	Fri.	Sat.	Sun.
			(CIRCLE ALL THAT APPLY)				
7 A.M. to 8 A.M.	1	2	3	4	5	6	7
8 A.M. to 9 A.M.	1	2	3	4	5	6	7
9 A.M. to 10 A.M.	1	2	3	4	5	6	7
10 A.M. to 11 A.M.	1	2	3	4	5	6	7
11 A.M. to 12 Noon	1	2	3	4	5	6	7
12 Noon to 1 P.M.	1	2	3	4	5	6	7
1 P.M. to 2 P.M.	1	2	3	4	5	6	7
2 P.M. to 3 P.M.	1	2	3	4	5	6	7
3 P.M. to 4 P.M.	1	2	3	4	5	6	7
4 P.M. to 5 P.M.	1	2	3	4	5	6	7
5 P.M. to 6 P.M.	1	2	3	4	5	6	7
6 P.M. to 7 P.M.	1	2	3	4	5	6	7
7 P.M. to 8 P.M.	1	2	3	4	5	6	7
8 P.M. to 9 P.M.	1	2	3	4	5	6	7
9 P.M. to 10 P.M.	1	2	3	4	5	6	7
10 P.M. to 11 P.M.	1	2	3	4	5	6	7
11 P.M. to 12 Midnight	1	2	3	4	5	6	7
Midnight to 1 A.M.	1	2	3	4	5	6	7
1 A.M. and later	1	2	3	4	5	6	7

3. Now, please think about what you do to decide which TV programs to watch. For *each* possibility listed below indicate if you never, practically never, occasionally, or very often do it by circling the appropriate code.

	(CIRCLE ONE CODE FOR EACH)			
	Never	*Practically Never*	*Occasionally*	*Very Often*
I watch shows picked by other family members	1	2	3	4
I look up TV shows several days in advance	1	2	3	4
I follow recommendations of friends	1	2	3	4
I switch channels until I find something interesting	1	2	3	4
I watch the same shows because I like them and know when they are on	1	2	3	4
I read listings each day in the newspaper	1	2	3	4
I select programs from ads on the radio, in the newspapers or magazines	1	2	3	4
I follow recommendations given to children by their teachers	1	2	3	4
I watch one program and then just leave the set on	1	2	3	4
I make selections from TV Guide, or from the weekly guides in weekend newspapers	1	2	3	4
I select programs from advertisements made for them on TV	1	2	3	4

4. The following is a list of possible reasons for watching television. When you watch TV, how often does each of these reasons apply to you? For *each* reason below circle the code that best represents how you feel, indicating whether the reason is never, rarely, occasionally, or usually true for you.

| | (CIRCLE ONE CODE FOR EACH REASON) | | | |
	Never True	Rarely True	Occasionally True	Usually True
I watch to see a special program that I've heard a lot about	1	2	3	4
I watch because there is nothing else to do at the time	1	2	3	4
I watch to get away from the ordinary cares and problems of the day	1	2	3	4
I turn on the set just "to keep me company" when I'm alone	1	2	3	4
I watch because I think I can learn something	1	2	3	4
I watch because I'm afraid I might be missing something good	1	2	3	4
I keep watching to put off doing something else I should do	1	2	3	4
I start watching because someone else in the household is watching and seems to be interested	1	2	3	4
I start on one show and then "get stuck" for the rest of the evening	1	2	3	4
I watch because everyone I know is watching and I want to be able to talk about it afterwards	1	2	3	4
I watch just for "background" while I am doing something else	1	2	3	4
I watch just because I feel like watching television	1	2	3	4
I watch mainly to be sociable when others are watching	1	2	3	4
I watch to see a specific program that I enjoy very much	1	2	3	4
I watch just because it is a pleasant way to spend an evening	1	2	3	4

5. What do you *usually* look at to find out what programs are on TV on a particular night? Circle the one code that best represents your answer.

	(CIRCLE ONE)
TV Guide	1
Sunday newspaper TV bulletin or magazine	2
Daily newspaper TV listing	3
Daily program listing shown on a TV channel	4
Other	5

6. How often do you discuss with someone else a television program that you watched?

	(CIRCLE ONE)
Very often	1
Sometimes	2
Rarely	3
Never	0

7. *When* do you most often discuss with someone else a TV program that you watch? You may circle more than one code if they apply.

	(CIRCLE ALL THAT APPLY)
During the program	1
Shortly after the program	2
The day after the program was on	3
More than one day after the program was on	4
Never discuss a TV program	0

8. The next few questions are about *radio*. On an *average* weekday, Saturday or Sunday, about how many hours do you listen to the radio? Write in the average number of hours per day, on each of the

three lines. If you don't listen to the radio at all on that day, write
"0." Try to give us an average number of hours, rather than a range.

	(WRITE IN NUMBER OF HOURS PER DAY)
Average weekday	_____
Average Saturday	_____
Average Sunday	_____

9.   Now please think about the time of day you spend listening to the
        radio during a typical weekday, Saturday and Sunday. In the space
        below, circle the codes of the time of day that you listen to the
        radio each "typical" day.

	(CIRCLE ALL THAT APPLY FOR EACH DAY)		
	Typical Weekday	Typical Saturday	Typical Sunday
Early morning – 6 A.M. to 9 A.M.	1	1	1
Morning – 9 A.M. to Noon	2	2	2
Early afternoon – Noon to 3 P.M.	3	3	3
Late afternoon – 3 P.M. to 5 P.M.	4	4	4
Early evening – 5 P.M. to 7 P.M.	5	5	5
Evening – 7 P.M. to Midnight	6	6	6
Late at night – Midnight to 6 A.M.	7	7	7
Do not listen to the radio this day	0	0	0

10.   Thinking about the time you spend listening to the radio, would you
        say you listen:

	(CIRCLE ONE)
Mostly while in a car	1
Mostly at home	2
About half the time in a car, and half at home	3
Usually some place other than in a car or at home	4
Never listen to radio	0

11. Do you listen:

	(CIRCLE ONE)
Only to AM	1
Mostly to AM	2
AM and FM, about equally	3
Mostly to FM	4
Only to FM	5
Never listen to radio	0

12. For each of the types of radio programs listed below, circle the code number that indicates how often you listen to that type of program. If you never listen to the radio, circle this code 0 and skip to Q.13.

		Never	Almost Never	Sometimes	Very Often
MUSIC	Classical	1	2	3	4
	Country Music	1	2	3	4
	Disco Music	1	2	3	4
	Golden oldies — from the 50's and 60's	1	2	3	4
	Jazz	1	2	3	4
	Mostly instrumental — "background music"	1	2	3	4
	Popular music — by popular vocalists, some current hits	1	2	3	4
	Rhythm and blues	1	2	3	4
	Rock music	1	2	3	4
	Top hits of the week	1	2	3	4
OTHER	All-news stations (local, national, international)	1	2	3	4
	Black programming	1	2	3	4
	Educational/instructional programming	1	2	3	4
	Farm programs	1	2	3	4

	Never	Almost Never	Sometimes	Very Often
Radio drama	1	2	3	4
Religious programs	1	2	3	4
Spanish programming	1	2	3	4
Sports programming	1	2	3	4
Talk, phone-in shows on radio	1	2	3	4

13. How interested would you be in listening to each of the following types of radio programs listed below? Circle the code which represents your degree of interest in each program type.

	Not at All Interested	Not Very Interested	Very Interested	Extremely Interested
Documentaries	1	2	3	4
Public affairs (i.e., interviews, panel discussions, etc.)	1	2	3	4
Radio drama	1	2	3	4
Children's programs	1	2	3	4
Coverage of local events	1	2	3	4
Public service information	1	2	3	4

14. How often do you listen to programs on a Public Radio station? Public Radio stations are non-commercial and are partially funded by listener contributions.

	(CIRCLE ONE)
Never	1
Almost never	2
Sometimes	3
Very often	4
Don't know	V

15. On the average, about how many days a week do you read a daily paper? That is, one that is published Monday through Saturday. If "none," write in "0."

NUMBER OF DAYS: _____ _____

16. Do you usually read the *Sunday* edition of a newspaper?

Yes	1
No	2

17. Do you usually read a local *weekly* newspaper? (That is, one that is published only once a week.)

Yes	1
No	2
There is no such paper where I live	3

18. Which sections in the newspapers you read do you read frequently? Circle the codes of all sections listed below that you read. If you don't read any newspapers, circle this code ⑨ and skip to Q.19.

World news	1	Social News	1
National news	2	Entertainment	2
Local news	3	Comics	3
Editorial pages	4	Personal advice	4
Gardening	5	Sports	5
Travel	6	Business	6
Cooking	7	Real estate	7
Advertising	8		

19. Approximately how many books have you read in the past year? Do not include books that you have read only in connection with school or work requirements. Try to give us an average number rather than a range. If "none," write in "0" and skip to Q.21.

NUMBER OF BOOKS: _____

20. Which of the following types of books do you read most frequently? Circle the codes of all types that apply.

		(CIRCLE ALL THAT APPLY)
FICTION	Mysteries	1
	Science fiction	2
	Historical novels	3
	Other fiction	4
NON-FICTION	Biography or autobiography	5
	Psychology, self-help	6
	Philosophy, religion	7
	"How to" books	8
OTHER NON-FICTION	Poetry	0
	Drama (plays)	1
	Humor	2
	Travel	3
	Other (SPECIFY): _____	0

21. And about how many times in the past year have you gone to the *movies*? Please give us an average number rather than a range.

NUMBER OF TIMES: _____

22. What kinds of movies do you most frequently attend? Circle the codes of all that apply.

	(CIRCLE ALL THAT APPLY)
Love and romance	1
Comedies	2
Westerns	3
Science fiction or supernatural	4
Horror	5
Religious	6
Musicals, opera or dance	7
Biographies	8
Children's movies	9

	(CIRCLE ALL THAT APPLY)
Crime or spy thrillers	0
Documentaries	1
Historical or adventure films	2
Disaster films	3
Other	0
Never attend movies	9

23. In the list of magazines below, please circle the codes of those that you read regularly. Even if you usually only glance through a magazine, if you do so almost every issue, that counts as "read regularly."

	CIRCLE IF READ REGULARLY		*CIRCLE IF READ REGULARLY*
American Home	1	Ladies Home Journal	29
Apartment Life	2	Mademoiselle	30
Argosy	3	McCall's	31
Baby Talk	4	Mechanix Illustrated	32
Better Homes &		Modern Romances	33
Gardens	5	Modern Screen	34
Black Enterprise	6	Money	35
Business Week	7	Moneysworth	36
Car and Driver	8	Mother's Manual	37
Cosmopolitan	9	Motor Trend	38
Ebony	10	Motorboating and	
Esquire	11	Sailing	39
Essence	12	Ms.	40
Family Circle	13	National Geographic	41
Field and Stream	14	National Lampoon	42
Flying	15	Nation's Business	43
Forbes	16	Natural History	44
Fortune	17	Newsweek	45
Glamour	18	New Times	46
Golf	19	New Yorker	47
Golf Digest	20	Outdoor Life	48
Good Housekeeping	21	Parent's Magazine	49
Gourmet	22	Penthouse	50
Guns and Ammo	23	People	51
Harper's	24	Photoplay	52
Hot Rod	25	Playboy	53
House Beautiful	26	Popular Mechanics	54
House and Garden	27	Popular Photography	55
Jet	28	Popular Science	56

	CIRCLE IF READ REGULARLY		CIRCLE IF READ REGULARLY
Psychology Today	57	*Sunday Newspaper*	
Reader's Digest	58	*Supplements*	
Redbook	59	Family Weekly	78
Road and Track	60	N.Y. Times Sunday	
Rolling Stone	61	Magazine	79
Scientific American	62	Parade	80
Smithsonian	63	Sunday	81
Sport	64	Tuesday at Home	82
Sports Afield	65	*National Newspapers*	
Sports Illustrated	66	Barron's	83
Tennis	67	Wall Street Journal	84
Time	68	None read regularly	0
Travel and Leisure	69		
True	70		
True Story	71		
TV Guide	72		
US	73		
U.S. News and World Report	74		
Vogue	75		
Woman's Day	76		
Yachting	77		

24.   Are you a male or a female?

(CIRCLE ONE)

Male	1
Female	2

25.   How old are you?

_____ YEARS

26.   What category best describes the level of your formal education?

(CIRCLE ONE)

Some grammer school	1
Grammer school completed	2

	(CIRCLE ONE)
Some high school or trade school	3
High school or trade school completed	4
Some college	5
College completed	6
Some graduate study	7
Graduate degree	8

27. Which one of the following best describes your current situation?

	(CIRCLE ONE)	
	Employed — full time	1
ANSWER	Employed — part time (less than 30 hours weekly)	2
Q.28	Temporarily unemployed	3
	Retired	4
	A student	5
GO TO Q.29 OF THIS BLUE SECTION	A homemaker	6

28. Which of the categories listed below includes your occupation? If you are temporarily unemployed or retired, indicate your *former* occupation. Here are some examples for each major occupation category.

	(CIRCLE ONE)
Sales or clerical (secretary, clerk, bookkeeper, bank teller, salesperson)	1
Professional or technical (doctor, lawyer, engineer, scientist, teacher, clergy, registered nurse)	2
Operatives (operate some kind of machinery, such as a truck/ cab driver, welder, textile weaver, mine worker, parking attendant)	3
Laborers (farm worker, longshoreman, warehouse worker)	4
Manager, official, proprietor (executive, store manager/owner, farm manager/owner, department manager)	5
Craftsmen, foremen (carpenter, electrician, radio/TV repairman, mechanic, baker, factory foreman)	6
Service worker (barber, beautician, police officer, practical nurse, stewardess, cook)	7

If you're not sure which group you're in, write in your occupation below and we will classify it.

Occupation: _____   Kind of Industry: _____

29. Which of the following groups do you consider yourself a member of?

	(CIRCLE ONE)
American Indian	1
Black	2
Oriental	3
Spanish (such as: Central or South American, Cuban, Chicano, Mexican, Mexican-American, Puerto Rican, other Spanish)	4
White	5
Other (EXPLAIN) _____	0

30. Are you:

	(CIRCLE ONE)
Single,	1
Married,	2
Divorced, separated or	3
Widowed?	4

SEGMENT #: _____ D.U. # _____

NATIONAL ANALYSTS   Study #1-923
A Division of Booz, Allen & Hamilton Inc.   Fall, 1977

SPECIAL INTERESTS STUDY

PART 5

WRITE YOUR NAME HERE: _____

INSTRUCTIONS FOR COMPLETING PART 5

This part of the questionnaire contains questions mostly about Public Television. By Public Television we mean stations which have no commercials for products or services, such as those shown on commercial television. We would like to know how often you watch a Public TV station and what you think about Public TV in general. There is also a question about commercial television, that is, the national networks (ABC, CBS and NBC).

(NOW PLEASE TURN THE PAGE AND BEGIN.)

NATIONAL ANALYSTS   Study #1-923
A Division of Booz, Allen & Hamilton Inc.   Fall, 1977

SPECIAL INTERESTS STUDY
PART 5

The following questions are primarily about Public Television. Even if
you have never watched Public Television, try to answer the questions as
best as you can.

1.   Is there a Public Television station in your area?

                              (CIRCLE ONE)

Yes	1
No	2

2.   How often do you usually watch programs on *Public Television*?

                              (CIRCLE ONE)

Every day	1
5 or 6 times a week	2
3 or 4 times a week	3
1 or 2 times a week	4
Once or twice a month	5
Few times a year	6
Once a year	7
Never	8
Don't know	V

3.   During what time of the day do you *usually* watch programs on a
      Public TV station?

                              (CIRCLE ONE)

Morning (7 A.M. to 12 Noon)	1
Afternoon (12 Noon to 4 P.M.)	2
Early evening (4 P.M. to 7 P.M.)	3
Evening (7 P.M. to 11 P.M.)	4
Late at night (11 P.M. or later)	5

(CIRCLE ONE)

Never watch	6
Don't know	V

4. Have you ever supported your local Public TV station with a donation?

Yes	1
No	2

5. As you know, Public Television currently has no commercial messages during programs. Consequently, funds for the operation of Public TV must come from other sources. The following is a list of some possible sources of funding for Public Television. Among these, what would you like to see as the major source of funding for Public TV? Circle the *one* code that best represents your answer.

	(CIRCLE ONE)
Use of Federal taxes to fund Public TV	1
State government funding of Public TV	2
Local community funds for Public TV	3
Television set tax – a tax placed on each new TV set purchased Revenue from this tax would be used to support Public TV	4
National networks taxed – commercial television networks would be taxed and these taxes would support Public TV	5
Commercial time sold *between* Public TV programs to support Public TV	6
Income tax checkoff – every individual would be given an option to designate a small portion of their income tax payment to be used for the support of Public TV	7

6. There are many different views about what types of programs Public TV should offer. The list below gives several alternatives. How interested would you be in having Public Television offer more of each of the types of programs listed below? Circle the code indicating your degree of interest in each of the program types.

	Not at All Interested	Not Very Interested	Somewhat Interested	Very Interested
Cultural programs (i.e., drama, opera, art, etc.)	1	2	3	4
Programs similar to those on commercial TV	1	2	3	4
Music only programs	1	2	3	4
Programs appealing to certain kinds of people (i.e., women, blacks, Spanish-speaking, older people, etc.)	1	2	3	4
Programs about local events and issues	1	2	3	4
News programs	1	2	3	4
Programs about special interests (i.e., home gardening, tennis, the stock market, etc.)	1	2	3	4
Educational programs	1	2	3	4
Children's programs	1	2	3	4

7. This question is about *commercial television*, such as the national networks (ABC, CBS and NBC). Please think only about commercial television when answering this question.

    Below is a list of some "opposites." Please read each pair quickly and circle a number someplace between them to indicate where you think it belongs to best describe *commercial television*. Just give us your off-hand impressions.

    For example:

| Pleasant | ⑥ | 5 | 4 | 3 | 2 | 1 | Unpleasant |

    If you feel that commercial television is very pleasant you would circle the "6," which is closest to the word pleasant — as shown in the example. If you feel that commercial television is just slightly more pleasant than unpleasant, you would circle the "4."

Don't spend a lot of time worrying about where to put your answer. Just give us your general, off-hand impression of where you think *commercial TV* belongs for each pair below.

ANSWER FOR COMMERCIAL TV ONLY

Exciting	6	5	4	3	2	1	Dull
In good taste	6	5	4	3	2	1	In bad taste
Important	6	5	4	3	2	1	Unimportant
Generally bad	6	5	4	3	2	1	Generally excellent
Lots of variety	6	5	4	3	2	1	All the same
Upsetting	6	5	4	3	2	1	Relaxing
Interesting	6	5	4	3	2	1	Uninteresting
Wonderful	6	5	4	3	2	1	Terrible
Nobody cares much	6	5	4	3	2	1	On everyone's mind
For me	6	5	4	3	2	1	Not for me
Too "simple minded"	6	5	4	3	2	1	Too "highbrow"
Getting worse	6	5	4	3	2	1	Getting better
Stays the same	6	5	4	3	2	1	Keeps changing
Informative	6	5	4	3	2	1	Not informative
Lots of fun	6	5	4	3	2	1	Not much fun
Serious	6	5	4	3	2	1	Playful
Imaginative	6	5	4	3	2	1	No imagination
Educational	6	5	4	3	2	1	Not educational
Stimulating	6	5	4	3	2	1	Boring

8. Now, we would like you to answer the same questions, but this time think only about Public TV when reading each pair of opposites. Even if you don't watch Public TV, try to answer the questions as best you can.

Below is the list of "opposites." Please read each pair quickly and circle the code of a number someplace between them to indicate where you think it belongs to describe Public Television. Just give us your general, off-hand impression for each pair.

ANSWER FOR PUBLIC TV ONLY

Exciting	6	5	4	3	2	1	Dull
In good taste	6	5	4	3	2	1	In bad taste
Important	6	5	4	3	2	1	Unimportant
Generally bad	6	5	4	3	2	1	Generally excellent
Lots of variety	6	5	4	3	2	1	All the same
Upsetting	6	5	4	3	2	1	Relaxing
Interesting	6	5	4	3	2	1	Uninteresting
Wonderful	6	5	4	3	2	1	Terrible
Nobody cares much	6	5	4	3	2	1	On everyone's mind
For me	6	5	4	3	2	1	Not for me
Too "simple minded"	6	5	4	3	2	1	Too "highbrow"
Getting worse	6	5	4	3	2	1	Getting better
Stays the same	6	5	4	3	2	1	Keeps changing
Informative	6	5	4	3	2	1	Not informative
Lots of fun	6	5	4	3	2	1	Not much fun
Serious	6	5	4	3	2	1	Playful
Imaginative	6	5	4	3	2	1	No imagination
Educational	6	5	4	3	2	1	Not educational
Stimulating	6	5	4	3	2	1	Boring

SEGMENT #: _____ D.U. # _____

NATIONAL ANALYSTS   Study #1-923
A Division of Booz, Allen & Hamilton Inc.   Fall, 1977

SPECIAL INTEREST STUDY
PART 6

WRITE YOUR NAME HERE: _____

INSTRUCTIONS FOR COMPLETING PART 6

In this part of the questionnaire we will describe some ideas for new television programs. We would then like you to tell us how you feel about these ideas.

Please turn the page and begin.

1. Below we have outlined a number of ideas for new television programs or series. We would like to know how interested you would be in watching these kinds of programs, based upon their descriptions.

   Please read each program description and then indicate your degree of interest in each by circling a number from 1 to 4 in the space provided. You may find it easier to rate each program if you look over all eight programs before rating the first one.

	Not at All Interested	Not Very Interested	Quite Interested	Extremely Interested

A. *"Just Plain Country"*

"Music City, U.S.A.," "City of ten thousand pickers," or "Music capital of the world" . . . call it what you might, Nashville, Tennessee, is the home of the Grand Ole Opry and a wealth of talent which has supplied the world with country music. This program takes advantage of this abundance of Nashville talent to appeal to television's blue collar viewers whose language is

	Not at All Interested	*Not Very Interested*	*Quite Interested*	*Extremely Interested*
spoken in every country song . . . the fans who fill the auditoriums around the country when the bus carrying their favorite star pulls into town.	1	2	3	4

B. *"Mother's Little Network"*

Mother's Little Network (MLN) offers something unique — a comedy born, bred, and rooted in America. Posing as an up-and -coming family-owned broadcasting company, MLN hits the air every week with its own brand of video humor — a series of fast-paced sketches, animations, parodies and personalities, with a format owing nothing to anyone or anything, including the meaning of its title.	1	2	3	4

MLN restores a freshness and regularity to your TV viewing. All new punchlines! All new accents! All new breaches of regional and national standards of good taste!

C. *"Sportlight"*

Sportlight gives viewers — in a regular, weekly 90-minute format of live or edited coverage — the chance to see and follow a variety of first-rate competitive amateur athletic events not to be found elsewhere on American television.	1	2	3	4

On-air hosts are top journalists or well-known participants in the field, men and women who speak colorfully and incisively on the event and the issues that surround it, e.g., Bud Collins, Arthur Ashe, Donald Dell, Kem Prince, Judy Dixon, and others, who go into the back-

	Not at All Interested	Not Very Interested	Quite Interested	Extremely Interested
ground of each sport and, where appropriate for a home audience, give instructional tips.				

D. *"Your Retirement Dollar"*

	Not at All Interested	Not Very Interested	Quite Interested	Extremely Interested
Your Retirement Dollar is a series of 13 half-hour programs based on the syndicated newspaper column, "Your Retirement Dollar," by Peter Weaver, who serves as the program's host and chief expert.	1	2	3	4

The series covers a variety of topics of interest and concern to the elderly, and those approaching retirement, in the areas of family finances, buying habits, good values, safe types of investments, personal pension plans, money management on a reduced income, retirement job opportunities, etc. Two guest experts assist Mr. Weaver in further exploring given subject areas. The series contains on-location footage demonstrating many of the traps facing the elderly in the areas of nutrition, personal health, nursing homes, personal loans and legal aid.

E. *"Hollywood Television Theatre: Habit"*

	Not at All Interested	Not Very Interested	Quite Interested	Extremely Interested
Habit is an originally created serial for *Hollywood Television Theatre*. Based upon a true story, Habit explores the human condition from a uniquely sensitive view.	1	2	3	4

It is based on a profound social change which occured as a result of the precedent breaking Vatican Council II, and the individual

	Not at All Interested	Not Very Interested	Quite Interested	Extremely Interested

struggle and change that came to a number of extraordinary women who suggested they should receive a small stipend for teaching; should choose their own form of government; shift their energies from church-related to social, economic, intellectual and spiritual needs of the family of man; and choose their own clothing to wear when working outside the College of the Immaculate Heart.

An uproar ensued, and this series tells the story in personal terms by focusing on the emotional struggles of four of five individual nuns.

F. *"The Fertile Crescent"*

A 13 part series on the history and culture of the Near East, demonstrating the accuracy of the term "Cradle of Civilization" by examining the enormous cultural contributions of the Near East to Western Civilization.

	1	2	3	4

It was filmed at important archaeological sites and monuments, reconstructions, and sites of custom and ritual. Also shown is the art, much of it now preserved in national museums in the Near East and in the British Museum and the Louvre, and in such fabled cities of the Near East as Baghdad, Damascus, Cairo, Jerusalem. It is safe to say that viewers will see moving sights of glory that they have never before beheld.

	Not at All Interested	Not Very Interested	Quite Interested	Extremely Interested

G. *"What In The World"*

"What In The World" is a panel game show which entertains and educates by using the artifacts and treasures of the Smithsonian Institution (Museum) as its subject. The format is deceptively simple: engage two panels of three people each in a friendly, witty debate over the identity of an object from the Smithsonian.

	1	2	3	4

The basic object of the game is for one panel to stump the other by weaving curious but true descriptions and stories about the object — two not fittting and one fitting the object per round — so there is a pitting of wills, wit and intellect in the process.

H. *"Woman's Place"*

What does being a woman mean today? What are the special problems that our age of change thursts into women's lives? Considering the shifts in the patterns of women's lives attending their new awakening (with responses ranging from Radical Feminism to Total Womanhood), what is *Woman's Place* . . . as it was, as it is, as it may become?

	1	2	3	4

This series of 13 hour-long TV programs attempts to answer these and many other questions as it presents a picture of the multiple activities and the flexible strength to be found among women who come from many backgrounds and diverse views.

2. In the space below, please *rank* the eight television programs in the order in which you are interested in them. Write a "1" next to the program that you are most interested in, a "2" next to the program that you are next most interested in and so on, until you have ranked all eight programs.

TELEVISION PROGRAMS	RANK (1 to 8)
Just Plain Country	____
Mother's Little Network	____
Sportlight	____
Your Retirement Dollar	____
Hollywood Television Theatre: Habit	____
The Fertile Crescent	____
What In The World	____
Woman's Place	____

SEGMENT # _____ D.U. # _____

NATIONAL ANALYSTS   Study #1-923
A Division of Booz, Allen & Hamilton Inc.   Fall, 1977

SPECIAL INTERESTS STUDY

PART 7

RESPONDENT'S NAME: _____

TO THE INTERVIEWER: THIS PART OF THE QUESTIONNAIRE
MUST BE ADMINISTERED BY YOU TO EITHER THE MALE OR
FEMALE HEAD OF HOUSEHOLD.

These next few questions are used to classify the answers of people in your
household with those of similar households.

1. How many television sets do you have in your home that are usually
    in working order?

                                              NUMBER OF WORKING
                 _____   TELEVISION SETS

2. Of the (*# IN Q.1*) television sets you have, how many are *color* sets?

                                              NUMBER OF COLOR
                 _____   TELEVISION SETS

3. Do you subscribe to *cable television*?

Yes	1
No	2
Not available in my area	3

The next few questions are about the channels that you receive on your television set. If you have more than one television set in your home, answer the questions for the set that is in the *best* working order and has the best reception.

4.   What channel numbers can you receive on your television set? First tell me the numbers of the channels for each of the major networks, such as ABC, NBC, CBS, then any Public TV channel numbers, and finally the UHF channels that you receive. RECORD CHANNEL NUMBERS IN APPROPRIATE SPACES UNDER COLUMN LABELED Q.4.

5.   For each major network channel number you gave me, tell me whether that channel represents the ABC, CBS, or NBC network. You may want to refer to a *TV Guide*, the Sunday newspaper TV bulletin, or a daily newspaper for the answers to this question.

    First, what network is channel (NAME FIRST NUMBER LISTED UNDER Q.4 – MAJOR NETWORKS)? RECORD NETWORK (ABC, CBS, NBC) UNDER COLUMN LABELED Q.5.

    REPEAT QUESTION FOR EACH CHANNEL LISTED FOR MAJOR NETWORKS.

6.   IF NO PUBLIC TV CHANNELS LISTED IN Q.4, SKIP TO Q.7. OTHERWISE, CONTINUE.

    Now for each of the Public TV channel numbers you gave me, please tell me what the call letters of that station are. What are the call letters of channel (NAME FIRST NUMBER LISTED UNDER Q.4 – PUBLIC TV CHANNELS)? RECORD CALL LETTERS UNDER COLUMN LABELED Q.6.

    REPEAT QUESTION FOR EACH CHANNEL LISTED FOR PUBLIC TV.

7.   How good is the reception you get at your home for each of the channels you listed? How about channel (*NAME FIRST CHANNEL NUMBER IN Q.4*) – is the reception you get very poor, poor, fair, good, or very good? REPEAT QUESTION FOR EACH CHANNEL LISTED IN Q.4 AND RECORD ANSWER FOR EACH CHANNEL UNDER THE COLUMN LABELED Q.7.

	Q.4 TV Channels Received	Q.5 Network (ABC, CBS, NBC)	Q.6 Public TV Call Letters	Q.7 Reception				
				Very Poor	Poor	Fair	Good	Very Good
Major Networks			▓	1	2	3	4	5
			▓	1	2	3	4	5
			▓	1	2	3	4	5
			▓	1	2	3	4	5
Public TV Channels		▓		1	2	3	4	5
		▓		1	2	3	4	5
		▓		1	2	3	4	5
UHF Channels		▓	▓	1	2	3	4	5
		▓	▓	1	2	3	4	5
		▓	▓	1	2	3	4	5
		▓	▓	1	2	3	4	5
		▓	▓	1	2	3	4	5

8. LOOK AT SCREENING FORM. IF NO CHILDREN UNDER AGE 12, SKIP TO Q.9 — OTHERWISE, CONTINUE. On the average, approximately how many hours per week do each of your children, ages 12 or under, watch programs on Public Television? Just tell me the first name of each of your children age 12 or under, that child's age, and the average number of hours per week that he or she watches Public Television.

First Name of Child 12 Years or Under	Child's Age	Average Number of Hours Per Week Watches Public TV
_____	_____	_____
_____	_____	_____
_____	_____	_____
_____	_____	_____
_____	_____	_____

9. Finally, which of these categories includes what your total family income will be for 1977, before taxes and other deductions? Will it be:

READ	*(CIRCLE ONE)*
Under $5,000,	1
$5,000 to $7,999,	2
$8,000 to $9,999,	3
$10,000 to $12,499,	4
$12,500 to $14,999,	5
$15,000 to $17,499,	6
$17,500 to $19,999,	7
$20,000 to $24,999, or	8
$25,000 or more?	9

Appendix B

SAMPLING FRAME

The sample design can be described as a customized multistage stratified area probability sample encompassing the universe of all private households in the coterminous United States.

National Analysts' basic sample design consists of three levels of stratification. This was accomplished by grouping all housing units in the United States, as given in the 1970 Census of population and housing and the corrections therein, into a two-way model. This stratification contains two levels—type of population (urbanization) and geographic divisions. Three types of population were defined, and nine geographic divisions. The third level of stratification was carried out within each of the 3 x 9 strata cells formed by the two-way model.

In setting up the strata, the 3103 counties and independent cities which comprise the total land area of the United States were then divided into two parts, central cities and the rest of the metropolitan area. The nonmetropolitan population was put into a third part. The three types of populations (zones) follow definitions from the 1970 Census of population and housing:

Zone I. The area comprised of the central city (or cities) in metropolitan areas (a central city is a city named in the metropolitan area title).

Zone II. The suburban area in standard metropolitan statistical areas (SMSA) outside Zone I (central city or cities).

Zone III. Nonmetropolitan areas.

The level of stratification based on Census geographic divisions and regions was accomplished by classifying every private household in the coterminous United States into one of the 9 Census divisions. Within each division, parts of the metropolitan areas, central cities, or "suburbia" were ordered geographically, and within each state, groups of state economic areas were ordered. This array provided the sampling frame such that 114 strata of approximately equal size could be identified by legal or census boundaries. The average stratum size is approximately 600,000 housing units.

Stratification and Selection
of the Metropolitan Primary Sampling Units

Those parts of metropolitan areas defined as central cities were formed into 38 strata. This was accomplished by grouping together within strata central cities which are alike in either size or geographical proximity. Some strata contain only one central city.

Primary sampling units (central cities) were given measures of size based on the 1970 Census housing counts. One city sampling unit was selected from each stratum with the chance of selection of any city unit being proportional to its 1970 housing units.

Random numbers were used to select a number between "one" and the stratum number of housing units. This gives each number between "one" and the stratum total number of housing units an equal chance of being selected. This same procedure was followed for each stratum. The probability of any central city within the stratum being selected is the quotient of its 1970 housing units and the total of the 1970 housing units within the strata. In the stratum where Worcester, Massachusetts, was selected, for example, the size of the city of Worcester is 58,589 housing units. The stratum size is 574,259 housing units. If we divide this into 58,589, the result is a probability of selection of .10202.

In Zone II, the remaining portions of each of the 243 metropolitan areas ("Suburbia"—that area outside of central cities) were grouped into 39 strata. This grouping was accomplished by placing in the same strata counties in the same geographic area. A primary sampling unit in Zone II is a metropolitan county, or that part of a metropolitan county less the central city if it contains only one county. The size of the primary sampling unit is the number of 1970 housing units in the county, or the county less the central city if it contains only one county. The size of each of the 39 strata is the sum of the housing units of all the primary sampling units it contains. Again, random numbers were used to select one primary sampling unit from each stratum.

Stratification and Selection
of the Nonmetropolitan Areas

In Zone III, the counties of the United States defined as nonmetropolitan in the 1970 Census were grouped into strata. State economic areas were used to form these 37 strata.

A primary sampling unit in Zone III is one or more counties. The reason for having more than one county in some primary sampling units is that a minimum county size of 10,000 housing units was established for each primary sampling unit. This was done for two reasons. First, we believe that any county of less than 10,000 housing units is quite homogeneous. Second, this sampling frame must "last" for ten years, and any primary sampling unit with less than 10,000 housing units would be completely surveyed before the ten years were up. All counties with less than 10,000 1970 housing units were combined with an adjacent county to form a primary sampling unit of two or more counties. This was done before any selection of primary sampling units was made.

The size of each of the 37 strata is the total of all the counties it contains. Random numbers were used to select 37 primary sampling units proportional to the 1970 housing units in the primary sampling unit.

Appendix C

SAMPLE COMPLETION RATES

Stage 1: Screening

Total dwelling units (DU's) assigned		7857
Vacant DU's	542	
Occupied DU's		7315
Total non-respondents		3174
Refused screening	1159	
Not at home	1223	
Other	467	
Unknown	325	
Household screened		4141
Eligible for interview	2061	
No T.V. set	179	
No children*	1901	

First stage completion rate: 4141/7315 = 56.6%

Stage 2: Interviewing

	Number Eligible in Household				
	1	2	3	4	Total
Number of household eligible	405	806	459	391	2061
Results of call					
Refused	98	218	99	66	481
Not together at same time	–	93	125	129	347
Other	25	46	14	14	99
Interviewed	281	449	221	182	1133
Stage 2 Completion Rate	69.4%	55.7%	48.1%	46.5%	55.0%

*Households with children were systematically oversampled. These 1901 households were systematically eliminated as a part of that process.

308

Appendix D

INTEREST FACTORS

Factor 1: Comprehensive News and Information (22%)*	Loadings
National Economy	.79
National Unemployment	.77
Tax Laws	.76
Legal Processes in U.S. Courts	.75
State Issues	.73
Morality in Politics	.72
Sources and Uses of Energy	.72
Social Security System	.70
Preventive Medicine	.69
Labor Unions in the U.S.	.67
Welfare System	.67
Wills and Estate Planning	.66
How and When to Use a Lawyer	.65
Nuclear Energy	.63
Managing Money (finances, taxes, etc.)	.62
Mental Illness and Its Treatment	.62
Conflict in the Middle East	.61
Foreign Policy	.61
Consumerism	.60
Causes and Prevention of Crime	.60
Community Issues	.60
Local History	.59
Balance of Trade	.59
Election Campaigns (funding, organizing, supporting)	.59
Health and Nutrition	.58
Conservation/Ecology	.57
Problems of Drug Abuse	.55
Aging and Retirement	.55
Capital Punishment of Criminals	.55
Real Estate Investment	.55
Education and Schools	.54
Psychology	.53
Medical Sciences (anatomy, physiology, etc.)	.51
Managing and Business	.50

*Percentage of total variance of entire set of 139 interest items accounted for by factor.

Rights of Minority Groups	.47
Arms Race	.47
The Stock Market	.47
Geology	.47
Advertising and Marketing	.46
Social Etiquette	.46
Divorce in the U.S.	.44
Career Guidance	.44
Abortion vs. Right to Life Issue	.41
Natural History (birds, fish, wildlife, etc.)	.41
Women's Rights/Roles	.40
Railroads	.39
Child Rearing Methods	.39
Mathematics	.39
Sexual Attitudes and Behavior	.39
Maintenance and Repair of the Home	.37
Space Travel	.37
Sex Education	.35

Factor 2: Athletic Activities—Participant (9%)	*Loadings*
Snow Skiing	.75
Water Skiing	.73
Tennis	.69
Volleyball	.69
Squash/Handball	.68
Soccer	.68
Jogging	.66
Table Tennis/Ping Pong	.65
Swimming	.61
Ice Skating	.59
Hiking	.59
Bicycling	.59
Judo/Karate	.57
Backpacking	.56
Motorcycles	.55
Boating (rowing, canoeing, sailing, etc.)	.52
Camping	.48
Photography	.45
Hockey	.44
Woodworking	.44
Modern Dance	.42
Foreign Languages	.40
Billiards/Pool	.39
Model Building	.38
Playing a Musical Instrument	.37
Movies (cinema)	.36
Bowling	.36

Factor 3: Household Activities and Management (6%)   *Loadings*

Housecleaning	.75
Meal Preparation	.69
Sewing (making clothes, drapes, etc.)	.69
Needlework (needlepoint, knitting, etc.)	.67
Household Management	.66
Indoor Plants	.64
Interior Decorating	.62
Shopping	.60
Gourmet Cooking	.51
Ceramics/Pottery	.46
Gardening	.41
Child Rearing Methods	.37
Health and Nutrition	.36
Child Related Activities (PTA, Scouts, etc.)	.35

Factor 4: Classical Arts (3%)   *Loadings*

Opera	.74
Classical Music	.72
Ballet	.63
Live Theater (plays, musicals, etc.)	.62
Literature	.56
Paintings	.53
Sculpture	.53
Poetry	.53
Local Cultural Activities	.51
Playing a Musical Instrument	.39

Factor 5: Reaping Nature's Products (2%)   *Loadings*

Fishing	.62
Hunting	.51
Agriculture and Farming	.51
Gardening	.51
Natural History (birds, fish, wildlife, etc.)	.42
Camping	.37

Factor 6: Professional Sports (2%)   *Loadings*

Baseball	.75
Basketball	.74
Football	.67
Boxing	.54
Golf	.39
Hockey	.37

Factor 7: Science and Engineering (2%)   *Loadings*

Chemistry	.58
Electronics	.47
Medical Sciences (anatomy, physiology, etc.)	.46
Engineering	.46
Geology	.43
Mathematics	.39
Foreign Language	.36

Factor 8: Popular Entertainment (2%)   *Loadings*

Visiting Friends	.56
Radio	.55
Travel/Sightseeing	.54
Popular Music (jazz, folk, rock, country, etc.)	.53
Dining Out	.52
Movies (cinema)	.51
Driving/Motoring	.50
Television	.43
Entertainment at Home	.39

Factor 9: Religion (1%)   *Loadings*

Religious Organization Activities	.73
Religion	.71

Factor 10: Popular Social Issues (1%)   *Loadings*

Sex Education	.70
Sexual Attitudes and Behavior	.67
Rights of Minority Groups	.43
The Occult	.41
Women's Rights/Roles	.39
Social Etiquette	.38

Factor 11: Indoor Games (1%)   *Loadings*

Board Games (Backgammon, Scrabble, Monopoly, etc.)	.66
Crossword/Jigsaw Puzzles	.59
Chess/Checkers	.53
Playing Cards (rummy, bridge, etc.)	.50
Party Games (Charades, Password, etc.)	.49
Coin or Stamp Collecting	.37

Factor 12: Community Activities (1%)   *Loadings*

Community Social Functions	.55
Charities and Civic Associations	.53
Local Cultural Activities	.42
Community Issues	.35

Factor 13: Investments (1%)   *Loadings*

Real Estate Investment	.48
Managing and Business	.42
The Stock Market	.39

Factor 14: International Affairs (1%)   *Loadings*

Arms Race	.55
Balance of Trade	.46
Conflict in the Middle East	.39

Factor 15: Camping Out (1%)   *Loadings*

Camping	.44
Backpacking	.44
Hiking	.38
Boating (rowing, canoeing, sailing, etc.)	.37

Factor 16: Crime and Society (1%)   *Loadings*

Capital Punishment of Criminals	.51
Abortion vs. Right to Life Issue	.50
Causes and Prevention of Crime	.48
Problems of Drug Abuse	.41
Career Guidance	.39

Factor 17: Mechanical Activities (1%)   *Loadings*

Auto Repair	.67
Auto Racing	.62
Model Building (cars, ships, etc.)	.55
Engineering	.47
Electronics	.46
Motorcycles	.45
Woodworking	.44
Hunting	.42
CB Radio	.41
Billiards/Pool	.41
Boxing	.38
Judo/Karate	.35

Factor 18: Contemporary Dancing (1%)   *Loadings*

Modern Dance	.48
Dancing (discotheque, ballroom, etc.)	.47

Appendix E

NEEDS FACTORS

Factor 1: Socially Stimulating (30%) *	*Loadings*
To find that my ideas are often shared by others	.61
To be interesting and stimulating to other people	.58
To do things which I am familiar with	.56
To feel good about life in general	.56
To meet new people	.55
To participate in discussion with my friends	.54
To be physically active	.54
To have interesting experiences which I can tell others about	.52
To spend time with friends	.52
To feel I am important to other people	.51
To experience again events and places I enjoyed in the past	.49
To have a sense of direction and purpose in life	.44
To have peace of mind	.42
To help other people	.41

Factor 2: Status Enhancement (7%)	*Loadings*
To impress people	.71
To feel more important than I really am	.63
To have more influence on other people	.64
To be like other people	.60
To compete against others	.58
To be more of a leader	.44
To be more like people I respect	.44
To feel more physically attractive	.44
To get away from the pressures and responsibilities of my home life	.43
To help me imagine other ways of living my life	.40
To know that other people have the same problems I have	.37
To feel I am important to other people	.37

*Percentage of total variance of entire set of 59 need items accounted for by factor.

Factor 3: Unique/Creative Accomplishment (4%)   *Loadings*

To really excel in some area of my life	.55
To be more of a leader	.54
To feel unique, different from other people	.52
To compete against others	.50
To feel creative	.49
To do unique things	.49
To get a feeling of adventure and excitement	.46
To feel independent, free from the authority of others	.41
To do things which are different from what I'm used to	.41
To further improve my skills and abilities	.38

Factor 4: Escape from Problems (3%)   *Loadings*

To get away from the pressures and responsibilities of my home life	.57
To get away from the pressures of work	.56
To relax	.53
To forget my problems for a while	.53
To escape from the reality of everyday life	.52
To be alone with my thoughts	.48
To be more in control of my own life	.39
To feel independent, free from the authority of others	.38
To get a better idea of how I want to live my life when I get older	.36

Factor 5: Family Ties (3%)   *Loadings*

To feel closer to my family	.77
To spend time with my family	.77
To help develop strong family ties	.76
To help other people	.35

Factor 6: Understanding Others (2%)   *Loadings*

To understand how other people think	.69
To better understand why people behave the way they do	.67
To get the most out of the daily experiences that life has to offer	.42
To know that other people have the same problems I have	.38
To participate in discussion with my friends	.38
To be interesting and stimulating to other people	.36

Factor 7: Greater Self-Acceptance (2%)   *Loadings*

To lift my spirits	.68
To understand myself better	.64
To overcome loneliness	.58
To feel I am using my time in the best way possible	.57
To develop good taste	.50
To be more like people I respect	.48
To have peace of mind	.40
To feel good about life in general	.36
To help other people	.36

Factor 8: Escape from Boredom (2%)   *Loadings*

To be entertained	.60
To kill time	.56
To escape from the reality of everyday life	.37
To experience again events and places I enjoyed in the past	.35

Factor 9: Intellectual Stimulation and Growth (2%)   *Loadings*

To find out more about how things work	.69
To learn new thoughts and ideas	.64
To learn about new things to do	.51
To learn about new places to see	.50
To learn more about what is going on in the world	.50
To help me imagine other ways of living my life	.42
To free myself from traditional roles	.42
To be more in control of my own life	.41
To further improve my skills and abilities	.41
To get a better idea of how I want to live my life when I get older	.35
To do unique things	.35
To feel creative	.35

Appendix F

TELEVISION PROGRAM VIEWING

TABLE F.1 Average Number of Times Viewed by Interest Segment for Adventure Programs

	Entire Population	Adult Male Concentration				Adult Female Concentration			Youth Concentration			Mixed			
		Mechanics and Outdoor Life	Money and Nature's Products	Family and Community Centered	Elderly Concerns	Arts and Cultural Activities	Home and Community Centered	Family Integrated Activities	Competitive Sports and Science/Engineering	Athletic and Social Activities	Indoor Games and Social Activities	News and Information	Detached	Cosmopolitan Self-Enrichment	Highly Diversified
Total	4.14	5.15	4.32	3.80	4.59	2.33	3.77	4.41	4.52	3.73	6.00	4.21	3.52	1.73	6.77
The Bionic Woman	.60	.91	.46	.58	.56	.25	.58	.61	.60	.64	1.06	.33	.63	.22	1.08
The Life and Times of Grizzly Adams	.91	1.13	1.56	1.04	1.40	.47	.83	.96	.66	.39	.54	1.24	.74	.36	1.23
Nancy Drew/Hardy Boys Mystery Show	.55	.65	.20	.27	.35	.28	.56	.75	.78	1.01	1.69	.47	.26	.30	.81
Six Million Dollar Man	.84	1.15	.60	.65	.69	.66	.76	.77	1.06	.92	1.62	.73	.86	.31	1.40
The Wonderful World of Disney	1.00	1.14	1.05	.97	1.20	.58	.83	1.21	1.21	.70	.96	1.02	.77	.47	1.76
Young Dan'l Boone	.24	.17	.44	.30	.38	.09	.21	.12	.20	.07	.14	.41	.25	.08	.49

TABLE F.2 Average Number of Times Viewed by Interest Segment for Children's Programs

	Adult Male Concentration						Adult Female Concentration		Youth Concentration				Mixed		
	Entire Population	Mechanics and Outdoor Life	Money and Nature's Products	Family and Community Centered	Elderly Concerns	Arts and Cultural Activities	Home and Community Centered	Family Integrated Activities	Competitive Sports and Science/Engineering	Athletic and Social Activities	Indoor Games and Social Activities	News and Information	Detached	Cosmopolitan Self-Enrichment	Highly Diversified
Total	1.36	1.12	.65	.62	.46	.62	1.51	3.04	1.62	1.64	1.80	1.10	.96	1.40	2.24
Captain Kangaroo	.21	.09	.17	.09	.15	.04	.35	.65	.10	.26	.12	.10	.16	.14	.29
Captain Noah	.01	.01	.01	–	–	.01	–	.01	–	–	.05	–	–	.01	.04
Children's Cartoons	.73	.91	.43	.44	.26	.37	.68	.88	1.25	.87	1.41	.75	.65	.42	1.32
Electric Company	.13	.06	.01	.03	.01	.07	.15	.44	.09	.16	.07	.10	.05	.24	.19
Mister Rogers	.07	–	–	.01	–	.01	.08	.36	.07	.13	.02	–	.02	.15	.09
Sesame Street	.21	.04	.04	.05	.03	.12	.25	.70	.10	.23	.13	.16	.09	.44	.31

319

TABLE F.3 Average Number of Times Viewed by Interest Segment for Crime Drama Programs

	Adult Male Concentration				Adult Female Concentration				Youth Concentration				Mixed		
	Entire Population	Mechanics and Outdoor Life	Money and Nature's Products	Family and Community Centered	Elderly Concerns	Arts and Cultural Activities	Home and Community Centered	Family Integrated Activities	Competitive Sports and Science/Engineering	Athletic and Social Activities	Indoor Games and Social Activities	News and Information	Detached	Cosmopolitan Self-Enrichment	Highly Diversified
Total	7.70	8.39	8.41	6.51	8.39	6.23	7.40	7.73	8.11	5.84	10.68	9.11	7.46	3.93	10.74
Baretta	.80	.92	.58	.65	.76	.51	.91	.88	1.18	.82	1.04	.79	.64	.44	1.22
Barnaby Jones	.66	.53	1.19	.63	.94	.69	.65	.50	.36	.32	.72	.97	.77	.28	.75
Charlie's Angels	1.03	1.16	1.00	.91	.79	.78	1.03	1.10	1.42	1.03	2.05	.96	.84	.42	1.46
Chips	.49	.82	.33	.32	.41	.37	.25	.52	.57	.75	.71	.28	.45	.27	.87
Hawaii Five-O	.68	.65	1.22	.57	1.01	.62	.50	.48	.38	.33	.72	1.07	.80	.35	.89
Kojak	.77	.89	1.05	.65	.96	.59	.74	.58	.65	.35	.68	.99	.89	.61	1.03
Police Woman	.60	.66	.86	.67	.75	.41	.49	.44	.50	.43	.79	.78	.62	.14	1.06
Quincy	.62	.63	.50	.40	.79	.56	.77	.95	.63	.15	.91	.82	.44	.25	.70
The Rockford Files	.65	.77	.67	.61	.97	.49	.55	.65	.77	.22	.84	.95	.52	.43	.66
Rosetti and Ryan	.23	.24	.15	.10	.14	.22	.22	.33	.18	.11	.27	.28	.21	.19	.44
Starsky & Hutch	.89	.91	.53	.80	.68	.65	.96	1.07	1.13	1.05	1.57	.87	.90	.36	1.30
Switch	.28	.22	.34	.19	.19	.34	.30	.24	.34	.28	.37	.35	.37	.17	.34

TABLE F.4 Average Number of Times Viewed by Interest Segment for Documentary Programs

| | Adult Male Concentration | | | | Adult Female Concentration | | | Youth Concentration | | | Mixed | | | |
	Entire Population	Mechanics and Outdoor Life	Money and Nature's Products	Family and Community Centered	Elderly Concerns	Arts and Cultural Activities	Home and Community Centered	Family Integrated Activities	Competitive Sports and Science/Engineering	Athletic and Social Activities	Indoor Games and Social Activities	News and Information	Detached	Cosmopolitan Self-Enrichment	Highly Diversified
Total	.34	.26	.44	.20	.30	.58	.31	.43	.32	.01	.15	.45	.20	.44	.43
Age of Uncertainty	.04	.01	–	–	.05	.10	–	.03	.10	–	.01	.11	.01	.06	.06
Last of the Wild	.20	.22	.39	.17	.16	.23	.21	.25	.14	–	.13	.28	.13	.18	.27
Nova	.10	.03	.05	.03	.09	.24	.09	.15	.08	.01	.01	.05	.06	.20	.10

TABLE F.5 Average Number of Times Viewed by Interest Segment for Drama Programs

Program	Adult Male Concentration				Adult Female Concentration				Youth Concentration				Mixed		
	Entire Population	Mechanics and Outdoor Life	Money and Nature's Products	Family and Community Centered	Elderly Concerns	Arts and Cultural Activities	Home and Community Centered	Family Integrated Activities	Competitive Sports and Science/Engineering	Athletic and Social Activities	Indoor Games and Social Activities	News and Information	Detached	Cosmopolitan Self-Enrichment	Highly Diversified
Total	4.42	3.60	4.83	3.98	5.91	3.58	5.01	5.71	3.20	3.85	4.64	5.55	3.65	2.92	5.25
Big Hawaii	.21	.32	.23	.15	.34	.09	.19	.11	.10	.11	.24	.40	.29	.05	.33
Family	.70	.41	.32	.45	.77	.63	.87	1.07	.65	1.03	1.11	.99	.49	.51	.74
The Fitzpatricks	.27	.25	.26	.05	.24	.18	.20	.34	.38	.38	.71	.23	.35	.13	.28
Little House on the Prairie	1.22	1.10	1.26	1.31	2.03	.93	1.38	1.72	.64	1.10	1.09	1.53	.93	.46	1.40
Lou Grant	.50	.42	.62	.46	.30	.55	.48	.47	.67	.35	.31	.58	.31	.82	.53
Oregon Trail	.26	.30	.51	.27	.36	.14	.26	.25	.21	.06	.12	.47	.13	.09	.43
Rafferty	.29	.26	.31	.09	.14	.30	.39	.56	.23	.12	.38	.19	.17	.39	.39
The Waltons	.98	.54	1.30	1.20	1.73	.78	1.25	1.19	.32	.70	.67	1.16	.99	.47	1.15

TABLE F.6 Average Number of Times Viewed by Interest Segment for Game Shows

	Entire Population	Adult Male Concentration			Adult Female Concentration				Youth Concentration				Mixed		
		Mechanics and Outdoor Life	Money and Nature's Products	Family and Community Centered	Elderly Concerns	Arts and Cultural Activities	Home and Community Centered	Family Integrated Activities	Competitive Sports and Science/Engineering	Athletic and Social Activities	Indoor Games and Social Activities	News and Information	Detached	Cosmopolitan Self-Enrichment	Highly Diversified
Total	3.56	2.14	2.45	2.20	6.03	3.16	4.29	4.37	3.66	2.07	5.91	5.03	2.82	1.71	4.39
Family Feud	.53	.23	.20	.32	.66	.53	.60	.91	.74	.18	1.16	.55	.44	.27	.63
Gong Show	.60	.68	.29	.38	.76	.44	.72	.73	.93	.72	.73	.58	.38	.39	.81
Hollywood Squares	.44	.21	.35	.37	.95	.56	.61	.46	.21	.14	.30	.74	.32	.31	.44
It's Anybody's Guess	.05	.02	.05	.01	.11	.01	.10	.05	.08	.01	.09	.04	.03	–	.12
Match Game '77	.42	.18	.24	.14	.73	.40	.35	.36	.49	.23	1.13	.73	.34	.40	.47
The Price Is Right	.59	.35	.61	.34	1.13	.31	.69	.79	.46	.26	1.17	.81	.49	.11	.91
Tattletales	.22	.05	.07	.05	.51	.33	.22	.22	.20	.29	.20	.47	.27	.03	.20
20,000 Dollar Pyramid	.40	.30	.25	.28	.45	.31	.53	.67	.38	.20	.95	.46	.33	.15	.44
Wheel of Fortune	.30	.14	.39	.30	.72	.28	.47	.18	.19	.04	.18	.67	.23	.04	.37

TABLE F.7 Average Number of Times Viewed by Interest Segment for Movies

	Entire Population	Adult Male Concentration			Adult Female Concentration				Youth Concentration			Mixed			
		Mechanics and Outdoor Life	Money and Nature's Products	Family and Community Centered	Elderly Concerns	Arts and Cultural Activities	Home and Community Centered	Family Integrated Activities	Competitive Sports and Science/Engineering	Athletic and Social Activities	Indoor Games and Social Activities	News and Information	Detached	Cosmopolitan Self-Enrichment	Highly Diversified
Total	5.45	5.87	5.01	4.20	4.44	4.60	4.60	6.73	5.26	5.88	4.92	7.27	5.05	4.33	8.01
Sunday Night Movie	1.14	1.51	1.07	.93	.88	1.00	.95	1.34	1.12	1.15	1.12	1.32	1.00	.84	1.70
Monday Night Movie	.86	.93	.70	.57	.88	.73	.82	1.24	.67	.81	.54	1.05	.84	.65	1.23
Wednesday Night Movie	.80	.66	.71	.64	.72	.67	.65	.97	.70	.75	.54	1.23	.94	.64	1.26
Friday Night Movie	.85	.88	.79	.66	.79	.66	.74	1.05	.81	1.09	1.06	1.09	.72	.63	1.11
Saturday Night Movie	.83	.80	.82	.82	.68	.76	.75	.93	.80	.79	.59	1.19	.71	.52	1.37
Late Night Movies	.63	.74	.71	.39	.26	.49	.48	.82	.72	.54	.56	.89	.68	.75	.79
The Big Event (varies)	.34	.36	.20	.18	.22	.29	.22	.37	.44	.76	.52	.50	.17	.29	.55

TABLE F.8 Average Number of Times Viewed by Interest Segment for Musical Performances

	Entire Population	Adult Male Concentration				Adult Female Concentration				Youth Concentration				Mixed		
		Mechanics and Outdoor Life	Money and Nature's Products	Family and Community Centered	Elderly Concerns	Arts and Cultural Activities	Home and Community Centered	Family Integrated Activities	Competitive Sports and Science/Engineering	Athletic and Social Activities	Indoor Games and Social Activities	News and Information	Detached	Cosmopolitan Self-Enrichment	Highly Diversified
Total	1.02	.53	.58	.31	.77	1.96	.92	.79	.90	.93	1.65	1.08	.73	.96	2.15
American Bandstand	.30	.16	.07	.10	.22	.15	.20	.30	.50	.61	.85	.40	.26	.11	.70
Evening at Pop's	.12	.06	.07	.05	.07	.45	.07	.05	.02	–	.05	.14	.09	.29	.09
Evening at Symphony	.13	.09	.15	.02	.12	.60	.10	.05	.01	–	.05	.05	.06	.26	.05
Music Hall America	.11	.13	.13	.07	.10	.10	.11	.15	.12	.03	.03	.17	.03	.09	.26
Opera (varies)	.09	–	.06	–	.06	.53	.08	.07	–	–	.04	.01	.04	.11	.10
Soul Train	.27	.09	.10	.06	.21	.14	.36	.16	.26	.28	.63	.31	.27	.11	.95

325

TABLE F.9 Average Number of Times Viewed by Interest Segment for News/Commentary Programs

| | Adult Male Concentration | | | Adult Female Concentration | | | | Youth Concentration | | | | Mixed | | |
	Entire Population	Mechanics and Outdoor Life	Money and Nature's Products	Family and Community Centered	Elderly Concerns	Arts and Cultural Activities	Home and Community Centered	Family Integrated Activities	Competitive Sports and Science/Engineering	Athletic and Social Activities	Indoor Games and Social Activities	News and Information	Detached	Cosmopolitan Self-Enrichment	Highly Diversified
Total	2.37	1.38	3.80	2.68	3.16	3.72	1.98	1.51	1.14	.83	.64	5.53	1.57	2.42	2.65
Black Perspective on the News	.07	.03	.01	.04	.09	.07	.08	.02	.02	.02	.05	.18	.08	.05	.24
Evening Magazine	.10	.05	.31	.19	.05	.14	.05	.05	.05	.02	.05	.07	.10	.19	.05
Face the Nation	.31	.05	.61	.38	.67	.33	.23	.12	.05	.02	.12	.91	.14	.29	.43
MacNeil/Lehrer Report	.11	—	.06	.06	.02	.36	.10	—	—	—	.01	.52	.04	.27	.18
Meet the Press	.33	.08	.71	.37	.75	.54	.14	.19	.06	.02	.07	.97	.09	.21	.39
Sixty Minutes	1.26	1.06	1.65	1.44	1.49	1.70	1.13	1.10	.94	.76	.33	2.30	1.02	1.28	1.20
Wall Street Week	.07	.06	.10	.08	—	.25	.07	.02	.01	—	.01	.24	.03	.04	.04
Washington Week in Review	.13	.05	.35	.13	.09	.34	.17	.02	.01	—	—	.35	.07	.10	.14

TABLE F.10 Average Number of Times Viewed by Interest Segment for News Shows/Daily

	Entire Population	Adult Male Concentration			Adult Female Concentration				Youth Concentration			Mixed			
		Mechanics and Outdoor Life	Money and Nature's Products	Family and Community Centered	Elderly Concerns	Arts and Cultural Activities	Home and Community Centered	Family Integrated Activities	Competitive Sports and Science/Engineering	Athletic and Social Activities	Indoor Games and Social Activities	News and Information	Detached	Cosmopolitan Self-Enrichment	Highly Diversified
Total	5.19	3.61	5.86	6.06	6.55	6.61	5.12	5.00	3.70	2.06	2.39	6.98	4.17	6.96	5.37
Local news (any station)	2.73	1.93	2.97	3.15	3.54	3.18	2.81	2.71	1.95	1.41	1.17	3.47	2.37	3.68	2.72
National network news (ABC, CBS, NBC)	2.46	1.68	2.89	2.91	3.01	3.43	2.31	2.30	1.75	.65	1.22	3.51	1.79	3.28	2.65

TABLE F.11 Average Number of Times Viewed by Interest Segment for Science Fiction Programs

	Entire Population	Adult Male Concentration			Adult Female Concentration				Youth Concentration			Mixed			
		Mechanics and Outdoor Life	Money and Nature's Products	Family and Community Centered	Elderly Concerns	Arts and Cultural Activities	Home and Community Centered	Family Integrated Activities	Competitive Sports and Science/Engineering	Athletic and Social Activities	Indoor Games and Social Activities	News and Information	Detached	Cosmopolitan Self-Enrichment	Highly Diversified
Total	1.25	1.59	.77	.93	.94	.88	1.00	1.07	1.64	1.53	2.30	1.18	1.16	.89	2.18
Logan's Run	.36	.55	.19	.24	.17	.28	.28	.18	.55	.43	.70	.46	.29	.40	.61
The Man from Atlantis	.40	.46	.25	.30	.37	.34	.34	.32	.52	.49	.74	.29	.33	.28	.80
The New Adventures of Wonder Woman	.48	.59	.33	.40	.40	.26	.38	.57	.58	.62	.86	.43	.54	.21	.77

TABLE F.12 Average Number of Times Viewed by Interest Segment for Situation Comedies

	Entire Population	Adult Male Concentration				Adult Female Concentration			Youth Concentration				Mixed		
		Mechanics and Outdoor Life	Money and Nature's Products	Family and Community Centered	Elderly Concerns	Arts and Cultural Activities	Home and Community Centered	Family Integrated Activities	Competitive Sports and Science/Engineering	Athletic and Social Activities	Indoor Games and Social Activities	News and Information	Detached	Cosmopolitan Self-Enrichment	Highly Diversified
Total	19.15	17.80	14.78	12.09	20.18	16.66	20.81	19.76	24.94	22.06	28.46	23.17	15.76	15.34	22.63
Alice	.74	.36	.66	.58	.99	.76	.79	.77	.87	.69	.90	1.15	.72	.47	.75
All in the Family	1.39	1.19	1.60	1.05	1.57	1.39	1.51	1.38	1.77	1.22	1.52	1.65	1.00	1.21	1.57
Barney Miller	.74	.89	.43	.41	.69	.70	.87	.70	1.14	.67	.98	.79	.45	.94	.81
The Betty White Show	.40	.22	.41	.12	.65	.34	.57	.43	.32	.22	.62	.42	.32	.50	.39
Bob Newhart	.58	.26	.70	.36	1.01	.92	.59	.56	.47	.18	.41	1.05	.52	.51	.40
Busting Loose	.27	.33	.13	.08	.21	.19	.23	.23	.50	.13	.50	.20	.24	.35	.47
Carter Country	.42	.43	.18	.21	.31	.29	.58	.41	.68	.42	.73	.55	.26	.60	.43
Chico and the Man	.48	.40	.68	.45	1.02	.26	.58	.40	.40	.16	.55	.63	.38	.05	.77
Eight Is Enough	.80	.62	.33	.62	.63	.68	.89	1.08	1.01	1.29	1.53	.89	.66	.52	.88
Fish	.55	.56	.45	.44	.80	.45	.55	.59	.58	.60	.62	.59	.43	.42	.70
Good Times	.80	.72	.66	.41	1.05	.54	.78	.63	1.17	.79	1.10	1.14	.77	.44	1.31
Happy Days	1.41	1.63	.93	.99	1.28	.87	1.41	1.61	2.08	1.89	2.44	1.75	1.09	.95	1.63
The Jeffersons	.91	.59	1.19	.53	1.37	.90	1.04	.55	.87	.76	.81	1.32	1.06	.62	1.17
Laverne & Shirley	1.16	1.19	.63	.75	1.11	.81	1.22	1.47	1.61	1.71	1.97	1.32	.90	.83	1.27

TABLE F.12 Average Number of Times Viewed by Interest Segment for Situation Comedies (Cont)

	Entire Population	Adult Male Concentration				Adult Female Concentration				Youth Concentration			Mixed		
		Mechanics and Outdoor Life	Money and Nature's Products	Family and Community Centered	Elderly Concerns	Arts and Cultural Activities	Home and Community Centered	Family Integrated Activities	Competitive Sports and Science/Engineering	Athletic and Social Activities	Indoor Games and Social Activities	News and Information	Detached	Cosmopolitan Self-Enrichment	Highly Diversified
The Love Boat	.70	.73	.38	.52	.42	.69	.84	1.05	.82	1.16	1.04	.51	.46	.43	.91
Mash	1.02	1.23	1.10	.75	.92	1.09	.79	.89	1.36	.95	.87	1.08	.97	1.42	.87
Maude	.54	.34	.56	.28	.82	.47	.69	.62	.44	.53	.99	.54	.34	.39	.71
Mulligan's Stew	.18	.17	.23	.21	.15	.05	.21	.16	.21	.15	.29	.34	.14	.05	.30
One Day at a Time	.68	.76	.65	.46	.58	.59	.56	.66	.82	.93	.92	.81	.66	.70	.72
On Our Own	.25	.14	.14	.08	.18	.30	.46	.31	.20	.30	.45	.49	.24	.08	.32
Operation Petticoat	.33	.40	.13	.33	.23	.24	.24	.26	.50	.64	.67	.34	.29	.24	.40
Rhoda	.68	.43	.56	.36	.92	.91	.84	.74	.57	.69	.87	.92	.64	.43	.75
Sanford Arms	.21	.17	.21	.07	.43	.13	.35	.11	.32	.10	.28	.26	.17	.01	.39
The San Pedro Beach Bums	.38	.43	.30	.26	.23	.30	.35	.21	.98	.77	.69	.18	.26	.19	.60
Soap	.56	.78	.29	.33	.30	.46	.61	.80	.59	.99	.70	.45	.49	.50	.64
Three's Company	.82	.94	.34	.44	.40	.54	1.05	1.21	1.17	1.68	1.65	.73	.53	.49	.98
The Tony Randall Show	.29	.22	.25	.14	.39	.56	.38	.19	.18	.12	.25	.46	.21	.34	.30
Welcome Back, Kotter	.92	.90	.30	.51	.69	.60	.89	.88	1.70	1.18	2.01	1.17	.75	1.05	.98
We've Got Each Other	.14	.01	.10	.06	.11	.19	.20	.15	.08	.06	.15	.49	.20	.06	.16
What's Happening	.78	.75	.25	.29	.71	.45	.70	.70	1.49	1.10	1.95	.96	.65	.57	1.05

TABLE F.13 Average Number of Times Viewed by Interest Segment for Soap Operas

	Entire Population	Adult Male Concentration			Adult Female Concentration				Youth Concentration				Mixed		
		Mechanics and Outdoor Life	Money and Nature's Products	Family and Community Centered	Elderly Concerns	Arts and Cultural Activities	Home and Community Centered	Family Integrated Activities	Competitive Sports and Science/Engineering	Athletic and Social Activities	Indoor Games and Social Activities	News and Information	Detached	Cosmopolitan Self-Enrichment	Highly Diversified
Total	3.64	.92	2.81	1.20	7.13	2.77	6.56	5.32	1.05	3.12	5.59	5.11	3.61	.93	4.63
All My Children	.41	.20	.18	.09	.54	.35	.70	.89	.11	.50	1.10	.43	.36	.17	.29
Another World	.33	.10	.20	.09	.60	.21	.52	.39	.12	.27	.43	.48	.34	.19	.63
As the World Turns	.40	.07	.52	.26	1.07	.28	.70	.34	.09	.38	.37	.73	.31	.11	.39
Days of Our Lives	.37	.15	.20	.20	.77	.39	.72	.45	.16	.15	.49	.41	.30	.08	.53
The Doctors	.27	—	.28	.14	.56	.17	.44	.30	.07	.12	.27	.42	.31	.04	.57
General Hospital	.30	.01	.23	.09	.40	.23	.84	.64	.09	.26	.36	.36	.30	—	.24
The Guiding Light	.27	.05	.30	.07	.62	.22	.43	.19	.10	.42	.26	.59	.21	.10	.38
Love of Life	.27	.07	.17	.07	.64	.12	.44	.40	.09	.13	.48	.34	.43	.04	.26
One Life to Live	.32	.12	.14	.04	.46	.26	.67	.66	.07	.25	.89	.26	.27	.02	.40
Search for Tomorrow	.34	.06	.34	.06	.76	.22	.60	.42	.09	.21	.41	.61	.41	.06	.42
The Young and the Restless	.37	.10	.24	.09	.71	.32	.49	.64	.04	.42	.53	.49	.36	.12	.53

TABLE F.14 Average Number of Times Viewed by Interest Segment for Specials

	Entire Population	Adult Male Concentration			Adult Female Concentration				Youth Concentration				Mixed		
		Mechanics and Outdoor Life	Money and Nature's Products	Family and Community Centered	Elderly Concerns	Arts and Cultural Activities	Home and Community Centered	Family Integrated Activities	Competitive Sports and Science/Engineering	Athletic and Social Activities	Indoor Games and Social Activities	News and Information	Detached	Cosmopolitan Self-Enrichment	Highly Diversified
Total	.89	.76	1.06	.63	.72	1.36	1.01	1.00	.58	.57	.85	1.05	.35	1.04	1.22
Kill Me If You Can (The Caryl Chessman Story)	.14	.18	.19	.10	.25	.20	.10	.15	.18	.02	.03	.12	.06	.12	.23
The Trial of Lee Harvey Oswald	.24	.20	.39	.17	.16	.29	.37	.19	.27	.30	.12	.28	.13	.20	.36
Washington Behind Closed Doors	.50	.38	.49	.36	.31	.87	.54	.67	.13	.26	.69	.66	.17	.72	.63

TABLE F.15 Average Number of Times Viewed by Interest Segment for Sports Programs

	Entire Population	Adult Male Concentration				Adult Female Concentration			Youth Concentration				Mixed		
		Outdoor Life and Mechanics	Money and Nature's Products	Family and Community Centered	Elderly Concerns	Arts and Cultural Activities	Home and Community Centered	Family Integrated Activities	Competitive Sports and Science/Engineering	Athletic and Social Activities	Indoor Games and Social Activities	News and Information	Detached	Cosmopolitan Self-Enrichment	Highly Diversified
Total	5.79	4.15	7.64	7.56	4.22	5.83	4.60	2.97	11.85	4.00	4.99	9.68	4.24	4.99	7.01
Baseball	.85	.51	1.18	1.02	.90	.86	.86	.59	1.68	.44	.94	.86	.67	.61	.97
Basketball	.55	.21	.66	.55	.56	.47	.48	.24	1.35	.28	.30	1.28	.39	.28	.85
Football	1.71	1.40	2.46	2.48	1.04	1.95	1.24	.75	3.27	1.43	1.21	2.85	1.39	1.56	1.72
Hockey	.23	.11	.20	.17	.19	.13	.31	.08	.78	.11	.33	.55	.12	.16	.27
NFL Football	1.31	1.13	1.87	1.97	.64	1.51	.95	.48	2.65	.95	1.03	2.15	.99	1.37	1.38
Wide World of Sports	.85	.61	.94	1.18	.64	.77	.61	.65	1.48	.54	.92	1.38	.52	.79	1.25
Other	.28	.18	.32	.19	.25	.14	.15	.18	.63	.24	.26	.61	.17	.23	.58

TABLE F.16 Average Number of Times Viewed by Interest Segment for Talk Shows

	Entire Population	Adult Male Concentration			Adult Female Concentration				Youth Concentration				Mixed		
		Mechanics and Outdoor Life	Money and Nature's Products	Family and Community Centered	Elderly Concerns	Arts and Cultural Activities	Home and Community Centered	Family Integrated Activities	Competitive Sports and Science/Engineering	Athletic and Social Activities	Indoor Games and Social Activities	News and Information	Detached	Cosmopolitan Self-Enrichment	Highly Diversified
Total	2.90	.85	3.28	1.97	4.03	4.15	3.44	2.79	2.21	1.21	2.21	5.29	2.27	3.69	2.67
Dialing for Dollars	.13	.04	.10	.10	.34	.08	.22	.04	.07	–	.17	.18	.02	.15	.26
Dinah	.25	.03	.21	.18	.39	.43	.15	.34	.26	.12	.18	.39	.22	.30	.25
Fernwood 2 Night	.09	.01	.16	.01	.05	.03	.12	.05	.16	.06	.12	.29	.03	.14	.18
Good Morning America	.32	.15	.36	.27	.33	.31	.50	.35	.07	.03	.54	.68	.20	.47	.29
Joel A. Spivak	.01	–	.02	–	–	.02	–	–	–	–	–	–	–	–	.02
Johnny Carson	.71	.30	1.06	.56	.60	.75	.63	.88	.99	.45	.62	1.13	.45	1.05	.54
Merv Griffin Show	.38	.07	.34	.24	.79	.58	.55	.23	.30	.24	.18	.72	.39	.41	.22
Mike Douglas	.31	.05	.24	.11	.68	.53	.38	.18	.13	.11	.20	.63	.38	.34	.28
Phil Donahue	.25	.04	.17	.05	.21	.59	.43	.40	.01	.13	.14	.56	.22	.18	.23
Today	.42	.14	.62	.44	.54	.82	.44	.31	.22	.08	.06	.67	.29	.64	.37
Woman	.03	–	.01	.02	.10	.02	.01	.02	–	–	.01	.04	.06	.01	.04

TABLE F.17 Average Number of Times Viewed by Interest Segment for Theatrical Performances

	Entire Population	Adult Male Concentration				Adult Female Concentration			Youth Concentration				Mixed		
		Mechanics and Outdoor Life	Money and Nature's Products	Family and Community Centered	Elderly Concerns	Arts and Cultural Activities	Home and Community Centered	Family Integrated Activities	Competitive Sports and Science/Engineering	Athletic and Social Activities	Indoor Games and Social Activities	News and Information	Detached	Cosmopolitan Self-Enrichment	Highly Diversified
Total	.63	.18	.43	.35	.46	2.43	.29	.44	.12	.12	.38	.78	.29	1.36	.63
The Best of Families	.07	.03	.04	—	.07	.16	.07	.08	.01	—	.09	.22	.07	.08	.12
Dickens of London	.09	.02	.04	—	.01	.47	.07	—	.01	.03	.03	.04	.03	.29	.03
Great Performances	.09	.01	.10	.03	.08	.43	.02	.01	—	.01	.05	.13	.02	.18	.13
In Pursuit of Liberty	.02	—	—	.01	.01	.04	.03	.03	—	—	.01	.14	.01	.01	.04
Masterpiece Theater	.16	.07	.13	.14	.15	.59	.11	.18	.08	.01	.12	.11	.04	.24	.09
Once Upon a Classic	.08	.03	.04	.03	—	.15	—	.15	.02	.06	.02	.04	.04	.30	.10
Upstairs, Downstairs	.10	.03	.08	.14	.13	.47	.02	.01	—	—	.04	.03	.05	.19	.08
Visions	.03	—	—	—	—	.12	.04	—	—	.01	.03	.08	.03	.06	.04

TABLE F.18 Average Number of Times Viewed by Interest Segment for Variety Shows

	Adult Male Concentration					Adult Female Concentration			Youth Concentration				Mixed		
	Entire Population	Mechanics and Outdoor Life	Money and Nature's Products	Family and Community Centered	Elderly Concerns	Arts and Cultural Activities	Home and Community Centered	Family Integrated Activities	Competitive Sports and Science/Engineering	Athletic and Social Activities	Indoor Games and Social Activities	News and Information	Detached	Cosmopolitan Self-Enrichment	Highly Diversified
Total	3.63	2.87	4.25	2.97	5.08	3.12	3.91	3.25	3.01	2.85	4.75	5.59	2.64	2.61	4.83
Andy Williams	.11	.06	.19	.14	.22	.10	.09	.12	.02	–	.09	.39	.08	.01	.14
The Carol Burnett Show	.64	.30	1.00	.46	1.13	.54	.73	.57	.45	.47	.70	1.21	.43	.50	.60
Donnie & Marie	.81	.69	.67	.65	1.02	.63	1.02	1.07	.58	1.07	1.29	1.02	.59	.41	.91
The Lawrence Welk Show	.64	.32	1.24	.86	1.49	.75	.72	.59	.08	.01	.31	1.19	.48	.25	.45
Redd Foxx	.70	.65	.74	.54	.78	.50	.84	.47	.73	.27	1.13	.93	.54	.62	1.21
The Richard Pryor Show	.36	.20	.22	.13	.32	.32	.29	.21	.51	.41	.63	.38	.27	.46	.84
Saturday Night Live	.38	.65	.19	.20	.12	.29	.21	.23	.64	.61	.59	.47	.26	.37	.68

TABLE F.19 Average Number of Times Viewed by Interest Segment for All Other Programs

	Adult Male Concentration					Adult Female Concentration			Youth Concentration				Mixed		
	Entire Population	Mechanics and Outdoor Life	Money and Nature's Products	Family and Community Centered	Elderly Concerns	Arts and Cultural Activities	Home and Community Centered	Family Integrated Activities	Competitive Sports and Science/Engineering	Athletic and Social Activities	Indoor Games and Social Activities	News and Information	Detached	Cosmopolitan Self-Enrichment	Highly Diversified
Total	.67	.09	.91	.89	1.28	.63	1.10	.32	.26	.43	.43	1.03	.67	.21	1.10
The French Chef	.04	—	.02	.02	.01	.06	.05	.03	.02	.02	.02	.03	.05	.09	.10
Any Religious Programs	.58	.09	.80	.87	1.24	.57	.91	.28	.19	.27	.35	.98	.52	.10	.90
Any Spanish Programs	.05	—	.08	—	.03	—	.14	.01	.04	.15	.06	.02	.10	.02	.11

Appendix G

MAGAZINE READERSHIP

TABLE G.1 Percentage of Regular Readers by Interest Segment for Automotive Magazines

	Entire Population	Adult Male Concentration			Adult Female Concentration				Youth Concentration			Mixed			
		Mechanics and Outdoor Life	Money and Nature's Products	Family and Community Centered	Elderly Concerns	Arts and Cultural Activities	Home and Community Centered	Family Integrated Activities	Competitive Sports and Science/Engineering	Athletic and Social Activities	Indoor Games and Social Activities	News and Information	Detached	Cosmopolitan Self-Enrichment	Highly Diversified
Nonreaders	91.2	70.4	93.3	92.1	93.8	97.3	97.6	97.9	68.4	94.2	97.4	98.9	96.9	96.5	83.6
Net readers of . . .	8.8	29.6	6.7	7.9	6.2	2.7	2.4	2.1	31.6	5.8	2.6	1.1	3.1	3.5	16.4
Car and Driver	4.6	16.6	3.6	3.2	2.4	2.3	1.9	0.5	16.3	0.6	1.5	0.6	1.8	2.0	9.3
Hot Rod	5.5	22.4	4.8	1.3	2.2	0.3	1.6	0.6	24.1	4.3	1.1	0.7	1.3	1.1	10.4
Motor Trend	3.2	9.0	1.9	3.7	1.3	0.1	0.8	0.9	15.5	1.5	0.4	0.9	1.3	1.3	5.4
Road and Track	2.8	10.9	3.6	0.3	0.6	0.4	0.4	0.5	13.4	1.2	0.5	0.4	0.1	1.6	4.6

TABLE G.2 Percentage of Regular Readers by Interest Segment for Black Magazines

	Entire Population	Adult Male Concentration				Adult Female Concentration			Youth Concentration				Mixed		
		Mechanics and Outdoor Life	Money and Nature's Products	Family and Community Centered	Elderly Concerns	Arts and Cultural Activities	Home and Community Centered	Family Integrated Activities	Competitive Sports and Science/Engineering	Athletic and Social Activities	Indoor Games and Social Activities	News and Information	Detached	Cosmopolitan Self-Enrichment	Highly Diversified
Nonreaders	93.2	96.9	98.1	94.8	95.3	92.8	90.3	96.3	95.1	97.7	87.4	94.1	94.5	98.2	73.0
Net readers of . . .	6.8	3.1	1.9	5.2	4.7	7.2	9.7	3.7	4.9	2.3	12.6	5.9	5.5	1.8	27.0
Black Enterprise	1.6	0.2	–	1.0	0.1	1.0	2.1	0.3	–	0.3	2.5	3.2	0.8	–	11.0
Ebony	5.4	0.4	1.7	3.9	3.8	6.6	8.5	3.1	2.5	2.3	11.1	5.8	4.1	1.8	20.7
Essence	2.8	–	1.5	0.8	1.5	3.0	6.3	0.9	1.4	1.5	4.3	3.4	2.4	1.3	10.5
Jet	4.1	2.7	1.1	3.2	2.0	3.7	6.1	1.1	4.4	1.0	5.8	4.4	2.9	1.2	16.8

TABLE G.3 Percentage of Regular Readers by Interest Segment for Business/Finance Magazines

	Entire Population	Adult Male Concentration			Adult Female Concentration				Youth Concentration				Mixed		
		Mechanics and Outdoor Life	Money and Nature's Products	Family and Community Centered	Elderly Concerns	Arts and Cultural Activities	Home and Community Centered	Family Integrated Activities	Competitive Sports and Science/Engineering	Athletic and Social Activities	Indoor Games and Social Activities	News and Information	Detached	Cosmopolitan Self-Enrichment	Highly Diversified
Nonreaders	89.6	94.8	89.1	87.5	97.9	83.6	88.5	92.9	91.5	93.5	95.6	90.4	91.0	79.5	82.6
Net readers of . . .	10.4	5.2	10.9	12.5	2.1	16.4	11.5	7.1	8.5	6.5	4.4	9.6	9.0	20.5	17.4
Business Week	4.6	3.6	3.1	6.6	0.3	8.6	2.7	2.9	4.0	2.8	0.6	5.2	5.8	10.6	5.3
Forbes	1.9	0.9	0.5	1.5	–	5.4	0.3	–	0.4	0.3	0.7	1.9	6.0	3.8	2.3
Fortune	2.0	0.3	1.2	1.4	–	4.7	1.1	0.7	0.7	–	0.8	4.3	5.0	2.4	4.1
Money	2.7	1.9	4.6	1.4	0.1	1.9	3.1	1.6	3.5	3.8	2.7	3.1	0.8	4.2	6.2
Moneysworth	2.4	1.5	2.3	4.4	1.1	0.9	6.2	2.6	0.8	–	0.4	–	1.2	5.3	5.1
Nation's Business	1.6	1.8	3.1	3.0	0.6	2.7	0.7	–	1.4	–	0.1	1.6	0.8	2.0	4.2

TABLE G.4 Percentage of Regular Readers by Interest Segment for Fashion Magazines

	Entire Population	Adult Male Concentration				Adult Female Concentration			Youth Concentration				Mixed		
		Mechanics and Outdoor Life	Money and Nature's Products	Family and Community Centered	Elderly Concerns	Arts and Cultural Activities	Home and Community Centered	Family Integrated Activities	Competitive Sports and Science/Engineering	Athletic and Social Activities	Indoor Games and Social Activities	News and Information	Detached	Cosmopolitan Self-Enrichment	Highly Diversified
Nonreaders	91.4	98.2	100.0	98.0	99.1	87.3	88.1	85.1	97.5	73.0	79.8	95.3	96.4	87.7	86.9
Net readers of . . .	8.6	1.8	—	2.0	0.9	12.7	11.9	14.9	2.5	27.0	20.2	4.7	3.6	12.3	13.1
Glamour	6.0	1.3	—	2.0	0.4	7.8	10.2	11.0	1.1	18.9	15.7	3.0	2.0	6.5	9.9
Mademoiselle	3.4	0.8	—	0.5	0.1	1.9	3.8	5.5	1.2	20.6	8.8	0.4	2.1	2.9	7.1
Vogue	2.7	0.1	—	—	0.3	6.4	3.6	4.1	0.9	6.8	6.2	1.7	1.1	5.7	2.8

TABLE G.5 Percentage of Regular Readers by Interest Segment for General Magazines

	Entire Population	Adult Male Concentration				Adult Female Concentration			Youth Concentration				Mixed		
		Mechanics and Outdoor Life	Money and Nature's Products	Family and Community Centered	Elderly Concerns	Arts and Cultural Activities	Home and Community Centered	Family Integrated Activities	Competitive Sports and Science/Engineering	Athletic and Social Activities	Indoor Games and Social Activities	News and Information	Detached	Cosmopolitan Self-Enrichment	Highly Diversified
Nonreaders	47.2	45.6	51.1	50.5	56.4	39.4	48.9	32.9	54.5	55.3	33.9	31.4	70.2	44.5	43.9
Net readers of …	52.8	54.4	48.9	49.5	43.6	60.6	51.1	67.1	45.5	44.7	66.1	68.6	29.8	55.5	56.1
People	13.7	10.5	1.4	6.0	7.0	16.7	15.8	21.7	12.4	23.3	15.8	16.9	5.7	25.3	13.7
Reader's Digest	31.5	23.5	39.3	33.0	30.8	36.9	33.2	47.9	19.3	17.7	27.9	44.5	16.5	35.6	28.1
TV Guide	29.4	30.1	16.8	25.6	21.6	31.4	24.5	35.8	36.8	29.2	51.3	43.6	14.1	22.7	41.0
US	0.7	0.1	—	—	—	—	1.0	2.8	0.6	0.3	1.4	0.2	0.5	0.8	1.1

TABLE G.6 Percentage of Regular Readers by Interest Segment for Home Service/Home Magazines

	Entire Population	Adult Male Concentration				Adult Female Concentration			Youth Concentration				Mixed		
		Mechanics and Outdoor Life	Money and Nature's Products	Family and Community Centered	Elderly Concerns	Arts and Cultural Activities	Home and Community Centered	Family Integrated Activities	Competitive Sports and Science/Engineering	Athletic and Social Activities	Indoor Games and Social Activities	News and Information	Detached	Cosmopolitan Self-Enrichment	Highly Diversified
Nonreaders	72.1	88.7	80.3	79.7	74.7	60.1	55.7	53.3	94.5	73.4	57.3	78.9	90.6	67.1	60.9
Net readers of . . .	27.9	11.3	19.7	20.3	25.3	39.9	44.3	46.7	5.5	26.6	42.7	21.1	9.4	32.9	39.1
American Home	7.4	2.5	3.9	3.2	7.2	9.6	9.6	16.8	2.4	2.1	8.3	8.1	2.6	7.9	13.3
Apartment Life	1.7	1.4	—	—	0.1	2.8	2.0	1.6	0.3	3.7	3.1	0.6	1.1	4.6	3.6
Better Homes & Gardens	21.7	8.3	14.0	16.2	21.6	29.7	37.8	40.7	4.7	19.7	28.4	18.8	6.1	20.6	29.3
House Beautiful	7.3	0.9	8.4	2.8	6.0	10.8	12.7	14.9	0.4	5.5	11.2	1.6	0.9	13.8	8.4
House and Garden	10.6	5.6	8.6	6.5	10.5	13.3	18.8	19.0	2.4	10.6	10.4	7.3	1.2	12.0	17.2

TABLE G.7 Percentage of Regular Readers by Interest Segment for Mechanics Magazines

	Entire Population	Adult Male Concentration			Adult Female Concentration				Youth Concentration			Mixed			
		Mechanics and Outdoor Life	Money and Nature's Products	Family and Community Centered	Elderly Concerns	Arts and Cultural Activities	Home and Community Centered	Family Integrated Activities	Competitive Sports and Science/Engineering	Athletic and Social Activities	Indoor Games and Social Activities	News and Information	Detached	Cosmopolitan Self-Enrichment	Highly Diversified
Nonreaders	89.0	73.4	86.3	83.5	96.3	94.0	98.6	94.4	71.7	96.6	95.6	93.8	87.8	95.7	81.5
Net readers of . . .	11.0	26.6	13.7	16.5	3.7	6.0	1.4	5.6	28.3	3.4	4.4	6.2	12.2	4.3	18.5
Mechanix Illustrated	6.7	19.7	9.2	9.5	2.5	2.5	0.9	4.5	14.4	1.0	0.4	4.9	7.7	3.3	10.1
Popular Mechanics	7.8	19.4	11.0	10.9	1.2	3.4	1.1	3.0	20.6	2.8	2.8	3.8	9.7	3.3	14.0
Popular Science	4.0	9.9	6.7	6.9	0.7	2.3	0.1	3.8	9.6	—	2.3	1.9	0.9	1.1	8.3

TABLE G.8 Percentage of Regular Readers by Interest Segment for Men's Magazines

	Entire Population	Adult Male Concentration				Adult Female Concentration			Youth Concentration				Mixed		
		Mechanics and Outdoor Life	Money and Nature's Products	Family and Community Centered	Elderly Concerns	Arts and Cultural Activities	Home and Community Centered	Family Integrated Activities	Competitive Sports and Science/Engineering	Athletic and Social Activities	Indoor Games and Social Activities	News and Information	Detached	Cosmopolitan Self-Enrichment	Highly Diversified
Nonreaders	75.8	46.7	74.7	78.7	90.5	80.7	88.6	81.7	66.9	88.7	73.0	72.2	84.1	69.2	67.0
Net readers of . . .	24.1	53.3	25.3	21.3	9.5	19.3	11.4	18.3	33.1	11.3	27.0	27.8	15.9	30.8	33.0
Esquire	4.1	4.3	4.4	3.4	1.7	3.3	2.7	6.6	4.6	1.2	3.1	3.2	2.4	5.8	7.8
Penthouse	7.4	21.5	2.1	7.9	–	5.1	1.1	5.3	11.4	3.2	12.8	7.5	0.5	11.7	14.5
Playboy	12.1	37.6	12.7	8.2	0.1	8.0	1.3	10.1	19.7	7.1	15.7	12.5	4.3	18.6	14.6
True	2.0	3.8	0.2	1.5	1.7	–	0.5	1.1	2.3	1.1	4.9	5.4	0.5	–	6.7

TABLE G.9 Percentage of Regular Readers by Interest Segment for News Magazines

	Entire Population	Adult Male Concentration				Adult Female Concentration			Youth Concentration				Mixed		
		Mechanics and Outdoor Life	Money and Nature's Products	Family and Community Centered	Elderly Concerns	Arts and Cultural Activities	Home and Community Centered	Family Integrated Activities	Competitive Sports and Science/Engineering	Athletic and Social Activities	Indoor Games and Social Activities	News and Information	Detached	Cosmopolitan Self-Enrichment	Highly Diversified
Nonreaders	73.9	86.6	82.1	77.0	86.9	61.4	80.7	77.4	65.4	84.8	83.8	60.2	79.6	43.4	70.7
Net readers of . . .	26.1	13.4	17.9	23.0	13.1	38.6	19.3	22.6	34.6	15.2	16.2	39.8	20.4	56.6	29.3
Newsweek	16.8	11.0	12.2	12.8	7.0	22.7	8.7	17.4	20.9	10.5	7.6	31.6	15.9	28.6	24.4
Time	11.9	6.4	4.5	8.2	2.1	21.0	6.4	13.1	21.9	5.7	13.3	12.9	3.5	33.7	12.0
U.S. News and World Report	7.6	6.3	11.0	11.7	5.2	12.1	8.1	4.4	6.1	1.0	2.0	13.5	7.7	7.6	7.8

347

TABLE G.10 Percentage of Regular Readers by Interest Segment for Outdoor Magazines

	Entire Population	Adult Male Concentration			Adult Female Concentration				Youth Concentration				Mixed		
		Mechanics and Outdoor Life	Money and Nature's Products	Family and Community Centered	Elderly Concerns	Arts and Cultural Activities	Home and Community Centered	Family Integrated Activities	Competitive Sports and Science/Engineering	Athletic and Social Activities	Indoor Games and Social Activities	News and Information	Detached	Cosmopolitan Self-Enrichment	Highly Diversified
Nonreaders	84.9	69.2	71.4	71.6	97.8	96.8	94.3	92.1	75.0	87.6	95.2	85.3	87.7	88.5	73.3
Net readers of . . .	15.1	30.8	28.6	28.4	2.2	3.2	5.7	7.9	25.0	12.4	4.8	14.7	12.3	11.5	26.7
Field and Stream	9.2	22.4	18.1	20.7	1.2	2.1	2.4	3.0	15.0	5.9	2.8	11.4	7.2	3.6	15.8
Guns and Ammo	4.0	18.4	3.1	9.3	1.2	0.1	0.4	1.4	9.7	0.4	0.3	0.8	1.0	0.2	7.5
Outdoor Life	6.7	12.6	17.3	12.6	0.8	0.7	2.6	4.4	8.8	7.6	2.0	5.0	6.9	3.0	11.9
Argosy	1.2	1.7	2.2	2.6	1.2	0.3	0.8	0.3	–	–	1.0	2.7	0.3	1.8	2.7
Sports Afield	6.1	7.7	9.2	13.5	0.2	2.0	1.3	1.2	14.1	7.6	1.5	5.9	8.0	6.6	9.3

TABLE G.11 Percentage of Regular Readers by Interest Segment for Romance Magazines

	Entire Population	Adult Male Concentration			Adult Female Concentration				Youth Concentration			Mixed			
		Mechanics and Outdoor Life	Money and Nature's Products	Family and Community Centered	Elderly Concerns	Arts and Cultural Activities	Home and Community Centered	Family Integrated Activities	Competitive Sports and Science/Engineering	Athletic and Social Activities	Indoor Games and Social Activities	News and Information	Detached	Cosmopolitan Self-Enrichment	Highly Diversified
Nonreaders	91.3	94.8	98.1	98.1	92.1	94.1	87.1	86.7	94.8	79.7	79.8	92.3	95.0	95.7	83.3
Net readers of . . .	8.7	5.2	1.9	1.9	7.9	5.9	12.9	13.3	5.2	20.3	20.2	7.7	5.0	4.3	16.7
Modern Romances	2.9	0.9	0.2	0.9	3.1	1.1	2.8	6.4	1.9	9.0	10.9	1.1	0.8	0.9	5.9
Modern Screen	2.0	0.8	–	0.6	1.7	2.3	6.4	2.9	0.3	4.2	4.2	0.8	0.9	0.9	2.6
Photoplay	2.9	0.8	1.4	–	1.5	3.7	4.0	4.2	0.7	5.4	2.6	4.9	2.2	3.4	6.1
True Story	5.0	4.2	1.3	1.6	7.1	0.3	5.9	9.8	2.7	12.8	11.9	2.2	2.5	0.9	10.6

TABLE G.12 Percentage of Regular Readers by Interest Segment for Select Magazines

	Entire Population	Adult Male Concentration			Adult Female Concentration				Youth Concentration			Mixed			
		Mechanics and Outdoor Life	Money and Nature's Products	Family and Community Centered	Elderly Concerns	Arts and Cultural Activities	Home and Community Centered	Family Integrated Activities	Competitive Sports and Science/Engineering	Athletic and Social Activities	Indoor Games and Social Activities	News and Information	Detached	Cosmopolitan Self-Enrichment	Highly Diversified
Nonreaders	70.5	78.1	78.0	73.3	83.8	46.8	80.3	75.2	74.0	79.9	76.3	71.5	81.8	34.2	64.0
Net readers of . . .	29.5	21.9	22.0	26.7	16.2	53.2	19.7	24.8	26.0	20.1	23.7	28.5	18.2	65.8	36.0
Harper's	1.4	0.3	–	0.3	1.5	5.0	1.1	0.8	0.2	1.0	1.8	1.6	0.7	2.2	2.5
National Geographic	19.5	14.4	17.5	23.6	8.9	39.2	12.0	19.0	14.6	7.2	4.9	21.8	12.5	48.4	15.8
Natural History	1.6	0.2	0.2	1.0	0.6	0.9	2.3	1.4	1.5	2.2	1.6	2.4	0.7	2.0	5.3
New Yorker	2.5	1.7	–	0.8	1.5	7.5	0.9	0.5	1.4	2.3	3.0	2.8	0.7	8.1	2.6
Psychology Today	4.3	2.0	0.2	1.7	1.3	8.3	3.2	7.5	3.5	2.1	0.6	1.6	1.2	12.7	8.4
Gourmet	1.3	0.2	–	–	0.5	2.4	1.4	1.1	1.0	–	1.5	1.2	0.6	4.9	1.9
Scientific American	1.8	1.9	0.7	1.1	–	4.0	0.2	0.9	1.4	1.8	0.9	1.3	0.7	9.2	0.9
Smithsonian	2.2	1.9	0.3	2.2	0.2	9.0	3.0	–	1.0	–	0.3	–	–	8.2	3.5
Travel and Leisure	2.4	0.7	6.8	0.2	1.3	6.3	1.5	0.9	2.4	–	–	1.1	3.2	2.8	2.2
Rolling Stone	3.3	4.7	–	0.3	1.2	0.4	–	2.6	7.4	9.8	6.0	0.4	1.2	7.1	6.7
New Times	3.4	3.7	2.0	3.2	1.9	3.0	4.1	2.9	2.5	3.0	12.5	1.7	0.2	4.1	6.4

TABLE G.13 Percentage of Regular Readers by Interest Segment for Sports Magazines

	Entire Population	Adult Male Concentration				Adult Female Concentration			Youth Concentration				Mixed		
		Mechanics and Outdoor Life	Money and Nature's Products	Family and Community Centered	Elderly Concerns	Arts and Cultural Activities	Home and Community Centered	Family Integrated Activities	Competitive Sports and Science/Engineering	Athletic and Social Activities	Indoor Games and Social Activities	News and Information	Detached	Cosmopolitan Self-Enrichment	Highly Diversified
Nonreaders	80.5	82.3	82.3	77.0	96.9	85.0	85.1	89.2	46.5	79.7	84.8	79.6	85.3	73.1	72.0
Net readers of . . .	19.5	17.7	17.7	23.0	3.1	15.0	14.9	10.8	53.5	20.3	15.2	20.4	14.7	26.9	28.0
Flying	2.1	6.7	0.7	1.7	0.1	—	0.4	0.5	8.8	—	0.8	—	0.5	4.8	3.5
Golf	2.7	0.3	4.0	4.1	—	1.8	6.3	0.8	7.1	0.6	2.2	4.5	2.7	1.9	2.3
Golf Digest	2.7	1.3	4.4	2.5	—	3.0	—	0.8	5.7	0.6	—	2.3	5.6	7.5	2.7
Sport	8.0	3.7	4.3	7.6	0.9	5.1	9.7	2.0	33.7	9.6	5.7	10.4	3.9	9.1	13.3
Sports Illustrated	12.4	6.4	7.4	19.7	3.1	10.1	6.0	6.2	40.2	14.6	7.0	17.0	8.3	17.4	17.3
Tennis	2.3	0.3	1.7	1.8	0.1	2.1	2.9	1.8	5.7	5.2	6.5	—	0.2	4.1	3.1
Yachting	0.9	3.1	2.8	—	—	—	—	—	2.8	—	0.2	—	—	2.8	0.6
Motorboating and Sailing	2.5	6.8	6.9	0.9	—	—	0.3	3.2	8.7	3.0	—	0.5	1.4	2.8	0.9

TABLE G.14 Percentage of Regular Readers by Interest Segment for Women's Services Magazines

	Entire Population	Adult Male Concentration				Adult Female Concentration			Youth Concentration			Mixed			
		Mechanics and Outdoor Life	Money and Nature's Products	Family and Community Centered	Elderly Concerns	Arts and Cultural Activities	Home and Community Centered	Family Integrated Activities	Competitive Sports and Science/Engineering	Athletic and Social Activities	Indoor Games and Social Activities	News and Information	Detached	Cosmopolitan Self-Enrichment	Highly Diversified
Nonreaders	58.2	86.8	80.2	73.1	59.5	45.7	39.4	23.4	90.1	43.0	42.0	63.5	84.6	45.0	45.0
Net readers of . . .	41.8	13.2	19.8	26.9	40.5	54.3	60.6	76.6	9.9	57.0	58.0	36.5	15.4	55.0	55.0
Cosmopolitan	7.0	1.6	1.3	4.7	2.3	4.8	5.6	8.3	2.9	24.0	17.5	5.0	1.9	18.2	10.7
Family Circle	23.1	7.9	11.8	14.6	18.7	29.5	35.5	55.1	2.2	19.0	31.0	14.6	8.8	32.1	28.0
Good Housekeeping	20.8	5.4	9.2	10.3	20.1	34.0	29.9	43.8	3.8	16.3	28.1	17.3	6.4	25.9	28.0
Ladies' Home Journal	15.0	0.6	6.7	4.3	14.5	20.4	23.8	37.2	1.8	17.3	15.5	15.4	5.2	18.2	19.5
McCall's	17.2	2.2	5.3	9.2	15.2	25.6	25.8	34.0	3.1	30.8	26.2	16.5	4.4	20.8	22.7
Ms.	1.4	1.4	0.3	0.8	–	2.3	0.8	0.9	0.4	4.5	2.9	1.3	0.5	2.2	2.5
Parents' Magazine	5.0	1.1	2.0	2.3	0.2	7.0	5.5	15.0	2.1	5.3	5.1	3.6	1.6	6.3	9.4
Redbook	9.1	1.4	1.7	3.1	4.5	9.7	12.4	24.5	3.0	14.0	5.4	10.4	1.8	17.9	12.3
Woman's Day	15.1	0.5	4.3	4.4	14.3	20.8	27.3	34.1	1.2	17.2	16.0	12.5	6.2	20.7	21.5
Baby Talk	2.4	1.3	0.6	0.7	–	1.9	4.7	5.5	–	0.5	12.8	0.2	2.3	–	4.5
Mother's Manual	0.9	–	–	–	–	1.6	0.6	1.9	–	5.2	0.9	0.2	0.2	1.3	1.1

352

TABLE G.15 Percentage of Regular Readers by Interest Segment for Miscellaneous Magazines

| | Adult Male Concentration | | | Adult Female Concentration | | | | Youth Concentration | | | | Mixed | | |
	Entire Population	Mechanics and Outdoor Life	Money and Nature's Products	Family and Community Centered	Elderly Concerns	Arts and Cultural Activities	Home and Community Centered	Family Integrated Activities	Competitive Sports and Science/Engineering	Athletic and Social Activities	Indoor Games and Social Activities	News and Information	Detached	Cosmopolitan Self-Enrichment	Highly Diversified
Nonreaders	95.3	88.7	97.6	98.5	97.3	96.2	97.9	97.1	91.1	94.7	98.2	97.2	99.2	90.6	91.5
Net readers of . . .	4.7	11.3	2.4	1.5	2.7	3.8	2.1	2.9	8.9	5.3	1.8	2.8	0.8	9.4	8.5
Popular Photography	2.8	5.5	0.2	1.5	2.7	3.2	2.1	2.5	3.0	4.7	1.0	0.4	0.8	6.4	4.2
National Lampoon	2.2	5.8	2.2	—	—	0.6	0.4	0.4	6.1	0.6	1.3	2.5	0.5	4.8	5.8

Appendix H

SHORT FORM QUESTIONNAIRE
AND SCORING PROCEDURE

This appendix describes a procedure which researchers can use in future studies to assign individuals to the same 14 interest segments described in this book. The procedure employs an abbreviated version of the battery of 139 leisure interest and activity items that were used as input to the clustering routine that developed the 14 segments.

The development of this abbreviated questionnaire makes use of multiple discriminant analysis, a technique yielding that linear combination of independent or predictor variables that best predicts membership in the set of mutually exclusive and exhaustive classes that constitute the dependent variable. More specifically, the algorithm used was The BMD, 1977 Version, Modification Level I Stepwise Multiple Discriminant Analysis.

The analytic sequence was as follows: .

(1) All 139 interest items were used as independent variables in an initial run of the stepwise program with the dependent variable being the 14 interest segments.

(2) The first 40 variables to enter were then selected to be used as independent variables for subsequent runs.

(3) Using only these 40 independent variables, stepwise discriminant analyses were run, and detailed output (classification data) was requested for the 30, 35, and 40 variable solutions.

The above steps were conducted using the interest data and the segment membership for each of the 2476 respondents in the study.

Clearly, the ability to classify respondents correctly into their proper segments increases with the length of the item battery employed. Because researchers may differ in their needs for efficiency in questionnaire administration and their needs for accuracy in classification, we describe below two short forms, one battery with thirty items and one with forty. The investigator who wishes to examine other alternatives can readily do so with a copy of the data tape for the study.*

Short Form—Thirty

The thirty items listed in Table H.1 constitute a battery that on the total sample classifies 64.8% of respondents into their proper segments

TABLE H.1   Thirty-Item Interest Battery

Item Number*	Interest
6	Baseball
8	Being a wine connoisseur
11	Board games
19	Child related activities
21	Classical music
27	Driving/Motoring
34	Hiking
36	Housecleaning
40	Hunting
45	Judo/Karate
49	Maintenance and repairs of the home
51	Model building
52	Modern dance
53	Motorcycles
56	Opera
63	Popular music
66	Sculpture
67	Sewing
70	Soccer
73	Table tennis/ping pong
74	Television
76	Travel/sightseeing
81	Abortion vs. right to life issues
86	Arms race
101	Engineering
105	Health and nutrition
125	Religion
128	Sexual attitudes and behavior
130	Social security system
134	Tax laws

*Item numbers correspond to those used in the code book accompanying the data tape.

*See Chapter 11 for information on availability of data tape and uses of short form versions of the interest battery.

(i.e., the segments into which they were classified using all 139 interest items).

The classification function is shown in Table H.2.

In order to assign an individual to one of the fourteen segments, his or her score on each of the four-point interest rating scales is multiplied by the corresponding weights for each of the fourteen segments and then adjusted by adding the constant for that segment. The individual is then assigned to that segment for which he or she had the largest score.

The segment codes are as follows:

   (1) News and Information

   (2) Competitive Sports and Science/Engineering

   (3) Detached

   (4) Arts and Cultural Activities

   (5) Mechanics and Outdoor Life

   (6) Athletic and Social Activities

   (7) Highly Diversified

   (8) Elderly Concerns

   (9) Money and Nature's Products

  (10) Home and Community Centered

  (11) Cosmopolitan Self-Enrichment

  (12) Family Integrated Activities

  (13) Family and Community Centered

  (14) Indoor Games and Social Activities

The classification matrix, showing how individuals in each of the fourteen segments are classified using this short form is presented in Table H.3.

The jackknifed classification, which estimates the accuracy one could expect in classifying a new sample of respondents, indicates that the percentage classified correctly would be expected to drop from 64.8% to 61.8%.

Short Form—Forty

The forty items listed in Table H.4 constitute a battery that on the total sample classifies 71.3% of respondents into the proper segments.

TABLE H.2 Classification Function for Thirty-Item Battery

GROUP =	*1.0000	*2.0000	*3.0000	*4.0000	*5.0000	*6.0000	*7.0000
Variable							
3 INT6	1.97782	1.70152	1.30475	1.70316	0.73159	1.19675	1.44014
4 INT8	1.10786	0.86041	1.43827	1.41661	1.74015	1.10760	1.20679
6 INT11	1.15504	1.60381	0.90405	1.61259	1.15023	0.77931	1.44559
9 INT19	-0.45140	-1.10374	-0.50184	-0.41735	-0.70203	-1.15050	-0.57730
10 INT21	0.60443	0.50613	0.51346	1.86840	0.62777	0.48485	0.78745
12 INT27	1.08545	1.60251	0.55029	1.10757	1.47887	1.25186	0.87649
13 INT34	-0.76568	-0.38390	-0.27614	-0.52329	0.13954	0.61632	-0.52328
14 INT36	0.93219	0.41456	0.86363	0.40104	0.59027	0.11395	1.09735
15 INT40	0.66750	0.53347	0.66204	0.51521	1.45945	0.50712	1.03514
16 INT45	-0.12009	0.32413	0.23310	0.06825	0.25541	0.82618	1.17556
17 INT49	0.57756	0.91708	0.51514	1.04059	1.22905	0.40808	1.26131
18 INT51	0.23788	1.65269	0.51773	0.47298	1.18614	-0.51396	1.49234
19 INT52	-0.11597	-0.92731	-0.15340	-0.25918	-0.41233	0.62479	-0.08186
20 INT53	0.51076	1.50183	0.68083	0.21943	1.88943	1.56304	0.92414
21 INT56	1.08905	0.71982	1.34936	4.15716	0.97490	0.95365	1.55687
22 INT63	2.14970	2.26379	1.15152	1.81708	2.26492	2.19079	1.84669
23 INT66	-0.42537	-0.26688	0.08676	1.06569	-0.34151	0.23430	0.88404
24 INT67	0.96694	0.58685	1.02879	0.53002	0.60193	1.02050	1.38773
25 INT70	0.40348	2.14619	0.67801	0.09136	0.14680	1.78717	1.40896
27 INT73	-1.20809	-0.11438	-0.83718	-0.80277	-1.22336	-0.43191	-0.68682
28 INT74	4.46638	4.37986	3.70173	3.75558	4.09032	4.10243	4.07113
29 INT76	1.62247	1.64465	0.64163	1.99557	1.64746	1.99060	1.59683
30 INT81	1.29411	0.75384	0.97308	1.16696	1.15487	1.96387	1.14560
31 INT86	2.02242	0.73178	0.53560	0.79836	1.02759	-0.13728	0.51953
32 INT101	0.75981	1.28354	0.65833	0.23451	1.42866	0.09268	1.01453
34 INT105	2.03236	1.67279	1.01579	1.64468	1.19760	1.41682	1.62143
35 INT125	1.38827	1.18617	1.24270	1.74039	1.02551	1.69034	1.53524
36 INT128	0.27170	0.31373	-0.14320	0.43416	0.08295	0.62305	0.45228
37 INT130	1.55112	0.96664	0.89776	1.06124	1.21491	1.10208	1.27973
39 INT134	1.10659	0.12594	0.00629	1.01120	0.45818	-0.07406	0.84079
Constant	-41.50487	-42.13715	-21.56479	-46.03284	-39.31609	-39.82951	-48.72578

TABLE H.2 Classification Function for Thirty-Item Battery (Cont)

GROUP =	*8.0000	*9.0000	*10.000	*11.000	*12.000	*13.000	*14.000
Variable							
3 INT6	1.43486	1.55518	1.48025	1.14385	1.10859	1.81368	1.48956
4 INT8	1.34751	0.90934	1.39784	2.33456	1.61087	0.73466	0.99644
6 INT11	1.02287	0.90526	1.19468	1.26730	2.53260	1.25859	2.26013
9 INT19	-1.22900	-0.92811	-0.51627	-0.82985	-0.37557	-0.07371	-0.66778
10 INT21	1.21750	0.60354	0.67382	1.61978	0.37234	0.79036	1.40746
12 INT27	0.59395	1.40720	1.67456	0.67628	1.20628	1.25093	1.23384
13 INT34	-0.48858	-0.18509	-0.32876	0.90715	-0.02127	0.09792	0.12318
14 INT36	1.16607	0.67285	1.47027	0.15236	1.18935	0.32007	0.42382
15 INT40	0.59438	1.65069	0.56186	0.24878	0.40626	1.55943	0.36500
16 INT45	0.40002	-0.22968	-0.15320	0.00057	-0.03722	-0.35880	0.36739
17 INT49	0.80609	1.23479	1.28878	1.02435	1.40001	1.32958	-0.04896
18 INT51	0.51561	0.22412	0.29336	0.33812	0.61876	0.73331	0.00017
19 INT52	-0.65024	-0.34738	-0.32903	-0.10570	-0.37483	-0.65149	0.81143
20 INT53	0.88023	0.33118	0.41901	0.58626	0.39761	0.34509	0.64882
21 INT56	0.90387	1.09047	1.20772	2.25352	0.84935	1.09054	1.10310
22 INT63	1.75744	1.28826	2.13570	2.10140	1.75858	0.94431	1.99730
23 INT66	-0.05111	0.01038	-0.08407	0.85992	-0.35735	-0.14298	-0.37869
24 INT67	0.75756	0.57111	1.17437	0.60024	1.43590	0.42180	1.23176
25 INT70	0.74538	0.56161	0.74262	0.75663	0.44501	0.42023	0.68666
27 INT73	-1.23289	-0.68140	-0.98253	-1.28398	-0.39900	-0.82412	-0.06415
28 INT74	4.70473	4.06727	4.24281	2.87314	3.90854	3.43448	4.47130
29 INT76	1.38609	2.01328	2.20564	2.23041	1.74376	1.77482	1.54803
30 INT81	1.15090	0.26394	1.19094	1.23204	1.56661	1.55272	0.72933
31 INT86	0.30799	0.28474	0.09991	0.64491	0.43677	0.54923	0.23059
32 INT101	-0.15579	0.21592	0.37114	0.15630	-0.01536	0.50209	0.36807
34 INT105	2.40264	1.53751	1.93384	2.21493	1.88503	1.42692	1.72888
35 INT125	1.99259	1.49253	1.65193	0.66014	1.00652	1.97379	1.93029
36 INT128	-0.62579	0.31224	-0.03246	0.77759	0.34896	0.69606	0.01845
37 INT130	2.30245	1.62607	0.82982	0.84955	1.27219	1.06559	1.24433
39 INT134	0.67211	1.43916	-0.10532	0.90879	0.95450	0.92013	0.41196
Constant	-36.23451	-33.97369	-37.72633	-38.63428	-40.41869	-35.70027	-39.96928

TABLE H.3 Classification Matrix for Thirty-Item Battery

Group	Percent Correct	Number of Cases Classified Into Group													
		*1.0000	*2.0000	*3.0000	*4.0000	*5.0000	*6.0000	*7.0000	*8.0000	*9.0000	*10.0000	*11.0000	*12.0000	*13.0000	*14.0000
* 1.0000	62.4	93	1	1	8	1	0	4	16	8	2	1	5	7	2
* 2.0000	76.6	6	144	1	1	10	9	5	0	3	1	1	3	2	2
* 3.0000	77.6	4	5	180	0	3	4	1	12	6	6	3	1	4	3
* 4.0000	75.3	4	0	1	125	0	0	3	3	3	3	13	2	4	5
* 5.0000	64.3	6	17	5	1	117	6	5	1	10	2	3	2	6	1
* 6.0000	72.5	2	5	0	2	1	95	2	0	0	6	1	2	2	13
* 7.0000	63.7	5	7	1	12	10	7	144	3	3	6	6	8	10	4
* 8.0000	59.5	11	1	5	1	1	1	4	110	18	17	0	9	5	2
* 9.0000	56.2	8	1	6	2	5	1	3	10	91	6	1	4	19	5
*10.0000	53.8	3	2	6	7	3	3	2	16	10	107	5	21	2	12
*11.0000	57.9	4	0	5	20	4	6	4	1	1	2	77	4	3	2
*12.0000	65.6	9	1	3	7	2	6	5	5	2	12	4	124	1	8
*13.0000	59.5	6	2	4	7	13	1	3	4	20	6	5	6	113	0
*14.0000	58.3	2	3	6	5	5	14	4	2	2	5	2	9	1	84
Total	64.8	163	189	224	198	175	153	189	183	177	181	122	200	179	143

TABLE H.4   Forty-Item Interest
Battery

Item Number*	Interest
2	Auto repair
5	Ballet
6	Baseball
8	Being a wine connoisseur
9	Bicycling
11	Board games
13	Bowling
18	Chess/checkers
19	Child related activities
21	Classical music
26	Dining out
27	Driving/Motoring
34	Hiking
36	Housecleaning
40	Hunting
45	Judo/Karate
49	Maintenance and repairs of the home
51	Model building
52	Modern dance
53	Motorcycles
56	Opera
63	Popular Music
66	Sculpture
67	Sewing
70	Soccer
71	Squash/handball
73	Table tennis/ping pong
74	Television
76	Travel/sightseeing
81	Abortion vs. right to life issue
86	Arms race
101	Engineering
103	Foreign policy
105	Health and nutrition
125	Religion
128	Sexual attitudes and behavior
130	Social security system
131	Sources and uses of energy
134	Tax laws
136	The stock market

*Item numbers correspond to those used in the code book accompanying the data tape.

The classification function is shown in Table H.5.

The classification matrix, showing how individuals in each of the fourteen segments are classified using this short form is presented in Table H.6.

The jackknifed classification indicates that the percentage classified correctly would be expected to drop from 71.3% to 66.4% on a new sample of respondents.

Those who feel that the percentage of individuals classified correctly by the short form versions is too low for their purposes may wish to employ additional items all the way up to the full 139-item battery. This can readily be done using the classification matrix that results from a stepwise multiple discriminant analysis, forcing into the solution as many variables as the researcher wishes to use.

TABLE H.5   Classification Function for Forty-Item Battery

Variable	GROUP = *1.0000	*2.0000	*3.0000	*4.0000	*5.0000	*6.0000	*7.0000
1 INT2	0.85084	1.48370	1.14736	1.20604	2.09696	0.74130	0.95123
2 INT5	1.30654	1.24156	1.40042	2.83425	1.43339	1.82185	1.59699
3 INT6	1.84277	1.55935	1.19395	1.57991	0.58202	1.16502	1.33550
4 INT8	0.72484	0.57255	1.11480	1.03625	1.50244	0.87127	0.81426
5 INT9	0.28846	0.37659	0.18641	0.29375	0.06068	0.77792	0.01934
6 INT11	0.95058	1.32068	0.76107	1.43176	1.12317	0.64488	1.29269
7 INT13	0.67491	0.56964	0.33356	0.52774	0.55848	0.16158	0.30688
8 INT18	-0.18596	0.21459	0.05810	-0.07532	-0.29089	-0.72594	0.08183
9 INT19	-0.57379	-1.29828	-0.66060	-0.61488	-0.85378	-1.25640	-0.74359
10 INT21	0.28970	0.27269	0.30479	1.51178	0.39261	0.24764	0.54152
11 INT26	1.50646	1.49401	0.98415	1.02024	1.13988	1.38085	1.08257
12 INT27	0.57552	1.06117	0.18562	0.70254	0.92118	0.85240	0.52521
13 INT34	-0.93325	-0.59685	-0.40610	-0.71422	0.08293	0.38604	-0.64559
14 INT36	1.14369	0.48373	0.96788	0.52468	0.72921	0.13400	1.24751
15 INT40	0.78954	0.51221	0.65264	0.56419	1.40985	0.61207	1.05192
16 INT45	-0.02328	0.29667	0.22015	0.15058	0.30161	0.82950	1.17191
17 INT49	0.42258	0.62909	0.30641	0.85194	0.85714	0.27581	1.07734
18 INT51	0.22545	1.40601	0.40218	0.43485	0.99142	-0.61016	1.42562
19 INT52	-0.28116	-1.10574	-0.30610	-0.52420	-0.51156	0.38509	-0.25742
20 INT53	0.51582	1.45438	0.60263	0.17097	1.81582	1.55390	0.87699

TABLE H.5   Classification Function for Forty-Item Battery (Cont)

GROUP =	*1.0000	*2.0000	*3.0000	*4.0000	*5.0000	*6.0000	*7.0000
21 INT56	0.55035	0.51773	1.01274	3.46221	0.70932	0.53863	1.08044
22 INT63	2.18226	2.22083	1.16706	1.83417	2.24831	2.17874	1.88656
23 INT66	-0.67157	-0.51452	-0.14284	0.76001	-0.52270	0.00772	0.58604
24 INT67	1.02951	0.69451	1.07461	0.50968	0.73443	1.02017	1.43153
25 INT70	0.39067	1.97688	0.51836	0.13956	0.38639	1.53284	1.13414
26 INT71	-0.51831	0.44574	0.33670	-0.45079	-0.70007	0.63467	0.59531
27 INT73	-1.41164	-0.36656	-1.00323	-0.88045	-1.25815	-0.57735	-0.89156
28 INT74	4.54069	4.40213	3.72545	3.79703	4.12451	4.13951	4.11975
29 INT76	1.31105	1.40914	0.50493	1.84028	1.50096	1.74859	1.42380
30 INT81	1.11425	0.64786	0.91197	1.02635	0.99762	1.83127	1.08079
31 INT86	1.60776	0.64075	0.42252	0.65218	0.91898	-0.22885	0.29286
32 INT101	0.28397	1.06091	0.44976	0.03481	1.10521	-0.00354	0.71956
33 INT103	1.55749	0.13280	0.32345	0.68231	0.28574	0.45010	0.66995
34 INT105	1.82422	1.54762	0.97271	1.52257	1.15178	1.29762	1.52203
35 INT125	1.30868	1.15166	1.20342	1.72175	0.98390	1.69108	1.47577
36 INT128	0.11808	0.15559	-0.20257	0.31589	-0.07440	0.48350	0.36711
37 INT130	1.29454	0.78311	0.85362	0.97161	1.07429	1.00801	1.15231
38 INT131	0.51659	0.78668	0.02650	0.24410	0.63835	0.34861	0.14901
39 INT134	0.51737	-0.01669	-0.08216	0.89323	0.26694	-0.07643	0.58325
40 INT136	0.87036	-0.41732	0.14722	0.01685	-0.11292	-0.41063	0.50263
Constant	-44.03497	-44.20720	-22.74191	-48.62553	-41.69691	-41.73230	-50.20865

TABLE H.5 Classification Function for Forty-Item Battery (Cont)

GROUP =	*8.0000	*9.0000	*10.0000	*11.0000	*12.0000	*13.0000	*14.0000
Variable							
1 INT2	0.97333	1.12313	1.00934	1.17289	1.13883	1.42105	0.76642
2 INT5	1.41749	1.19305	1.30302	2.52092	1.24179	1.29359	2.08072
3 INT6	1.39192	1.50165	1.43138	1.16749	0.95358	1.69536	1.38643
4 INT8	1.21205	0.57212	1.10408	2.05176	1.30425	0.48954	0.47228
5 INT9	0.01382	0.09992	0.06464	0.78600	0.69667	0.30763	1.31818
6 INT11	0.88015	0.86490	1.09583	1.12479	2.24775	1.13598	1.69757
7 INT13	0.03841	0.19427	0.33578	-0.34605	0.85668	0.45120	0.29949
8 INT18	0.22068	-0.28436	-0.38568	-0.32339	-0.06188	-0.10869	0.82712
9 INT19	-1.35018	-1.05613	-0.62259	-0.98533	-0.53914	-0.21598	-0.93483
10 INT21	1.01062	0.38076	0.47575	1.24061	0.13904	0.58188	1.00772
11 INT26	0.83279	1.29632	2.03168	1.37504	1.48974	1.06871	1.73401
12 INT27	0.31713	0.92241	1.10508	0.19825	0.64695	0.80328	0.66245
13 INT34	-0.58726	-0.24719	-0.41363	0.68251	-0.27142	-0.03076	-0.32918
14 INT36	1.19410	0.79875	1.49947	0.17801	1.25750	0.40432	0.44198
15 INT40	0.58382	1.68654	0.61950	0.35873	0.45394	1.55022	0.48265
16 INT45	0.44937	-0.22202	-0.05079	0.05357	-0.02240	-0.34051	0.35690
17 INT49	0.61948	1.03137	1.10564	0.83314	1.20721	1.08057	-0.15466
18 INT51	0.40752	0.11854	0.21166	0.22026	0.44986	0.57960	-0.16831
19 INT52	-0.78714	-0.44578	-0.52625	-0.31963	-0.56653	-0.78297	0.52682
20 INT53	0.90414	0.30336	0.41190	0.60086	0.32628	0.27482	0.54684

TABLE H.5 Classification Function for Forty-Item Battery (Cont)

GROUP =	*8.0000	*9.0000	*10.0000	*11.0000	*12.0000	*13.0000	*14.0000
21 INT56	0.63451	0.75769	0.91273	1.70594	0.59764	0.83945	0.63994
22 INT63	1.73781	1.29216	2.13106	2.07453	1.71875	0.92955	1.96021
23 INT66	-0.23177	-0.22943	-0.26460	0.57669	-0.54101	-0.31462	-0.68517
24 INT67	0.80934	0.70224	1.23192	0.67769	1.48586	0.49315	1.25562
25 INT70	0.75689	0.56214	0.76799	0.83481	0.44203	0.47651	0.55117
26 INT71	0.04370	-0.15337	-0.02150	-0.39250	-0.30193	-0.25873	-0.24500
27 INT73	-1.26072	-0.73949	-1.05008	-1.21664	-0.62662	-0.92489	-0.31600
28 INT74	4.73670	4.09991	4.16750	2.95073	3.89980	3.45043	4.47369
29 INT76	1.29491	1.79610	1.91818	2.03947	1.47047	1.62406	1.27100
30 INT81	1.04799	0.15589	1.04777	1.04334	1.44127	1.44325	0.63344
31 INT86	0.21093	0.16367	0.13392	0.51484	0.39654	0.48165	0.17383
32 INT101	-0.27303	-0.09982	0.29391	-0.04072	-0.18729	0.30151	0.23836
33 INT103	0.34687	0.11256	0.00604	0.47341	0.17805	0.22244	0.27663
34 INT105	2.29905	1.42355	1.93866	2.01194	1.78311	1.38046	1.55286
35 INT125	1.97506	1.41804	1.62531	0.61580	0.98805	1.94629	1.87317
36 INT128	-0.75998	0.12501	-0.09880	0.50348	0.24191	0.59708	-0.09280
37 INT130	2.15632	1.39587	0.84877	0.60429	1.18758	0.99932	1.19043
38 INT131	0.66592	0.74819	-0.20973	1.12403	0.35475	0.29788	0.21708
39 INT134	0.62111	1.00972	-0.07113	0.68298	0.83065	0.84118	0.28837
40 INT136	-0.73333	0.91415	0.01304	-0.33290	0.03351	-0.13040	0.16637
Constant	-37.36687	-35.63731	-39.63498	-41.44812	-42.31540	-37.10323	-42.78137

TABLE H.6 Classification Matrix for Forty-Item Battery

| | | | | | | | | Number of Cases Classified Into Group | | | | | | | |
Group	Percent Correct	*1.0000	*2.0000	*3.0000	*4.0000	*5.0000	*6.0000	*7.0000	*8.0000	*9.0000	*10.000	*11.000	*12.000	*13.000	*14.000
* 1.0000	67.8	101	0	1	7	2	0	3	10	8	4	0	5	6	2
* 2.0000	81.9	1	154	1	0	10	6	5	1	3	0	1	3	2	1
* 3.0000	77.2	3	4	179	1	4	4	2	11	6	10	3	4	0	1
* 4.0000	75.3	4	0	1	125	0	0	4	2	0	2	10	7	8	3
* 5.0000	69.2	3	17	3	1	126	4	4	0	11	1	3	3	5	1
* 6.0000	78.6	0	3	0	2	2	103	3	0	0	6	1	2	1	8
* 7.0000	69.5	4	8	2	8	6	5	157	4	7	3	4	7	7	4
* 8.0000	71.4	5	1	8	1	0	0	4	132	7	12	1	6	5	3
* 9.0000	63.6	5	2	4	2	5	2	0	13	103	5	2	5	12	2
*10.0000	66.3	0	2	4	1	4	2	1	12	6	132	4	23	1	7
*11.0000	71.4	2	0	1	13	2	5	2	2	1	0	95	5	2	3
*12.0000	68.8	7	1	0	6	2	3	5	7	3	9	3	130	3	10
*13.0000	67.9	3	4	6	6	11	2	0	3	10	5	2	8	129	1
*14.0000	68.8	2	4	6	3	0	9	6	2	1	5	2	5	0	99
Total	71.3	140	200	216	176	174	145	196	199	166	194	131	213	181	145

About the Authors

RONALD E. FRANK is Professor of Marketing at The Wharton School, where he has previously served as Vice Dean and Director of Research and Ph.D. Programs as well as Chairman of the Marketing Department. He has also served as founding editor of the *Journal of Consumer Research*. He received his Ph.D. in Marketing from the University of Chicago, and an M.B.A. from Northwestern. He has previously taught at the Harvard Business School and the Stanford University Graduate School of Business, as well as Northwestern's Business School. Dr. Frank has engaged in a wide range of consulting activities on marketing research and management problems with ATT, ATT-Long Lines, Coca Cola, General Foods, Nestle, Schlitz, the Management Analysis Center, the Market Research Corporation of America, and National Analysts. In addition, he is actively engaged in consulting on several antitrust cases. He has authored numerous articles and books. His most recent books include *Market Segmentation, An Econometric Approach to a Marketing Decision Model* and *A Manager's Guide to Market Research.*

MARSHALL G. GREENBERG is currently a Senior Vice President of Booz·Allen & Hamilton, National Analysts Division. He received his B.A. from Haverford College and his M.S. and Ph.D. degrees in Mathematical Psychology from the University of Michigan. Before joining Booz·Allen in 1970, he taught psychology at the University of Minnesota and the University of Cincinnati and was manager of the Professional Services Department at the Procter & Gamble Company. He is a former Vice President of the Market Research Division of the American Marketing Association and a current member of the editorial boards of the *Journal of Marketing Research,* the *Journal of Consumer Research,* the *Journal of Marketing,* and *Management Science.* He has published numerous articles in psychology and marketing research journals on applications of mathematical and statistical models to the understanding of behavior.

mago 145   CO   137-139